SOCIOANALYTIC METHODS

SOCIOANALYTIC METHODS

Discovering the Hidden in Organisations and Social Systems

Edited by Susan Long

Routledge
Taylor & Francis Group

LONDON AND NEW YORK

First published 2013 by
Karnac Books Ltd.

Published 2018 by Routledge
2 Park Square, Milton Park, Abingdon, Oxon OX14 4RN
711 Third Avenue, New York, NY 10017, USA

Routledge is an imprint of the Taylor & Francis Group, an informa business

British Library Cataloguing in Publication Data

A C.I.P. for this book is available from the British Library

ISBN 9781780491325 (pbk)

Cover design by Jason Long of Fingergraphics: jl@fingergraphics.com

Edited, designed and produced by The Studio Publishing Services Ltd
www.publishingservicesuk.co.uk
e-mail: studio@publishingservicesuk.co.uk

CONTENTS

To Gordon Lawrence, whose discovery of social dreaming led me to an articulation of the associative unconscious and whose work has stimulated creativity in a generation of socioanalysts

ACKNOWLEDGEMENTS

The descriptions of the chapters presented in the Introduction are provided by the chapter authors. As editor, I thank them for this and for their contributions to this volume.

Chapter Three was first presented as a paper to the "From Baby to Boardroom" conference on observing organisations, 18–19 October 2008, at the Tavistock Clinic, London.

Burkard Sievers (Chapter Seven) is grateful to Rose Mersky for her help in editing, and, of course, to all the participants in the matrices, who—for obvious reasons—have to remain anonymous.

The final section of Chapter Nine was first published as Stapley, L. (2003), "Britain and the world at the dawn of 2003: report of a New Year's Listening Post", in *Organisational and Social Dynamics*, London: Karnac.

The work described in Chapter Twelve, "Concepts, methods and case material", has been developed over time with the author's colleagues at Innovative Practice Consulting Pty Ltd and further afield. In particular, the author, Jinette de Gooijer, thanks Brigid Nossal, Rob Cairns, and Mary Burgess for their valuable and valued contributions to her working practice. An earlier version of this chapter was published in *Socioanalysis*, Volume 14, in December 2012, and will be published in Spanish in *Socio-analytical Approaches for the Study and Change of Groups and Organizations* by Editorial Universitaria, Santiago, Chile.

Alastair Bain would like to pay tribute to Joshua Bain for typing his chapter, for his advice and encouragement, and, most importantly, for his insight some years ago that wonder is at the heart of socioanalysis.

The editor is grateful to Jason Long for his help in formatting and with the cover design.

Eliat Aram, PhD, MSc, CPsych, is the CEO of the Tavistock Institute of Human Relations. She also works with other change agents. She is informed by concepts of emergence and self-organisation as well as power dynamics/dialogue, including developing skills and attitudes for working in conditions of uncertainty and ambiguity. She helps, supports, and challenges change and learning agents through their journey of growth by inviting them to think about and reflect upon their flow of experience as leaders in their organisations. She is regularly on staff of group relations conferences nationally and internationally. Since 2007, she has directed, and made innovations to, the TIHR's Leicester Conference: Authority Role & Organisation, the Institute's annual two-week group relations experiential learning conference.

Lilia Baglioni is a member of the Italian Psychoanalytic Society (SPI), the International Psychoanalytic Association (IPA), and the International Association of Group Psychotherapy and Group Processes (IAGP). She has been a director of Socialdreaming Ltd, UK and is co-founder of Socialdreaming.it, the Italian association for the study and research on social dreaming and creative processes. She is in private practice as an individual and group psychoanalyst and organisational consultant, and has taught and researched about specialised groups' techniques at La Sapienza University. With Franca Fubini and Gordon Lawrence, she has organised an International Experiential Seminar on Social Dreaming and Creativity for seven consecutive years in Rome, and has conducted with them the first training programme for SDM hosts.

Alastair Bain is a socioanalyst. He trained and worked as a consultant at the Tavistock Institute before returning to Australia in 1983. His main work interests at the moment are in organisational and social dreaming, the work of Wilfred Bion, and the exploration of wonder in socioanalytic practice. Alastair has two children; Josh, who lives with him in Carlton, and Lauren, who is based in Canberra with the diplomatic service. She and her husband have two children, Katharina, who is four, and Alexander, who is two.

Bruno Boccara, PhD, the founder of socioanalytic dialogue, is an economist with extensive policy experience worldwide in development assistance and financial markets. He graduated from Ecole Nationale des Ponts et Chaussées in France and has two PhDs (Civil Engineering and Economics) from the Massachusetts Institute of Technology (MIT) in the USA. He completed academic psychoanalytic training at the NYU School of Medicine Psychoanalytic Institute, and also trained in organisational behaviour and leadership coaching at the Institute for Psychoanalytic Training and Research. He is a member of the American Psychoanalytic Association.

Franca Fubini works as a psychoanalytic psychotherapist, group analyst, and organisational consultant. She is a member of IL NODO group (Italy), of OPUS (UK) and of the Group Analytic Society, London (GAS). She has taught at Rome and Perugia Universities in the field of Psychology and Human Resources. She is a senior Fellow of University College of London (UCL), and has been member and director of the staff of the Italian Group Relations conferences. She has been a Director of Social Dreaming Ltd (UK) and is co-founder of Socialdreaming.it , the Italian association for the study and research on social dreaming and creative processes. With Lilia Baglioni and Gordon Lawrence, she has organised an International Experiential

Seminar on Social Dreaming and Creativity for seven consecutive years in Rome and has conducted with them the first training programme for SDM hosts.

Jinette de Gooijer, PhD, consults to organisations on understanding the hidden aspects of organisational culture and their effects on business performance, with the view to developing work cultures that promote creativity and prosperity for the organisation, the individual, and wider society. She is a principal consultant with Innovative Practice, an independent consultancy firm specialising in systems psychodynamic approaches to understanding organisational work cultures and the leadership of organisational change. She is a founding member and Past President of Group Relations Australia, Member, ISPSO, and Associate and National Representative (Australia) of OPUS. Recent publications include *The Murder in Merger: A Systems Psychodynamic Exploration of a Corporate Merger* (London: Karnac, 2009); "Drawing down the blinds on reflection: what is to be shut out or in?", in L. J. Gould, A. Lucey, and L. Stapley (Eds.), *The Reflective Citizen* (London: Karnac, 2011); "Murderous mergers", in H. Brunning (Ed.), *Psychoanalytic Reflections on a Changing World* (London: Karnac, 2012).

Wendy Harding, PhD, has been actively involved in the field of organisation dynamics in Australia for twenty years. She has been an educator for fifteen years, first at Swinburne University and, since 2002, at RMIT. Wendy currently directs the Organisation Dynamics Master program at RMIT and is a founding member of NIODA (National Institute of Organisation Dynamics Australia). Wendy has undertaken action research and consultancy in a broad span of settings from hospitals and prisons to a variety of smaller organisations. Since completing her PhD in 2006, she has published a number of research-based articles. Wendy is particularly interested in the interface of object relations and intersubjective theories and relevance to organisational functioning, large group theory and practice, and systems psychodynamics education.

Maurita Harney, MA, PhD, is Honorary Senior Fellow in Philosophy at the University of Melbourne. She has taught philosophy at a number of Australian universities, and has held positions of Visiting Research Fellow at a number of local and overseas universities. She has also taught philosophically related subjects to students in management and in organisation dynamics. Her publications cover a range of topics in the philosophy of mind, mainly from the phenomenological/ hermeneutic perspective. Her recent research interests include the intersection of phenomenology and neuroscience, and the role of American philosopher C. S. Peirce in the newly emergent area of enquiry known as biosemiotics.

Robert D. Hinshelwood works in the Centre for Psychoanalytic Studies, University of Essex, and was previously Clinical Director, The Cassel Hospital, London. He is a Fellow of the British Psychoanalytical Society, and a Fellow of the Rotal College of Psychiatrists. He has authored *A Dictionary of Kleinian Thought* (1989) and other books and articles on Kleinian psychoanalysis. *Observing Organisations* (2000) was edited with Wilhelm Skogstad and is among a number of texts on psychoanalytic applications to social science. He founded the *British Journal of Psychotherapy*, and *Psychoanalysis and History*. Currently, he is completing *Research on the Couch: Single Case Studies, Subjectivity and Psychoanalytic Knowledge*, to be published in 2013.

Olya Khaleelee is a psychoanalytic psychotherapist, corporate psychologist, and organisational consultant, with a particular interest in organisational transition and transformation. She has worked with the Tavistock Institute for over thirty years in developing group relations, both in the UK and abroad, has been on the staff of many conferences, and was the first female director of the Leicester Conference, which explores authority, leadership, and organisation from a psychoanalytic and systemic perspective. She is also a past Chairwoman of the Council of the London Centre for Psychotherapy, and was for many years Director of OPUS, An Organisation for Promoting Understanding of Society.

James Krantz, PhD) is an organisational consultant and researcher from New York City. He is a Principal of Worklab, which concentrates on strategy implementation, senior team development, and work process design. Dr Krantz has a PhD in Systems Sciences from the Wharton School and a BA in Philosophy and Economics from Wesleyan University. He is a past president of the International Society for the Psychoanalytic Study of Organizations (ISPSO), a Fellow of the

A. K. Rice Institute, member of OPUS, and currently Director of the Socio-Analytic Program in Organizational Development and Consultation at The Institute for Psychoanalytic Training and Research (IPTAR). His writing has focused on the unconscious background of work life and on the socio-psychological challenges posed by emerging forms of organisation.

Susan Long, PhD, is an organisational consultant and researcher. Formerly Professor of Creative and Sustainable Organisation, she is now an adjunct professor at RMIT in Melbourne, Australia, where she conducts courses for senior managers, supervises research students, and conducts organisational research. As an organisational consultant she works with organisational change, executive coaching, board development, role analysis, team development, and management training. She is a member of Comcare's advisory board for the Center of Excellence for Research into Mental Health at Work and a member of the Board of the Judicial College of Victoria. She is currently President of the Psychoanalytic Studies Association of Australasia, was the founding President of Group Relations Australia, and a past president of the International Society for the Psychoanalytic Study of Organisations. Her research interests involve participatory action research projects in industry, government organisations, health, education, and correctional services, and have attracted grants through the Australian Research Council and industry. She has published five books and many journal articles, is on the editorial board of *Organisational and Social Dynamics* and is editor of the journal *Socioanalysis*. Her most recent is a book with Burkard Sievers, *Towards a Socioanalysis of Money, Finance and Capitalism: Beneath the Surface of the Financial Industry* (Routledge, 2012).

Rose Redding Mersky, MS, has been an organisational development consultant and executive coach for over twenty years. She conducts workshops in social dreaming, social dream-drawing, organisational role analysis, social photo-matrix, and organisational observation in Europe and the USA. She is a senior associate with Inscape International in Cologne, Germany and has been a member of the International Society for the Psychoanalytic Study of Organizations (ISPSO) (www.ispso.org) since 1988. She was elected as its first female president in 1995, and served as a board member for thirteen years and as Director of Professional Development from 2001 to 2006. She has taken roles as member, training group member, and staff member of group relations conferences in Israel, USA, and Australia. In June 2000, she was awarded the first annual prize for the best paper on applied psychoanalysis by the William Alanson White Institute in New York City. She is in her third year of doctoral studies at the Institute for Psycho-Social Studies at the University of West England in Bristol. She lives and works in Germany. Email: rosemer@earthlink.net; website: www.rrm-consulting.com.

John Newton, BBus, MA, PhD, is formerly Associate Professor in Organisation Dynamics at RMIT University and is now a freelance consultant and author. He is currently president (2012–2013) of Group Relations Australia, and a member of ISPSO and NIODA. He is the lead editor of J. Newton, S. Long, and B. Sievers (Eds.) (2006) *Coaching in Depth: The Organisational Role Analysis Approach* (London: Karnac), and he serves on the editorial boards of *SocioAnalysis* and *Organisational and Social Dynamics*.

Brigid Nossal, PhD, is a principal consultant at Innovative Practice and has worked as a consultant to organisations for the past nineteen years. She brings a systems psychodynamic approach to her practice. Brigid is a sessional lecturer in the Master of Applied Science in Organisation Dynamics at RMIT University and a founding member of Group Relations Australia (GRA) and the National Institute of Organisation Dynamics Australia (NIODA). She is also a member of the International Society for the Psychoanalytic Study of Organisations (ISPSO) and the Organisation for Promoting Understanding in Society (OPUS).

Mannie Sher, PhD, TQAP, FBAP, is a principal social scientist and Director of the Group Relations Programme at the Tavistock Institute of Human Relations, London. He manages organisational development and change projects and consults to top teams of organisations on the role of leadership in effecting strategic change. His research and consultancy work focuses on the impact of thought on the dialectic relationship between social constructivism, the unconscious and liberal democracy. He is a Fellow of the British Association of Psychotherapists and a practising psychoanalytical psychotherapist. Mannie has published on subjects of consultancy, leadership, organisational development, ethics, and corruption. He is a former member of the Board of the International Society for the Psychoanalytic Study of Organisations (ISPSO), and Member of the Israel Association for the Study of Group and Organisational Processes (OFEK).

Burkard Sievers, Dipl. Soz., is Professor Emeritus of Organization Development in the Schumpeter School of Business and Economics at Bergische Universität Wuppertal in Germany. In his research he focuses on unconscious dynamics in management and organisation from a socioanalytic and systemic perspective. In 1995, he was awarded the international price for participation by the HBK Bank in Antwerp, Belgium, for his book *Work, Death and Life Itself: Essays on Management and Organisation* (Berlin/New York: de Gruyter, 1994). He is Past President of The International Society for the Psychoanalytic Study of Organizations (ISPSO). His most recent book, edited with Susan Long, is *Towards a Socioanalysis of Money, Finance and Capitalism: Beneath the Surface of the Financial Industry* (London: Routledge, 2012).

Lionel Stapley (PhD) is the Director of OPUS, a world leader in providing a psycho-social understanding of societal dynamics; and which exists to promote "the reflective citizen". He is also an organisational consultant working with individuals, groups, and organisations in the public and private sectors, in both the UK and in other countries. He heads the OPUS Group Processes Programme that includes a one day, four day, and three day Advanced Training in Small Group Processes events; and is the Chair of the Listening Post Steering Group. He is the Chair of the Editorial Management Committee of the OPUS International Journal *Organisational & Social Dynamics*, a Chartered Fellow of the Chartered Institute of Personnel and Development (FCIPD), a Chartered Fellow of the Chartered Institute of Management (FCIM), and a Member of the International Society for the Psychoanalytic Study of Organisations (ISPSO). Recent books include: *Individuals Groups and Organisations: Beneath the Surface* (London: Karnac, 2006), and, with Larry Gould and Aideen Lucey, *The Reflective Citizen: Organisational and Social Dynamics* (2011). London: Karnac.

Socioanalytic methodology

Susan Long

Psychoanalysis has been around for over a hundred years and many books have been written about its method with particular emphasis on the clinical encounter. But what about the methodology used in the exploration of unconscious processes in social groups and organisations (i.e., socioanalytic methodologies)? Numerous articles have appeared in scholarly journals such as *Human Relations, Organisational and Social Dynamics, Organizational Studies, Journal of Management Development, Journal of Management Education, Social Psychiatry, Psychodynamic Practice, Socio-Analysis,* and various journals of psychotherapy and group analysis, among others, and books on specific methods have appeared (for instance, the series recently produced on the group relations method Aram, Baxter, & Nutkevitch, 2009, and Aram, Nutkevitch, & Baxter, 2012, the book on organisational observation by Hinshelwood & Skogstad, 2000, and those focused on the work of particular theorists/researchers such as Isobel Menzies Lyth, 1988, 1989). However, a book focused on a broad range of socioanalytic methods, together with an underlying philosophy to link these methods, has not until now been available. This book does just that.

Socioanalysis is the study of human social phenomena from a perspective combining systems theory and psychoanalysis. Systems theory examines the properties and dynamics of entities as complex systems where each part interacts with other parts and the system as a whole to produce behaviour. Psychoanalysis studies the hidden and repressed aspects of systems, whether individual or collective, and ascertains how these "beneath the surface" aspects influence the system dynamics and behaviours.

This perspective was developed at the Tavistock Institute in London after the Second World War and was initially based in Kleinian psychoanalysis, following also the work of Bion and linked to the socio-technical work of Eric Trist (see Gould, Stapley, & Stein, 2001; Menzies Lyth, 1988, 1989; Trist & Murray, 1990). It also developed a parallel life in the USA, integrating the work of Kurt Lewin (Fraher, 2004). In addition to the research work of the Tavistock Institute and, later, the Tavistock Clinic Consultancy Service, this perspective also became central to the group relations conferences run out of Leicester University since 1957 (Miller, 1990) and to the now worldwide group relations movement (Aram, Baxter, & Nutkevitch, 2009; Aram, Nutkevitch, & Baxter, 2012). It might be said the "study group" central to group relations work is the forerunner of the methods described in this book, in so far as its task is to look at "here-and-now" subjective experience within the culture and dynamics of the group.

Socioanalysis—a term coined by the then Australian Institute of Social Analysis in Melbourne, Australia (Bain, 1999) and now used more extensively (Long & Sievers, 2012 for example)—has extended also to include many different psychoanalytic theoretical perspectives alongside complex systemic perspectives. This has occurred in parallel with developments in the International Society for the Psychoanalytic Study of Organizations (ISPSO www.ispso.org) (see, for example, Lacanian, Jungian, and interpersonal articles in the journal *Socio-Analysis* and in the ISPSO library).

Socioanalytic practice has been primarily taken up by organisational consultants and researchers, although its methods have been used to study social movements and even the dynamics of countries (see Chapter Fourteen of this book). Over the past sixty years several different methods have emerged for accessing the underlying systems psychodynamics or socio-dynamics of organisations and, increasingly, of wider social movements. These methods have developed out of curiosity about unconscious social processes as expressed through dreams (e.g., social dreaming, see Lawrence, 2010), attempts to apply learning from group relations conferences to the workplace (organisational role analysis—see Reed, 2001 and Newton, Long, and Sievers, 2006), training students to observe organisational dynamics (organisational observation—see Hinshelwood & Skogstad, 2000), using organisational drawings to illuminate workplace issues (Gould, 1987; Nossal, 2010), examining societal dynamics (Listening Posts—see Khaleelee & Miller, 1985), and understanding workplace cultures (cultural diagnosis—see Levinson, Molinari, & Spohn,1972). These methods and others more recently developed each have in common the attempt to surface and utilise the hidden dynamics of social systems. While there are overlaps between socioanalytic investigations and other social science research methods, both psychoanalysis and socioanalysis are based in primarily ideographic and subjective frameworks. It can be argued that they involve the scientific study of subjectivity, individually and collectively (Long, 2001).

It is now timely that these socioanalytic methods be brought together around an understanding of their commonality. This book is an attempt to do that. The term socioanalysis will be used throughout, although it is recognised that others might use the terms "systems psychodynamics" or "psychoanalysis of organisations". Socioanalysis seems more appropriate, however, as it implies a more specific and yet broader field. It is the study of groups, organisations, and society using a systems psychoanalytic framework. It "combines and synthesises methodologies and theories derived from psychoanalysis, group relations, social systems thinking, organisational behaviour, and social dreaming" (Bain, 1999). In simple terms, socioanalysis studies social groupings and phenomena by looking beneath the surface (and the obvious) to see the underlying dynamics and how these dynamics are interconnected. Even though the beginnings of socioanalytic investigation lay in the mid-twentieth century, a broad look across several methodologies has not been done before, despite separate publications dealing with particular methods (for example, Hinshelwood & Skogstad 2000; Hollway & Jefferson 2000; Mersky 2011, the latter of whom does encompass some four of the methods in her chapter). This book will present and examine several of the methods used in socioanalytic work and will, perhaps for the first time, present a methodological basis for all those methods that have developed within the socioanalytic framework.

A philosophy of science for socioanalytic study

The philosophy of science supporting socioanalytic study is different from traditional empiricist or positivist philosophies, although some socioanalytic researchers might at times also work with these traditions. A primary philosophy of science supporting socioanalysis is that propounded by Charles Sanders Peirce, a late nineteenth century philosopher who introduced the idea of "abductive logic" (Burch, 2010; also see Chapter One of this book). He conceived of scientific discovery as moving through stages of abductive, deductive, and inductive logic. Abductive logic is involved in the early stages of hypothesis creation. At this stage, argument by metaphor leads to the creative development of "working hypotheses" that can then be examined against new cases. This underlies the method of "negative case analysis" as practised in many sociological investigations (Patton, 2001). Socioanalysis relies heavily on abductive logic. This might be due to its "youth" as a discipline, but it is also due to the nature of its subject—the unconscious dynamics of groups and organisations, where exploration of the unknown in systems is paramount.

> Abduction is not always inference to the best explanation, but it is always inference to some explanation or at least to something that clarifies or makes routine some information that has previously been "surprising," in the sense that we would not have routinely expected it, given our then-current state of knowledge. (Burch, 2010)

This seems apt to socioanalytic discovery, where the unconscious is, by definition, "surprising".

A major research methodology in this discipline is the case study. The reasons for this include the complexity of concepts with non-linear causality, the use of narrative, qualitative, descriptive methods rather than experimental, quantitative methods, the use of action research which—because of the changing, systemic nature of organisations—utilises a social and political intervention alongside an exploratory method, and the use of abductive logic in the development of working hypotheses that aid in thinking through case material and organisational change. But within case studies, several different methods ranging from observation through social dreaming and drawings to work culture analyses have been used.

Connecting all these methods is their aim of "tapping into" the dynamic operation of the associative unconscious within and between social systems. The associative unconscious is the unconscious at a systemic level. It refers to Bion's notion of the "infinite", discussed latterly by Gordon Lawrence, and stands in contrast to the individual repressed unconscious described by Freud. The associative unconscious covers all those associations available and potential within and among interacting social systems. It is a rich vein of golden insight into the underlying dynamics of the system. The totality of such associations are available to the system but not to any one individual. In Lacanian linguistic terms, the associative unconscious contains that network of existing and potential signifiers that create the way the organisation or social system is experienced. And, somewhat like Hopper's "social unconscious", it points beyond that network to "the existence and constraints of social cultural and communicational arrangements of which people are unaware or are denied" (Hopper, 2003, p. 127), but, I add, become available through exploratory methods that use the association and amplification of free associations made in social contexts. More simply though, it is that network of thoughts, ideas and feelings that create the social system as it is and, more creatively, as it might become. The potentiality lies in what Bohm (1980) calls the implicate order.

Each of the methods discussed in this book accesses the associative unconscious in different ways. They help to bring hidden dynamics to the surface for people to see how they influence, aid, or inhibit their activities. Excitingly, they can show what we know at some level, but have not yet been able to use. And, because the methods explore social systems, they can contribute to new collaborative endeavours for thinking the future.

An outline of the book

The book sets out initially in Chapter One to explain the idea of the associative unconscious, elaborating the description given above. Maurita Harney, a philosopher, and myself, a socioanalyst, provide an outline of the Peircean philosophy of abductive logic (Charles Sanders Peirce) that helped give a basic philosophical underpinning to the associative unconscious as an underlying concept for the

methodology presented in this book. A logic of association stands at
the basis of abductive logic—a form of logic proposed by Peirce as
fundamental to scientific creativity and process. As we argue, abduction presents us with *possibilities*: its conclusions give us something
novel or different although not yet probabilities. These are established
later through the work of normal science (Kuhn, 1962). Socioanalytic
methods exemplify a logic of association following Freud's psychoanalytic method of free association. In work with groups, organisations, and other social systems, this free association takes place across
many minds.

Chapter Two, by James Krantz, begins with the idea that "reflection" is the goal that underlies all socioanalytic methods, that the various social technologies that comprise socioanalytic method are
ultimately aimed at reflective practice. It explores what reflective practice means from a socioanalytic viewpoint, emphasising both the
importance of reflection in today's organisations as well as the considerable barriers to incorporating it in ongoing work life. An overview
of the place of reflective practice in the socioanalytic tradition is
presented, followed by an exploration of the conditions of contemporary organisational life that underscore the importance of integrating
reflection into organisational life. Some of the defensive manoeuvres
that have emerged in response to the anxieties stimulated by reflective
practice are then discussed.

Chapters Three to Fourteen deal with specific socioanalytic
methods.

Chapter Three describes a method of observing organisations
derived from the psychoanalytic method evolved by Esther Bick in the
training of child psychotherapists and psychoanalysts. In this chapter,
Robert Hinshelwood concentrates on observational material that he
has encountered in nearly three decades of supervising this training
exercise. Various aspects of an organisation can be exposed, he argues,
including the immediate experience of the atmosphere, the impact of
the task, finding oneself in a role, cultural schism, personal desires and
organisational duties, joining in unconscious phantasies, the importance of subjectivity, and of unconscious-to-unconscious communication.

Chapter Four argues for the enduring power and utility of drawing as a tool in socioanalytic and systems psychodynamic consultancy
and research. Through presenting a summarised version of some

earlier research with experienced practitioners in the field and some detailed case examples of its application, Brigid Nossal documents the use of drawing. In so doing, it serves as a guide to practice. The idea is presented that this method for engaging clients in socioanalytic exploration generates important data about the emotional dimension of experience in organisations, offers a way to promote a "mind" in the client for socioanalytic work, and, most significantly, creates opportunities for learning and transformation.

The socioanalytic interview is the focus of Chapter Five. Here, the practicalities of interviewing from a socioanalytic perspective are discussed by Wendy Harding and Susan Long, taking into account both the systemic and psychoanalytic theoretical bases of socioanaly-sis. The chapter covers interview design, beginning and conducting the interview, interviewer skills, and creating and analysing data. Particular focus is on understanding the unconscious material in the interview found not simply in the content, but in the interview process and through the projective dynamics between the partici-pants. While the chapter is primarily aimed at examining the socioan-alytic research interview, it is also applicable to organisational consultancy.

In Chapter Six, the idea of social dreaming (SD) as a method of cultural enquiry and evolution is traced by Lilia Baglioni and Fran-cesca Fubrini back to its origins in psychoanalysis and group processes and to Gordon Lawrence's preoccupation with illuminating and fostering unconscious creative processes in social contexts. The Social Dreaming Matrix (SDM) methodology is described in detail as the best way to capture the potential of SD and a short clinical vignette from a case study is offered. An account is given of where SD is at this time, and hypotheses are advanced on where it is going as far as its application in diverse societal contexts is concerned. For instance, SD developments in Italy, *vs.* SD developments in the UK are discussed as examples of the interaction between a new idea and the cultural container that receives it. Dreams from SDMs are occasionally used in the text to capture the essence of a concept or of an experience as only dreams and poetry can do.

Burkard Sievers describes the social photo-matrix (SPM) in Chap-ter Seven. This is an experiential method for promoting the under-standing of the unconscious in organisations by viewing digital photos taken by participants. Using association, amplification, systemic thinking, and reflection, the hidden meaning and deeper experience of what usually remains unseeable can be perceived and put into thoughts. This method is based on the assumption that *photographs* are the medium for new thoughts and thinking, while the photographer remains in the background and is usually unknown. This chapter provides a description of the method, design, process, learning, and insights into what it means to use photos as a means of understanding what might be below the surface of an organisation. The author uses two case examples. The first one is a seminar with post-graduate students in a Department of Business and Economics at a German university and the second is from an SPM in a penal institution for remand prisoners in Germany. While a university setting, with students who are familiar with searching for the unconscious in social systems by using experiential learning methods, may be an almost ideal situation for a SPM, the penal institution gave ample evidence of the impediments for such work. Derived from these cases, he elaborates several issues that have a decisive impact on the role of host and for a good-enough success of an SPM.

Social dream-drawing is the socioanalytic method described by Rose Mersky in Chapter Eight. It is designed to illuminate unconscious issues in organisations and systems. Based on the theoretical formulation that dreaming is a form of unconscious thinking and that dreams can be expressions of the social unconscious, participants bring drawings of recent dreams to each session. These drawings provide a physical representation of the original illusive and often fantastic dream images, which can often be more resonant and closer to the original unconscious source than verbal renditions. Using a theme, such as "What do I risk in my work?", participants in this method freely associate to the drawings and offer amplifications, that is, parallel events in the world at large, such as political or artistic activities, that are activated by the drawing. This combination of internal processes of free association with the external context brings the unconscious thinking alive. A shift to a reflective element allows for thinking applied to the theme and for a deeper insight into current organisational reality.

OPUS: an Organisation for Promoting the Understanding of Society, was set up in 1975 by Sir Charles Goodeve, who wanted to encourage workers to have a better understanding of the dynamics of the system in which they operated, because he felt that this would help them be more reflective when considering industrial action. The concept of the Listening Post emerged as one element of the research programme established by OPUS. Chapter Nine is in two sections. In the first, Olya Khaleelee describes the early history of the Listening Post and the conceptual development of the idea, and demonstrates how OPUS explored, through its work in British society, how society is an intelligible field of study at both conscious and unconscious levels. The second section, by Lionel Stapley, describes the Listening Post methodology as it is practised today and gives an example of the method in practice.

Chapters Ten and Eleven both consider ways of working with organisational roles as part of their wider organisational systems and contexts. John Newton describes the conceptual underpinnings of organisational role analysis from its beginnings in group relations conferences through to innovations in the method. His descriptions are illustrated by two case studies that detail the work done by consultant and client. In Chapter Eleven, Susan Long outlines the method of role biography. This method helps clients to examine the various work roles they have taken up through their lives, starting in childhood through to their current work role. From examining the arising themes, consultant and client together develop hypotheses about how past roles influence current roles. The context is also found in the role history, that is, how the current organisational role was shaped through past incumbents. Finally, she describes a method using a reflection group, the members of which give access to the associative unconscious underlying the role. This provides further information to the client or client organisation about how roles are taken up and work towards organisational tasks and purposes.

Assessing the health of organisational work cultures through a socioanalytic approach takes into consideration the social context, primary task, the way the task is performed, and the lived experiences of people who work at the task. Chapter Twelve, by Jinette de Gooijer, describes the conceptual basis for a socioanalytic work culture diagnostic and the principal investigative techniques employed for interpretive assessment. Techniques described include reflexivity, workplace observation, interviews, drawing, use of metaphor, working note, and design of the feedback workshop. Two cases are described that illustrate application of the approach in a law firm and a health service. It is shown that a socioanalytic work culture diagnostic, when coupled with a programme of organisational change, is a meaningful tool for the transformation of insight into action.

"Group relations" (GR) was the phrase coined in the late 1950s by staff working at the Tavistock Institute of Human Relations to refer to the laboratory method of studying relationships in and between groups. Chapter Thirteen, by Eliat Aram and Mannie Sher, describes the nature of group relations conferences and some of the major concepts underpinning them. They describe these conferences as providing for "the accelerated study of the connections and discontinuities of person and role, of role and group, of group and group, of group and organisation, of organisation and environment". These authors discuss the history of GR conferences, their current form, and some of the recent innovations that have occurred in this method.

In Chapter Fourteen, Bruno Boccaro takes socioanalytic methods beyond groups and organisations to a country level of analysis and a method for working at this level. Socioanalytic dialogue is motivated by policy failures and discontent. Disagreements on policies provide a fertile ground for large group unconscious dynamics. As manifestation of unconscious dynamics, social defences are likely to be poorly understood, despite their impact being significant precisely when policy makers are at a loss in understanding resistance to change and disaffection with policies. As most societies face issues that might not have been sufficiently worked through, facing unfinished mourning likely to complicate the psychosocial environment in which policies are chosen and implemented, socioanalytic dialogue might allow various constituencies to internalise the nature and role of existing social defences, the internalisation then becoming a potential catalyst to a national conversation on these issues. Country case studies are examined in this chapter.

> The problem with knowledge is that it can become, as Bion noted, a carapace or shell from which the world is made sense of. While knowledge is indispensable for our functioning, unless it is cleansed and bathed in wonder it can stifle us. (Bain, Chapter Fifteen, this volume)

Fitting with Peirce's philosophy of examining the "surprising", this quote from Alastair Bain (Chapter Fifteen) reminds us that socioanalytic methods should not be treated as static pieces of knowledge, but as living processes dependent on those who work with them. His chapter discusses the experience of wonder as a transformative process at the basis of socioanalytic work.

While socioanalytic methods engage people in exploring their immediate experience, in the final chapter I (Susan Long) explore the tension between direct experience and its transformations in thinking as relevant to socioanalytic methods. The creative marriage of psychoanalysis and systems thinking by the Tavistock in the 1950s has this tension at its very heart. I also offer some points to hold in mind when creating new socioanalytic methods.

References

Aram, E., Baxter, R., & Nutkevitch, A. (Eds.) (2009). *Adaptation and Innovation: Theory, Design and Role Taking in Group Relations Conferences and their Applications.* London: Karnac.

Aram, E., Nutkevitch, A., & Baxter, R. (Eds.) (2012). *Group Relations Conferences: Tradition, Creativity and Succession in the Global Group Relations Network.* London: Karnac.

Bain, A. (1999). On socioanalysis. *Socio-Analysis, 1*(1): 1–17.

Bohm, D. (1980). *Wholeness and the Implicate Order.* London: Routledge.

Burch, R. (2010). Charles Sanders Peirce. In: E. N. Zalta (Ed.), *The Stanford Encyclopedia of Philosophy* (Fall 2010 edn). Accessed July 2012, at http://plato.stanford.edu/archives/fall2010/entries/peirce/.

Fraher, A. L. (2004). *A History of Group Study and Psychodynamic Organizations.* London: Free Association Books.

Gould, L., Stapley, L., & Stein, M. (Eds.) (2001). *The System Psychodynamics of Organizations.* New York: Karnac.

Gould, L. J. (1987). A methodology for assesssing internal working models of the organisation: applications to management and organisational development programs. Paper presented at the Annual Meeting of the International Society for the Psychoanalytic Study of Organisations, New York.

Hollway, W., & Jefferson, T. (2000). *Doing Qualitative Research Differently: Free Association, Narrative and the Interview.* London: Sage.

Hinshelwood, R. D., & Skogstad, W. (Eds.) (2000). *Observing Organisations.* London: Routledge.

Hopper, E. (2003). *The Social Unconscious: Selected Papers.* London: Jessica Kingsley.

Khaleelee, O., & Miller, E. (1985). Society as an intelligible field of study. In: M. Pines (Ed.), *Bion and Group Psychotherapy* (pp. 354–385). London: Routledge and Kegan Paul.

Kuhn, T. S. (1962). *The Structure of Scientific Revolutions*. Chicago, IL: University of Chicago Press.

Lawrence, W. G. (Ed.) (2010). *The Creativity of Social Dreaming*. London: Karnac.

Levinson, H., Molinari, J., & Spohn, A. G. (1972). *Organizational Diagnosis*. New England: Harvard University Press.

Long, S. D. (2001). Working with organizations: the contribution of the psychoanalytic discourse. *Organisational and Social Dynamics*, 2: 174–198.

Long, S. D., & Sievers, B. (Eds.) (2012). *Towards a Socioanalysis of Money, Finance and Capitalism: Beneath the Surface of the Financial Industry*. London: Routledge.

Menzies Lyth, I. E. P. (1988). *Containing Anxiety in Institutions: Selected Essays, Vol. 1*. London: Free Association Books.

Menzies Lyth, I. E. P. (1989). *The Dynamics of the Social: Selected Essays, Vol. 2*. London: Free Association Books.

Mersky, R. (2011). Social dreaming, social photo-matrix, role biography and social dream drawing: structure, facilitation capacities and fundamental value to organizations. Paper given at the Annual Meeting of the International Society for the Psychoanalytic Study of Organisations. Melbourne, June 2011.

Miller, E. J. (1990). Experiential learning in groups 1: the development of the Leicester model. In: E. Trist & H. Murray (Eds.) (1990). *The Social Engagement of Social Science Volume 1: The Socio-Psychological Perspective* (pp. 165–185). London: Free Association Books.

Newton, J., Long, S., & Sievers, B. (2006). *Coaching in Depth*. London: Karnac.

Nossal, B. (2010). The use of drawing in socio-analytic exploration. *Socio-Analysis: the Journal of the Australian Institute of Socio-Analysis*, 12: 77–92.

Patton, M. Q. (2001). *Qualitative Research and Evaluation Methods*. Thousand Oaks, CA: Sage.

Reed, B. (2001). *An Exploration of Role as Used in the Grubb Institute*. London: Grubb Institute.

Trist, E., & Murray, H. (Eds.) (1990). *The Social Engagement of Social Science Volume 1: The Socio-Psychological Perspective*. London: Free Association Books.

PART I
BACKGROUND

CHAPTER ONE

The associative unconscious

Susan Long and Maurita Harney

C harles S. Peirce defines his famous concept of "abduction" as follows: "Abduction is the process of forming an explanatory hypothesis. It is the only logical operation which introduces any new idea" (Peirce, 1903, *CP*, 5.171,[1] cited in Hoffman, 1997).

In this chapter, we describe the idea of an "associative unconscious", differentiated from the repressed dynamic unconscious so well articulated through Sigmund Freud and his followers. In looking at an associative unconscious, we will explore some of the ideas of the philosopher Charles S. Peirce, whose concept of "abductive logic" not only provides a logic to underpin psychoanalytic and socioanalytic thinking, but also provides a conceptual framework for the associative processes that we believe are central to the unconscious, especially as it is evidenced in social groupings.

A clear philosophy of science has never fully been articulated for psychoanalysis. Much discussion has centred on debates about whether or not psychoanalysis can be considered a science, given traditional views of science (Grunbaum, 1984; Webster, 1995). Following Ricoeur and Habermas, and in defence of psychoanalysis, hermeneutic definitions appeared in the mid-twentieth century,regarding psychoanalysis more as an art and a linguistic interpreter of human experience (e.g., Steele, 1979). In addition, psychoanalysis is some-times claimed to be a philosophy in itself: *sui generis*, not fitting into other categories such as psychology or social science or medicine "because in the end, if psychoanalysis develops as a mature science, it will find that the successful models are those proper to it and not those developed by analogy to other disciplines" (Etchegoyen, 1999, p. 501). Indeed, its resistance to categorisation and difficulty in finding an established place as a discipline in universities worldwide might be due to its not having a clear or established philosophical partner. While challenged from within a positivist scientific perspective for its lack of laboratory experimental confirmation, the concepts of repres-sion and the unconscious are still compelling as explanatory tools: clinically with patients, socioanalytically with groups and organisa-tions, in art and literature, in social and political analysis, and in the popular imagination. Moreover, recent neurological work questions the challenge to the scientific status of psychoanalysis (Carhart-Harris & Friston, 2010), suggesting a neurological basis for the effects of unconscious processes.

Socioanalysis is psychoanalysis linked to systems thinking in order to explore individuals (as social animals), groups, organisations, and society. We argue that the associative unconscious is as vital to under-standing socioanalytic phenomena as the repressed unconscious. The idea of an associative unconscious brings forward the notion that all human thought and meaning is implicate within human symbolic form and capacity (Bohm, 1980, 1996). This essentially means that all past, present, and future thought exists in potentiality within the capa-city to use and interpret signs and symbols. We will return to this idea later in the chapter when discussing the philosophy of Peirce. For now, because much of human thought is implicate rather than expli-cate, it is argued that it is unconsciously present to humans: that is, implicit in their symbolising capacities and processes but not realised because of multiple factors. These are factors such as: repression of unwanted thoughts; psychotic exclusion or destruction of thinking capacity; social and cultural constraints on thinking; historical progression of thoughts; developmental factors in individuals; inher-ent restrictions on thinking capacities. As with the traditional idea of the unconscious (both repressed and inherent) the associative uncon-scious influences conscious thinking, feelings, desires, and behaviours in ways of which we are unaware. Just as free association is a method of accessing the individual unconscious, there are methods of accessing the unconscious as an associative field. The methods described in this book attempt to do this.

The unconscious in psychoanalysis

Freud was the first to systematically describe and explain unconscious processes and functioning. He focused primarily on the process of repression, a process whereby unwanted or highly distressing thoughts and associated emotions are deliberately forgotten or forbidden entry to consciousness (Freud, 1915d). And yet, they are not totally forgotten, because their influence continues even while the thinker or actor is unaware of their so doing. For psychoanalytic thinkers, consciousness is just the tip of that vast iceberg that is the human mind.

In early psychoanalytic thinking, following Freud's structural theories of id, ego, and superego, the unconscious became regarded as a kind of storehouse of thoughts and feelings that are either unwanted (repressed) or unable to be consciously articulated. This is echoed in some aspects of Jungian theory, where, as well as a personal unconscious, there is a collective unconscious replete with archetypes that are unconscious thought representations of fundamental collective social experiences that transcend specific cultures.

However, the unconscious has always been considered as much more than a repository for the unwanted. Freud was well aware of this. For him, it also included inherited tendencies and many ego processes. He called it "the system Uncs" even before he developed the structural theory, implying systemic processes in thought rather than a limited store of ideas. And his dynamic theories have explored how unconscious processes permeate everyday life as well as being in the aetiology of mental illnesses. The later concept of the "id" (the "it") indicates an otherness of the unconscious apart from the human ego. Freud saw this as a system of inherited tendencies and desires, where biological drives were represented in psychic terms.

Thus, we see that the unconscious is less a "place" in a topography of the mind and more a set of processes within cognitive and emotional functioning. This view becomes clearer in Lacanian psychoanalysis, where stress is placed on the operation of the unconscious in terms of linguistic phenomena (Lacan, 1977). Metaphor and metonymy, for instance, are regarded as the basic linguistic processes found in the psychological processes of displacement and condensation: the main unconscious processes described in dream work, jokes, slips of the tongue, and in the forming of neurotic symptoms. Briefly, to clarify this: (i) metaphor = whereby one signifier takes the place of another to create new meaning (underlies displacement); for example, in Shakespeare's sonnet, the line "Shall I compare thee to a summer's day" displaces the meaning of a summer's day on to the woman concerned; (ii) metonymy = whereby one signifier stands alone for several others that are then implied (underlies condensation). The whole meaning is condensed into one word, as when "the crown" in "the Crown *vs.* Smith" is used for all functions of the law pertaining to the head of state.

But the Lacanian formulation does not mean the unconscious is just another natural language. To regard unconscious functioning as a linguistic process is not to call it another natural language, but to emphasise the symbolic basis of thought.

Symbolic functions are the very basis of human thought, whether in mathematics, the syllogisms of formal logic, natural languages and musical forms, or common sense and colloquial logic. (It should be noted here that even so-called illogical thought, as found in neurosis or even in everyday life, in fact has a symbolic logic of its own; this is one of the great discoveries of psychoanalysis and modern therapeutic "talking" treatments where a "hidden logic" is uncovered.) It is only when the symbolic function remains uncreated or destroyed, as in psychotic functioning, that the boundary between conscious and unconscious dissolves. Without the symbolic function, neither distinctly conscious nor unconscious functioning occurs, only a kind of mishmash, where "dreams" invade waking experience and words and sentences fail to hang well together but invade each other's meanings. Psychic processes, such as splitting and projective identification, dominate. The central point here is that symbolic capacity allows the unconscious (as well as consciousness beyond simple awareness) to exist. The unconscious (a distinctly human phenomenon), seemingly totally illogical with its disregard of the passing of time, its naming one thing as another, and its interference with conscious will and logic is the product of the human capacity to symbolise and to create meaning.

Beyond the individual

More correctly, this section might be called "before the individual", because our premise here is that "thought" is a social rather than an individual process. In essence, this means that the functions and bases of thought are social, even though individual thinkers are the vehicles by which ideas, thoughts, words—all of symbolic activity—are articulated and extended. Wilfred Bion talks of "thoughts in search of thinkers" (Bion, 1984). Although formulated as an aid to understanding the ways in which patients attack their own mental links and acquire the thoughts of others as their own, this hypothesis captures the notion that thoughts exist unconsciously within the infinite of a thinking community without being the sole creation or property of any of its specific individuals. Symbolic processes and their products, such as language, music and song, money, mathematics, calendars, and formalised time, belong, as it were, to the group or community. Their specific meanings are co-created and co-evolve rather than simply reflecting changes instigated by individuals.

Individuals have the capacity for conscious thinking, so they are able to draw upon thoughts (ideas/symbolic formations) available in the social field in habitual or creative ways, to utilise them in conjunction with their experience. They may gain access to this social field or network of thoughts through interactions with others or through utilising the thought tools provided in the network, such as, for example, syntactic, formal, logical, mathematical, or cultural rules and logic. In terms of their own personal histories or capacities, some part of these available thoughts might not "gain entry" to consciousness because they have been previously repressed or because local cultural mores or beliefs, or even habits of thinking, prevent this.

Bion's theory of thinking (1984) outlines how the precursors of thought—beta elements derived from direct experience—become transformed through alpha function (or not) into more sophisticated thoughts (Grotstein, 2007). The process of forming and transforming alpha elements is modulated by the cultural container in which the individual lives and experiences. It is modulated by the behaviour of the parents towards their infant, the ethical and cultural beliefs of teachers, the actions and decisions of politicians, the creativity of artists, and the creative functioning or perversity of corporations. Moreover, Bion's (1961) theories of group dynamics explain how basic assumptions in the group culture shape the experiences, thoughts, and feelings of group members. This influence occurs in the symbolic functioning of the group and the individual out of conscious awareness. The simile here is that of a fractal where the same pattern is repeated at every level of magnification of a form: in this case, society, group, individual, alpha function.

Following these ideas, we argue here that the unconscious or, more correctly, the totality of unconsciousness, is a social phenomenon. A metaphor might work here; one that is understandable in the twenty-first century. We can say the unconscious is like the "world wide web" (www). It is a network of thoughts, symbols, or signifiers, able to give rise to many feelings, impulses, and images and, importantly, able to give rise to meaning. This network is not static, but constantly changing, with new connections being made by the thinkers who are a part of it. Here, we should make a correction. By talking of "access" to the unconscious social field of thought, it could sound as if the individuals are outside the network. This is not so. The social field (or parts of it) are "*in* the individuals", which gives an impression altogether different from the individuals being "in the social field". The social field of the unconscious is in each individual in the sense that it is in the connections and the mental associations between them (Long, 1992). The boundary marked by the word "individual" is not adequate. Mind is social (Harré, 1984). The boundary between individuals is more extensive when we speak of the associative unconscious. By talking of an individual "accessing" the associative unconscious, we refer to those processes whereby the unconscious social field of thoughts can be articulated or utilised in thinking.

The associative unconscious

Here, then, is a formulation of the unconscious as a mental network of thoughts, signs, and symbols or signifiers, able to give rise to many feelings, impulses, and images. The network is between people, but yet within each of them. The boundary of the unconscious does not coincide with the boundary of the individual, despite the necessity of the boundary of "individual" for other functions, including the functions described by Bion in his theory of thinking: the functions of the thinker, or, as we shall discuss later, the functions of the interpretant in Peirce's philosophy.

The associative unconscious might be conceptualised as a "pool of thoughts", much as Darwin's pool of genes, but that is too static. We have used the term "network", but that too readily gives an idea of a combination of "things" in physical space, whereas we conceptualise it as in psychic space. The associative unconscious might be seen as similar to Jung's idea of the collective unconscious, but there are differences. Jung says:

> My thesis then, is as follows: in addition to our immediate conscious-ness, which is of a thoroughly personal nature and which we believe to be the only empirical psyche (even if we tack on the personal unconscious as an appendix), there exists a second psychic system of a collective, universal, and impersonal nature which is identical in all individuals. This collective unconscious does not develop individually but is inherited. It consists of pre-existent forms, the archetypes, which can only become conscious secondarily and which give definite form to certain psychic contents. (Jung, 1969, p. 43)

Despite similarities, in contrast to the idea of the collective uncon-scious, the associative unconscious is not "identical in all individuals" because each individual holds *only a part of the vaster whole*. A metaphor here is that of a jigsaw puzzle where each individual part is shaped very differently, yet the picture as a whole has its own unique integrity. In this case, the whole network is supra-individual, with the system-as-a-whole capable of producing, for example, archetypes as system-wide symbols (the whole puzzle put together) that are then able to be introjected by individuals. Hence, such symbols may appear in different parts of the system (for instance, in individuals, groups, or cultures) contemporaneously. The idea of an associative unconscious does refer to shared representations, but not necessarily representa-tions that are inherited and held identically in each individual, as with Jung's collective unconscious. What is in common between individu-als is the capacity to symbolise and to co-create meanings, not the specific representations that *as a result of* co-creation thus are held within the culture.

The dynamics we hypothesise as involved here are akin to those described by Freud in his paper on narcissism (Freud, 1914c). He describes the infant at first in a state of primary narcissism or auto-eroticism. Self-love (secondary narcissism) only occurs with the devel-opment of the ego after the infant comes to love another (e.g., the mother). Then, having once loved another, the infant can love herself (her own ego) *as if* she were another. This, one could say, is a social relation to the self. This social relation implies an essentially split or "double" self, an "I" that loves and a "me" or ego that is loved.

Similarly, then, individuals have shared representations, that is, co-created meanings as part of a social relation. Each contributes and relates to others and, in so doing, is able to relate to the co-created associative system through its introjection. Here, we are not hypothesising an inherent associative unconscious, only an inherent, almost automatic, capacity to become part of a broader systemic process.

The associative unconscious as a system holds a set of processes of symbolisation constrained only by current expressions. Bion talked of the "infinite" rather than the unconscious (Bion, 1984). This allows for this social, mental network to be infinitely expanded beyond what explicitly it now is. This implies that all possibilities of thought are "implicate" when articulating the idea that all potentialities in a given system exist contemporaneously as the system exists and, it would seem, as it expands. Such possibilities simply need the conditions to unfold.

So, the associative unconscious is the infinite of human thought in all its possibilities. For individuals, their capacities and histories might cause repression of that portion of the associative unconscious that they might have gained access to initially but are now unable to tolerate. At times, a psychotic function or process might deny access or, alternatively, swamp the individual or group in the network such that normal thinking is precluded. For many, the constraints of particular cultures such as national, corporate, gender, or familial cultures pose barriers to access. However, because of the associative unconscious (that which is implicate but not yet conscious) new thoughts and new combinations of thought are possible. Hence, the associative unconscious is the crucible of creativity.

A philosophy of science for socioanalysis and psychoanalysis

In his paper "The unconscious" (1915e), Sigmund Freud argues a justification for the concept.

> It is *necessary* because the data of consciousness have a very large number of gaps in them; both in healthy and in sick people psychical

acts often occur which can be explained only by presupposing other acts, of which, nevertheless consciousness affords no evidence. These not only include parapraxes and dreams in healthy people, and everything described as a psychical symptom or an obsession in the sick; our most personal daily experience acquaints us with ideas that come into our head we do not know from where, and intellectual conclusions arrived at we do not know how. All these conscious acts remain disconnected and unintelligible if we insist upon claiming that every mental act that occurs in us must also necessarily be experienced by us through consciousness; on the other hand, they fall into a demonstrable connection if we interpolate between them the unconscious acts that we have inferred. (Freud, 1915e, p. 160)

Here, the father of psychoanalysis has argued that the concept of the unconscious is necessary because it explains certain effects that otherwise seem inexplicable.

The idea of making sense of puzzling and disconnected "symptoms" by inferring a hypothesis that connects those items into a coherent explanatory narrative is not unlike the work of the fictional detective using clues to infer a hypothesis connecting those clues to events which have occurred in the past. This similarity has not gone unnoticed by followers of Charles Sanders Peirce, an early twentieth century American philosopher of science. Peirce introduced the term "abduction" to describe the initial, creative phase in scientific enquiry, the phase of discovery sometimes described as "a flash of insight" whereby a hypothesis is formed to explain some surprising fact. Peirce saw abduction as a form of logic, alongside but different from, and irreducible to, induction and deduction. Elsewhere, he calls it a method of enquiry. It has the following form:

A surprising fact, C, is observed.

But if H were true, then C would be a matter of course

So, . . . (hypothetically) . . . H is true. (Peirce, 1903, CP 5.189)

An example of this is Kepler's observation of anomalies in the path traced out by the planet Mars, leading him to the hypothesis that Mars travels an elliptical orbit (rather than the circular orbit habitually believed by the astronomers of his day).

To satisfy the norms of scientific method and give us confidence in the truth of our hypothesis, that hypothesis must be tested. But this is a later, and separate, stage in the process of scientific enquiry. It is here that the methods of deduction and induction come in to play. Prior to testing, the hypothesis can only be held tentatively "as an interrogative" (Peirce, 1901, *HP* 2.898–899; also *CP* 2.544*n*) without any confidence in the probability of its truth. Abduction presents us with *possibilities*: its conclusions give us something novel or different, but not yet *probabilities*. Our hypothesis is subjected to testing by induction, which consists in accumulating data or instances that confirm the hypothesis, or by deduction, which tests the hypothesis by applying it to further cases. Deduction gives us certainty. For example, a valid deduction has the following form: "All dogs are mammals; Fido is a dog; so, Fido is a mammal." Here, the conclusion can be held with confidence. However, it produces no new knowledge, since the conclusion is already contained in the premises. As Peirce puts it, across the three forms of abduction, induction, and deduction, *uberty* decreases as *security* increases: "uberty" means "fruitfulness, productiveness", also rich growth, fertility, copiousness, abundance; security means the degree of confidence we can have that our hypothesis is true.

While "uberty" usefully characterises the products of abduction, "ubiquity" best describes its application. Abduction can be seen to operate in a vast array of contexts, ranging from the mundane, everyday interactions with the world to the truly spectacular creations of science and art. Cultural historian Carlo Ginzburg describes a method of enquiry that serves to connect the insights of Sherlock Holmes, Freud, and nineteenth-century art connoisseur Giovanni Morelli, all of whom are sharp observers of detail (either anomalous or seemingly trivial), and all of whom are responsible for discoveries regarded as highly creative.

"Morelli's method", as it was known, consisted in authenticating paintings by focusing not on the large stylistic features, but on the minor, seemingly irrelevant details such as fingernails, earlobes, etc., that served as clues to establish authorship of the work. These revealing "clues" have been left by the artist, in Morelli's words, "almost unconsciously". As Ginzburg remarks, "What is striking here is the way that the innermost core of the artist's individuality is linked with elements beyond conscious control" (Ginzburg, 1983, p. 87).

There are actual historical connections between Freud and Morelli: in *The Moses of Michelangelo* (1914b), Freud reports his great interest in meeting an art connoisseur who turned out to be none other than Morelli. While this is interesting in light of Morelli's reference to the concept of the "unconscious", what really impressed Freud was Morelli's method:

> It seems to me that his method of inquiry is closely related to the technique of psychoanalysis. It too, is accustomed to divine secret and concealed things from despised or unnoticed features, from the rubbish-heap, as it were, of our observations . . . (quoted in Ginzburg, 1983, pp. 84–85)

Indeed, the quotation at the beginning of this section shows that Freud is no stranger to the practice of abduction, not only in his actual use of the psychoanalytic method, but also by the fact of the very reasoning he uses in this quotation to infer that there is such a thing as the unconscious.

While Ginzburg himself does not use the term "abduction", it is clear that the method shared by Morelli, Sherlock Holmes, and Freud is an elaboration of Peirce's abductive method of enquiry. This method is evident in the practices of hunters, trackers, and even diviners of ancient times, as well as palaeontologists, historians, and medical practitioners. It is traceable to early forms of "knowledge acquisition", such as divination and astrology, any form of enquiry that proceeds as an inference from puzzling disconnected scraps of information— clues, hints, traces, symptoms—to the formation of a hypothesis which would explain those items by connecting them to a reality that is otherwise opaque and inaccessible. For Peirce, abduction characterises our day-to-day perceptions, for example, my perceptual recognition of the object in my garden as an azalea (Peirce, 1901, *HP* 2.899–2.900). These commonplace abductions are continuously inductively confirmed so that they become habitual and unnoticed. At the other end of the spectrum are those scientific discoveries, like Kepler's, that yield bold, highly creative new hypotheses.

Ginzburg links this method to "a cognitive model that is at once very ancient and very new" (Ginzberg, 1983, p. 102). He calls this the conjectural model of knowledge. "Conjecture" is often used to mean guess. However, the conjectural model serves to show that what we often categorise as "mere guesswork" can, on closer reflection, turn out to be an abductive process, although not necessarily recognised as such.

The autonomy of abduction as a logical form irreducible to deduction and induction means we can focus on the structural aspects of the creative phase of enquiry (which is still important, although only one stage in scientific enquiry). This is important in considerations of how abduction might be fruitfully used as a "respectable" method of psycho- and socioanalytic enquiry. For it means that questions about "scientific status" can be put on hold while we examine features of enquiry in "the conjectural paradigm" as a domain of interest in its own right.

Psychoanalysis seeks an understanding of a reality that is individual, particular, unique, just as socioanalysis seeks an understanding of the unique social system. The "clues" it works from are often produced unconsciously. Moreover, the events that are causally responsible for these clues are non-repeatable. In this respect, psychoanalysis shares a methodological orientation with other fields of enquiry such as crime detection, history, palaeontology, and medical diagnosis. In all of these cases, the object of the enquiry is knowledge about events—causes—which are unique, singular, deeply individual, often produced unconsciously or involuntarily, and are accessible only through their effects: "When causes cannot be repeated, there is no alternative but to infer them from their effects" (Ginzburg, 1983, p. 103).

But what of the status of abduction as a research methodology? Is it a form of logic or a method of enquiry? A flash of insight or an inference? Reasoning or instinct? Inference or creative leap? Peirce, at various times, described it in all of these ways.

Making sense of these seemingly contradictory characterisations involves some abductive work in its own right. While this is not the place to expound Peirce's broader philosophy of science, there are aspects of it that help to dismantle what appear to be mutually exclusive disjunctions and dichotomies. These include: his process-based metaphysics (characterised as creative evolution), which makes his methodological ideas particularly suitable for the analysis of complex systems; his (non-Cartesian) view of cognition as mediated and as encompassing perceptual experiences more generally; his view of scientific enquiry as a communal process; his "pragmaticist" philosophy which, like other forms of philosophical pragmatism, casts central philosophical concepts like "truth", "meaning", and "knowledge" as forms of doing, that is, action-related.

Insisting on the *logical* status of abduction is partly motivated by Peirce's anti-psychologism, that is, his resistance to the idea that the laws of logic, a normative discipline, can be reduced to the descriptive, empirical generalisations of psychology. However, it also indicates that his notion of logic is somewhat broader than those usually espoused (Hoffman, 1997). But, it might be objected, to qualify as "logic", a process of reasoning or thinking must have norms, and this is something that abduction appears to lack, yielding, as it does, some untested hypothesis. To this, we might respond by asking whether the norms in the case of abduction need to be the same as for other aspects of scientific enquiry? As the creative phase in the process of discovery, it seems reasonable to suppose that the norms governing abductive logic might be of a kind more appropriate to narrative, that is, norms of an aesthetic nature, employing notions such as "elegance", "coherence", and subject to constraints relating to imagination rather than "reason" (in its conventional sense). Indeed, the plausibility of this suggestion is strengthened when we notice that, for Peirce, logic and mathematics, as well as scientific enquiry, are ultimately subordinate to the aesthetic.

When we think about the purposes of human enquiry more generally, we can draw on Peirce's philosophy to question whether there is such a gulf between the scientific and the creative. Are aesthetic norms totally different from scientific ones? For Peirce, the requirement of science is that it be "truth-conducive" in a non-positivistic sense. Peirce, as a pragmatist, espoused a notion of truth tied to efficacy of action. That is to say, truth is to be understood in terms of what we *do* rather than "correctness or accuracy of representations": truth-conduciveness must be understood in terms of process or action.

While rejecting psycholog*ism*, Peirce clearly had no problem in allowing that abduction involved both psychological and logical elements. For Peirce, abduction is *both* insight (or instinct) *and* inference, and *both* inference *and* creative aesthetics (Anderson, 1987). He was able to claim this because of his non-Cartesian approach to cognition. Unlike Descartes, Peirce never subscribed to the view that the mind or consciousness is transparent to itself. Even self-knowledge in the form of self-awareness is not an indubitable immediate "given" (what Descartes called "intuition"), but is based on an inference. Cognition is always mediated. On this basis, the notion of the unconscious presents no conceptual problems for Peirce's philosophy of mind.

Related to this is the consideration that the "surprising fact" that initiates the abduction can be a perception in any sense-modality: a smell, a taste, a sound, etc. For Peirce, it can be argued, there is no inconsistency in claiming that abduction is "insight", "instinct", *and* "inference". Paavola suggests "there is some sort of continuum from animal instinct that is determinate and well adapted for certain purposes, to human instinct that is more flexible but at the same time more fallible" (Paavola, 2005, p. 22). In fact, for Peirce, reason *is* a sort of instinct (Peirce, 1913, *EP*,[1] p. 472). He even suggests that newly hatched chickens display something like this "rational instinct" in their ability to successfully find food among random barnyard scraps (Peirce, 1901, *HP*[1] 2.900). It has not gone unnoticed that, had Peirce been able to access the ideas of later writers such as Michael Polanyi, David Bohm, Francesco Varela, and Hubert Dreyfus, he might well have gone on to consider the possibility of "implicit or embodied" abduction.

A "logic of association" is present at the very beginning of the abductive process. The first premise of the abduction is the feeling of surprise which involves the breaking of "some habit of expectation" (Peirce, 1908, *CP* 6.469):

> I ask you whether at that instant of surprise there is not a double consciousness, on the one hand of an Ego, which is simply the expected idea suddenly broken off, on the other hand of the Non-Ego, which is the Strange Intruder, in his abrupt entrance. (Peirce, 1903, *EP*, p. 154)

This has echoes of the suggestion that ideas may emerge strangely from the unconscious as from "another place" (Lacan, 1977).

The second premise is the synthesising of this surprising fact with a "like" state of affairs, a situation recognised as similar, either known or invented, which would make sense of that fact:

> This synthesis [which] suggest(s) a new connection or hypothesis, is the Abduction . . . It is recognised that the phenomena are like, i.e., constitute an Icon of, a replica or a general conception, or Symbol. This is not accepted as shown to be true, nor even probable in the techni-cal sense . . . but it is shown to be likely, in the sense of being some sort of approach to the truth, in an indefinite sense. The conclusion is drawn in the interrogative mood. (Peirce, 1903, *EP*, p. 287)

For Peirce, an icon is a technical term defined as a sign that is related to its object by virtue of a similarity, likeness, analogy, or resemblance. It serves to position abduction in relation to Peirce's own system of logic, known as "semiotics". This is a logic of meanings rather than truth conditionality (although meanings are a vehicle to truth in Peirce's sense).

Peircian semiotics: inference, interpretation, and natural systems

Fundamental to Peirce's semiotics is the notion of the sign, understood as a triadic unity of something (a *sign-vehicle* or *representamen*, such as a footprint) which stands to somebody (the *interpretant*) for something (the *object*—the person, animal that had passed by). So, if I see smoke on the horizon, I take this to be a sign of fire. The relationship here is a triadic one of sign-vehicle (smoke), object (fire) and interpretant (myself). For Peirce, *semiosis* is the process of generating signs; *semiotics* is the study of signs. Peirce stated that "the universe is perfused by signs, if not entirely composed of them" (Peirce, *CP* 5.488*n*), a point we will return to later.

Peirce gives us a rich taxonomy of signs and the different kinds of associations they make, beginning with a threefold classification of signs, based on their *ground*: an *iconic* sign stands for its object by virtue of some similarity or likeness, for example, a map, a picture, a drawing; an *indexical* sign stands for its object by means of an existential or causal relationship, for example, smoke, weather vane, medical symptoms, footprints, animal droppings. A *symbolic* sign stands for its object by virtue of convention, habit, or rule, for example, a life-saver flag; "cat". All language is symbolic. These classifications are not mutually exclusive. For example, a footprint can be an icon (resembles the shape of a foot), or an index (is causally related to the actual foot), or a symbol (when used on the sand to form a letter, e.g., "Help").

Peirce's semiotic theory and his classification of signs offer a rich resource for developing a logic of association. Umberto Eco's semiotic approach to linguistics (Eco, 1984) combines literary tropes such as metaphor, metonymy, and synecdoche with Peircean signs and with abductive reasoning. His novel, *The Name of the Rose*, is a flamboyant game of abductive reasoning that complements his more technical academic work. So, for Eco, an indexical sign, such as hoof-prints being a sign that a horse has passed by, exhibits a metonymic association, in this case, a relation of contiguity between the clue and its inferred cause (Harney, 1994).

There are significant differences between Peirce's *semiotics* and the Saussurean-based *sémiologie* which is the theoretical basis of Lacan's ideas: Saussurean signs are dyadic, a direct pairing of *signifier* and *signified* (of word and object or concept), whereas, for Peirce, signs are irreducibly triadic (*sign-vehicle–object–interpretant*). A Peircean sign, like a clue or symptom, embodies an inference from the observed clue or symptom to its cause. For example, "red spots" as a sign of measles involves an inference from the observed symptom (*sign-vehicle*) to the causally related medical condition (*object*). It is a process mediated, in this case, by the diagnostician's interpretation (*interpretant*). In this respect, for Peirce, language is no different. It is not just the juxtaposition of sign, "cat", with the object, cat, as Saussurean approaches suggest. For Peirce, the word "cat", if it is to mean anything, implies an inference from the mere sound or visual percept, "cat", to the object, cat. In this case, unlike the case of red spots or hoof-prints, the inference is so habitual and familiar as to be "quasi-automatic", but none the less inferential or mediated for all that. In a very broad sense, we might say that Saussurean signs are referential, and Peirce's are inferential. This does not mean Peirce denies the *symbolic* function of human language. In the example just discussed, the ground of the association of the word "cat" with the actual cat is a matter of linguistic rules or conventions rather than a causal relation (as for indexes) or a likeness relation (as for icons). Recognition of the conventional nature of linguistic meaning is something shared by both Peirce and Saussure.

Saussure's theory of signs as a dyadic unity or direct pairing of signifier and signified belongs to a theory of culture which in turn is built on a theory of language: culture is like language. For Peirce, however, signs belong to a philosophy of nature, with human culture and human symbolic thought being but a sub-class of this (Hawkes, 2003).

For Peirce, signs pervade the universe. Peirce offers the example of the sunflower bending towards the sun as an instance of semiosis in nature (Peirce, 1902, *CP* 2.274). In this case, the interpretant is the genetic makeup of the plant, which represents a kind of "frozen past" to become part of a new semiosis for future generations (Hoffmeyer,

1998). The interpretant of a process of semiosis can become the sign-vehicle for a further act of semiosis, extending *ad infinitum*. So, although "the interpretant" in Peirce's triadic unity can be a human agent, it is not necessarily so. Cognition is an instance of semiosis, or meaning generation, but it is not the source. Ransdell suggests that an interpreter's interpretation can be seen "primarily (as) a perception or an observation of the meaning exhibited by the sign itself" (Ransdell, 1997, par. 2).

The context for these somewhat puzzling ideas is Peirce's philosophy of nature and its underlying ontology of processes and relations rather than a static, atomistic one. It has much in common with the *Gaia* hypothesis (Lovelock, 1995), which conceptualises nature as a vast interconnected organism. For Peirce, signs as vehicles of communication connect all of nature into a dynamic system of relationships that, for him, are semiotic relations. So, for example, the dance of the bees communicates the location of food, the sun communicates the source of light to the plant, etc., and these are all instances of semiosis or meaning generation (Sebeok, 1991). While Peirce himself did not elaborate on semiosis in nature, subsequent writers have extended his insights by showing that semiosis is exhibited in biotic systems generally. Through this, a new field of enquiry known as *biosemiotics* has been spawned.

Bion's idea of "thoughts without a thinker" finds surprising parallels in Peirce's philosophy of nature, where we find the suggestion that meaning generation is not necessarily the product of a human mind, perhaps not even of collective human minds, but located in natural living systems. In Peirce's semiotics, meaning is decoupled from the conscious individual mind ("the cogniser"). Even when semiosis is operative in the cognitive domain, there is no reason to suppose that it is the operation of a *conscious* mind (Ransdell, 1997).

The associative unconscious as a crucible for abductive logic and creativity

The unconscious as a field of associations is fertile ground for the social researcher and the organisational consultant, whose task is to tap these interconnections, using only chaotic, seemingly disconnected "bits and pieces" of human phenomena as clues. Understood semiotically, the "associative unconscious" is part of a dynamic system of meaning-generating processes (semiosis), both conscious and unconscious, which, being evolutionary processes, extend back in time and project forward infinitely into the future. These processes include, but are not restricted to, the cognitive processes, both conscious and unconscious, of individuals, groups, and societies.

If there is a logic of enquiry associated with this way of understanding unconscious processes, then Peirce's abduction seems to provide the appropriate model. Abduction, as a logic of creativity, discovery, or insight, is well suited to enquiries governed by the aesthetic norms associated with narrative and imagination. Dreams, drawings, metaphors, and idiosyncratic musings can all serve as vehicles of the unsettling feeling, the "surprising fact", which motivates the abductive process which "break(s) into" and disrupts our habits of expectation. The abductive "reasoning" then proceeds by way of a logic of association which sustains the process of "making sense" of what had been puzzling, unsettling, disturbing.

The abductive model of enquiry can fruitfully encompass or frame those applied methodologies in organisational research that aspire to be "scientific", and which require the further step of testing by induction and deduction. In such cases, Peirce's philosophy invites us to reflect carefully on what we mean by "scientific", and our understanding of the norms of "truth", "proof", and "evidence".

Peirce's abduction gives us a result that is risky: it can only be held tentatively, awaiting further confirmation. It leaves us with an *interrogative*—a further question. Abduction results in a "working hypothesis", and this suggests a "work in progress". There is even a sense in which we might want to claim that it is the interrogative, the "existential" working hypothesis, rather than a final answer, that is the ultimate goal of psychoanalytic and socioanalytic enquiry.

Note

1.   Peirce citations for *CP* and *HP* (see References, below) give volume and paragraph numbers, together with original date, where available. Citations for *EP* give page numbers.

References

Anderson, D. R. (1987). *Creativity and the Philosophy of C. S. Peirce*. Dordrecht: Martinus Nijhoff.

Bion, W. R. (1961). *Experiences in Groups*. London: Tavistock.

Bion, W. R. (1984). *Second Thoughts*. London: Karnac.

Bohm, D. (1980). *Wholeness and the Implicate Order*. London: Routledge and Kegan Paul.

Bohm, D. (1996). *On Creativity*. London: Routledge.

Carhart-Harris, R. L., & Friston, K. J. (2010). The default-mode, ego-functions and free-energy: a neurobiological account of Freudian ideas. *Brain*, *133*: 1265–1283.

Eco, U. (1984). *Semiotics and the Philosophy of Language*. Bloomington, IN: Indiana University Press.

Etchegoyen, R. H. (1999). *Fundamentals of Psychoanalytic Technique*. London: Karnac.

Freud, S. (1914b). *The Moses of Michelangelo*. S.E., *13*: 211–238. London: Hogarth.

Freud, S. (1914c). On narcissism: an introduction. *S.E. 14*: 67–102. London: Hogarth.

Freud, S. (1915d). Repression. *S.E.*, *14*: 141–158. London: Hogarth.

Freud, S. (1915e). The unconscious. *S.E.*, *14*: 161–215. London: Hogarth.

Ginzburg, C. (1983). Clues: Morelli, Freud, and Sherlock Holmes. In: U. Eco & T. A. Sebeok (Eds.), *The Sign of Three: Dupin, Holmes, Peirce* (pp. 81–118). Bloomington, IN: Indiana University Press.

Grotstein, J. S. (2007). *A Beam of Intense Darkness: Wilfred Bion's Legacy to Psychoanalysis*. London: Karnac.

Grunbaum, A. (1984). *The Foundations of Psychoanalysis: A Philosophical Critique*. Berkeley, CA: University of California Press.

Harney, M. (1994). Clues to creativity. In: T. Dartnall (Ed.), *Artificial Intelligence and Creativity* (pp. 195–208). Dordrecht: Kluwer.

Harré, R. (1984). Social elements as mind. *British Journal of Medical Psychology*, *57*: 127–135.

Hawkes, T. (2003). *Structuralism and Semiotics* (revised edn). London: Methuen.

Hoffman, M. (1997). Is there a "logic" of abduction? In: *Proceedings of the 6th Congress of the IASS-AIS, International Association for Semiotic Studies*, Guadalajara, Mexico, July, 13–18.

Hoffmeyer, J. (1998). The unfolding semiosphere. In: G. Van de Vijver, S. Salthe, & M. Delpos (Eds.), *Evolutionary Systems: Biological and*

Epistemological Perspectives on Selection and Self-Organization (pp. 281–293). Dordrecht: Kluwer.

Jung, C. G. (1969). The archetypes and the collective unconscious, *C.W., 9*. London: Routledge and Kegan Paul.

Lacan, J. (1977). *Ecrits*. London: Tavistock.

Long, S. D. (1992). *A Structural Analysis of Small Groups.* London: Routledge.

Lovelock, J. (1995). *Gaia: A New Look at Life on Earth.* Oxford: Oxford University Press.

Paavola, S. (2005). Peircean abduction: instinct, or inference? *Semiotica, 153*(1/4): 131–154. References are to online draft.

Peirce, C. S. (1931–1935 & 1958). *Collected Papers of Charles Sanders Peirce (CP)*, Volumes I–VI, C. Hartshorne & P. Weiss (Eds.) 1931–1935, and Volumes VII–VIII, A. W. Burks (Ed.), 1958. Cambridge, MA: Harvard University Press.

Peirce, C. S. (1985). *Historical Perspectives on Peirce's Logic of Science: A History of Science (HP)*, 2 vols., C. Eisele (Ed.), Berlin: Mouton-DeGruyter. References are to volume and page numbers.

Peirce, C. S. (1992–1998). *The Essential Peirce. Selected Philosophical Writings (EP), vol. 2, 1893–1913*, The Peirce Edition Project (Ed.). Bloomington, IN: Indiana University Press. References are to page numbers.

Ransdell, J. (1997). Teleology and the autonomy of the semiotic process. www.cspeirce.com/menu/library/aboutcsp/ransdell/autonomy.htm [03.03.2012].

Sebeok, T. A. (1991). *A Sign Is Just a Sign*. Bloomington, IN: Indiana University Press

Webster, R. (1995). *Why Freud Was Wrong: Sin, Science and Psychoanalysis.* Oxford: Orwell Press.

CHAPTER TWO

Work culture analysis and reflective space

James Krantz

Introduction

T he task of this chapter is to discuss work culture analysis, case study, and working hypotheses as part of the overall constellation of socioanalytic methods. This brings to mind a wonderful story told by my colleague, Tom Gilmore, about the little boy sitting in class, learning about different cloud formations: nimbus, cirrus, cumulus, and so on. Excitedly, he runs out after class to identify them, but is disheartened to discover that in reality they are not so distinct. The harder he looks, the more they blur and the more difficult it is to distinguish them: so, too, with many of the topics addressed in this volume.

This is, I believe, because there are some underlying commonalities to all socioanalytic approaches. My attempt here is to discuss these three "technologies", and to put them into the broader context of the socioanalytic paradigm with its underlying unifying elements. Only then, I think, does it really make sense why we do what we do in the way that we do it.

First, I discuss culture analysis, recognising that there is no fixed definition of this method. I will identify some of the qualities that distinguish it from other approaches, such as the use of working hypotheses and working notes as a basis for establishing collaborative enquiry. Organisational analysis or cultural analysis is *prima facia* a case study, since it is an attempt to understand a single organisation. As a result, the culture analysis has a dual role as both an intended catalyst for change as well as a method of enquiry.

Ultimately, though, what distinguishes socioanalytic culture analysis is that it is a way of creating reflective space for clients to understand their own systems, to recognise unseen forces that affect their ability to accomplish work, and ultimately enable them to take action. I see "socioanalytic methods" as an array of intellectual technologies aimed at the discovery of relevant and meaningful knowledge about the shared work world, knowledge that resides below the surface. Equating "technology" with machines or computers constricts a deeper appreciation of its meaning. The word technology originates in Greek ($\tau\epsilon\chi\nu o\lambda o\gamma\iota\alpha$ or technología) and is derived from $\tau\acute{\epsilon}\chi\nu\eta$ (*téchñ*), meaning "art, skill, craft," and -$\lambda o\gamma\iota\alpha$ (*-logía*), meaning "study of". Technology refers to the tools, processes, and systems that humans discover and develop to get things done. From this perspective, socioanalytic methods can be considered as technologies.

All socioanalytic methods have one thing in common: they are aimed at creating the conditions for reflection. Reflection, in general, and work culture analysis in particular, excavates this knowledge. Just as dreams might be the royal road to the unconscious, shared reflective practice is the socioanalytic pathway to understanding work cultures, the unconscious background of organisations, and for the development of meaningful working hypotheses that serve as a platform for reflective enquiry.

Given the central place of reflection and reflective practice in the socioanalytic approach to culture analysis, the second part of this chapter is a discussion of reflection in organisations, again from a socioanalytic perspective, and an effort to identify some challenges in creative reflective space. The challenges to creative reflective space are, given my working hypothesis here, equivalent to the challenges of conducting culture analysis.

But this poses several questions: what do we mean by culture, by cultural analysis, and by working hypotheses, or by "reflection"? What is case study methodology and how does it fit into all of this? This chapter is an attempt to explore these questions.

Culture has been studied and analysed from many different perspectives. Culture is a system of symbols and signs that people use to make sense out of their experience in organisations (Geertz, 1973). It is the symbolic context through which they think and feel. Building on this approach, Schein developed a widely used set of specific ideas about organisational culture as:

> the pattern of basic assumptions that a given group has invented, discovered or developed in learning to cope with its problems of external adaptation and internal integration—a pattern of assumptions that has worked well enough to be considered valid and, therefore, to be taught to new members as the correct way to perceive, think, and feel in relation to those problems. (Schein, 1985, p. 28)

These basic assumptions, says Schein, can be categorised into five dimensions: humanity's relationship to nature; the nature of reality and truth; the nature of human nature; the nature of human activity; the nature of human relationships.

It is important to emphasise that culture is not the overt behaviour or the surface reality of an organisation. And it is certainly not the stated mission, values, or vision statement, or other efforts to articulate a desired self-image. It refers to what is "under the surface", the assumptions and beliefs that underlie surface reality and that determine much of what occurs.

Socioanalysis, however, adds a particular dimension to understanding culture because it builds on the systems psychodynamic tradition that understands the organisational world from the perspective of the "seam" between systems theory and psychodynamics. The open systems framework refers to concepts that provide an understanding of the structural and formal aspects of an organisation. These include its design, division of labour, levels of authority, and reporting relationships; the nature of work tasks, processes, and activities; its mission and primary task. The "socio" dimension also conveys the fact that psychoanalytic perspectives are being applied in group, organisational, and social contexts.

The analytic refers to those psychoanalytic concepts that provide an understanding of irrational and often unconscious aspects of individual, group, and social processes. Because these processes often function outside of conscious awareness, they might have a significant impact on an organisation's work, and simultaneously on the emotional and psychological well-being of those who work within it. These are largely derived from Freud, Winnicott, and Kleinian object relations theory.

Understanding irrationality and ameliorating covert conflicts and anxieties can affect how well the organisation functions and performs its tasks and, at the same time, enhances the emotional well-being of those who live and work within the ever widening circles of families, groups, organisations, and communities. Socioanalytic enquiry demonstrates that what appears on the surface as simple organisational problems actually express unrecognised emotional conflicts. As a result, addressing surface problems, or symptoms, in systemic terms, either does nothing or actually aggravates the situation, because symptoms often function as a defence against the anxieties stimulated by the underlying problems. I recently came across a quote of Heraclitus, who pointed in this direction with the statement that: "Whoever cannot seek the unforeseen sees nothing for the known way is an impasse" (cited in Kahn, 1979).

Socioanalytic cultural analysis is an effort to get to those problems, and to do so in a way that enables client systems to take developmental steps. Another important point of differentiation is the *methodology* of socioanalytic cultural analysis. Consultants typically work from an "expert" position, are regarded as possessing superior knowledge about the client organisation's problems, and issue a report recommending reorganisation of one sort or another. Most of the consulting industry is based on this approach. Vast amounts of money are directed to these kinds of solutions. I believe there is an important place for this kind of consulting, especially because the rapid increase in complexity and the rate of change leads to many situations where the knowledge necessary to solve problems does not reside within the organisation itself.

Often, though, this model is deployed defensively, as if the problem resides entirely outside of the clients themselves. Also, frequently, the desired effects never materialise precisely because underlying cultural and socio-psychological factors are neglected or avoided.

Socioanalytic analysis takes a dramatically different approach. This approach takes the position that the consultant and client each bring a particular expertise to the challenge of problem solving and what ultimately matters is how the thinking of the client evolves through this engagement. Both consultant and client are learning through joint exploration. Anyone who has worked from this stance for any length of time has experienced powerful forces to induce him or her into the expert role. Resisting is difficult; the underlying defensive idealisation can be very gratifying. Ideally, one can keep—or regain—one's wits enough to identify this dynamic as an expression of the underlying anxieties and put it to the service of learning with the client. All transferential and countertransferential patterns offer rich opportunities for furthering understanding, if they can be harnessed to the task at hand.

The tension between these two models of consulting, the "expert model" and, shall we say, the "reflective model", can be found in a longstanding debate in the philosophy of science between two kinds of "knowing": explanation and understanding. With explanation, the authority for confirming or disconfirming hypotheses comes from data that are generated independently of the hypotheses. For the "understanding" model, also known as interpretative or hermeneutic methods, the authority for refining and replacing hypotheses arises from within the field of enquiry itself, whether it is a text, group, or organisation. It is self-reflexive.

The "explanation" model has the upper hand. This positivist approach is very handy when it comes to technology and the physical sciences, but when it comes to human affairs, positivist approaches have been found sorely lacking. Many practitioners today see a modest swing of the pendulum in organisations because of the (often desperate) searching for meaning at work. Socioanalytic methods, and cultural analysis in particular, are particularly well suited to meet that desire while, at the same time, helping organisations improve their overall functioning. Socioanalysis has long recognised that individual and organisational development are inseparable.

Creating the conditions for this kind of mutual exploration is the first and greatest challenge. I would like to put forward the idea that there are two distinct, though related, planes on which this must rest. One is the conduct of the cultural analysis with the client system. This involves the "social technologies" of data gathering, hypothesis generation, working note development, and subsequent dialogue. The second is a more general and elusive question of creating a reflective space. As I mentioned above, underlying culture analysis (and all socioanalytic methods) is the creation of reflective space in organisations. This allows for the creative function discussed in Chapter One of this book. Following a discussion of the social technology of cultural analysis, I shall discuss this second plane.

The social technology of socioanalytic culture analysis

There are many ways to conduct the "data gathering" phase. Most commonly, a series of interviews (possibly both group and individual) serves as the foundation (see Chapter Five). This can be complemented by review of archival material, observation of meetings and other important events, understanding the challenges posed by the technologies utilised, etc. Projective methods such as "mental maps" and social photo matrices can also be used to good effect. The dimensions of the data gathering phase need to be carefully negotiated at the start of any engagement.

Personally, I find stories the most illuminating source of data. Rather than ask interviewees about how they see the organisation and its dilemmas, when they are describing their roles to me there is almost always reference to some occurrence that was troubling or confusing. I pick up on this and engage them in telling me the story, which then leads to other stories, and so on.

Whatever specific data gathering methods are used, they are aimed at the development of a series of "working hypotheses" designed to stimulate thought and animate a productive dialogue about those aspects of the situation about which the client has been previously unaware. Working hypotheses are similar to psychoanalytic interpretation because they identify discrepancies or heretofore unrecognised patterns and offer a kind of "because clause" designed to invite the client to think about the situation from a different perspective. Again, though, it is important to emphasise that working hypotheses are not answers or explanations of a problem. Irrational dynamics can lead to situations where "answers" are disguised as "working hypotheses". The tone of a genuine working hypothesis is tentative and exploratory, inviting clients to disagree and provide deeper, richer ideas. They are works in progress, never final.

Typically, these initial hypotheses are delivered in a working note, which is written for the client system. The hypotheses are offered to provide new ways of linking the data in such a way that it stimulates dialogue with the client system. It also leaves open—often it actually invites—the introduction of new data to build on what has been gathered. Whether the new data confirm or disconfirm the working hypotheses, the development of richer and more compelling hypotheses from the dialogue is a sign of success. In other words, there is no need for the consultant to be right, though it is helpful if the consultant is able to illuminate important issues. Ultimately, the goal is to arrive at a fuller understanding of the challenges faced by a client system and to help clients arrive at shared understanding that becomes a basis for either resolution or for taking meaningful steps towards it.

Because the purpose of the working note is to generate dialogue, it endeavours to embody the same tone as the working hypotheses that serve as the centrepiece of the note. Every working note I have seen includes at the beginning language to emphasise the tentativeness of the hypotheses and invites clients to refine and improve them. Here are introductory comments to three working notes, each written by a different practitioner:

1. "On the basis of such a limited study, I could not pretend to offer firm recommendations. In this working note I have the more limited objective of offering some hypotheses and suggesting the direction of more detailed exploration by X and others."

2. "The following working note is based on the interviews conducted . . . as well as a review of financial statements and a survey of partner opinions about the nature of the challenges facing the firm. The note is divided into four sections: *The Changing Marketplace, Y's Leadership, The firm's Current Conflicts, and The Key Challenges Ahead.* Please read the note actively, noting where you agree and disagree, and where you think I have omitted or overlooked important issues. The purpose of this note is to provide a platform for reviewing the firm's recent history since Y's departure and developing strategies for moving forward."

3. "This working note is an attempt to summarize the key themes which emerged from interviews conducted with a group of Headquarters staff from xxx to xxx. It also puts forward some tentative hypotheses which may be useful in accounting for the reality I perceived in speaking with people about Xxxxxxxxx. Together these hypotheses and observations are offered as the basis for further discussion rather than as an attempt to provide any definite answers."

The subsequent note contains any preliminary findings and working hypotheses that are offered as the basis for dialogue. One of the notes introduced above goes on to say: "My working assumption throughout is that any understanding of organizational life and its problems must look first to the social and structural dimensions. By this I mean the shared milieu that is collectively created, but at the same time independent of any single member's control. It is this which creates the conditions within which people work." It then contains a series of sections summarising the data: "The Role of the Associate Director"; "The Absence of xxxxx"; "Atmosphere of Learning and Collaboration"; "The xxxx career"; "Xxxx as an open system".

This sort of analysis actually constitutes a "case study". It is an approach to research that is action orientated and is based on Kurt Lewin's recognition that the best way to study a system is to try to change it. As the consultant and client try to address an issue of concern to the client system, the change process (which includes discussion of issues previously avoided) inevitably raises defences and resistances. In systems terms, the homeostatic mechanisms (which maintain the status quo) appear and can be addressed. This research method came to be known as "action research". In the vast majority of research institutions, this approach is considered inferior to the detached research model, which often tries to emulate the positivist approach to objectivity. But the knowledge and insight that comes from this kind of study can be of general interest and importance as well as useful for client systems. Take, for example, Isabel Menzies' study of the nursing system (1960). Not only was it of great value to the client system that was attempting to address problems with morale and productivity among student nurses, but it provided insights and ideas that have had a profound effect on the systems psychodynamic tradition and several generations of practitioners.

Reflection in organisations

Socioanalytic methods and technologies are, in my view, all aimed at the same goal: creating reflective spaces in groups and organisations that enable people to achieve insightful recognition of the systemic factors and unconscious psychic realities that are contributing to a current situation. This kind of work needs to be distinguished from psychotherapeutic work aimed at uncovering important unconscious factors. Socioanalytic methods, as with all systems psychodynamic work, are geared toward organisational functioning. While the resolution of personal conflicts or an increase in happiness might be the outcome of psychotherapy, it is strictly a side effect if it occurs at all in socioanalytic intervention. Socioanalytic work is about increasing a system's capacity to confront challenges by bringing variables into the decision-making equation that are difficult to discover in other ways.

An important example of the practicality of reflective practice can be found in Bion's famous comment that anxiety serves as the "shadow of the future". At one level, it is a reminder that we know more than we know, so to speak, as Ken Eisold has discussed in his recent book of that name (Eisold, 2010). It brings to mind an illustration from the devastating tsunami in Asia. Almost no dead animals were found among the vast number of bodies. Somehow, their flight responses had been activated by some subtle change in the ambient environment. In the second vignette, a tourist had rented a fishing boat for the day. The captain sensed that something was wrong several hours before the tsunami hit. He did not know what it was, but he was intuitively alarmed, so he decided to curtail the fising expedition. He did exactly the wrong thing, though. Safety would have been found by heading out where the tsunami was not much more than a swell, not in where it took on such deadly proportions.

I have always felt that Bion's poetic statement contains an insight of enormous usefulness to managers. It provides an avenue to deciphering as yet tacit changes in the context of work that, if decoded, can provide invaluable information about emergent issues and forces. However, being able to "harvest" the knowledge that is conveyed through the experience of anxiety requires—as with all interpretative understanding—reflection.

I want now to address some of the dilemmas surrounding and pertaining to reflection in modern organisations. My point of reference is the idea that while reflection, and reflective practice, is more crucial than ever in contemporary organisations, it is common to encounter norms and practices that effectively prohibit occupying "reflective space", thus making inaccessible the outlines of the shadow of the future and other valuable system-level data that are conveyed through this channel. Many social defences are erected against the kind of reflective practice required to bring socioanalytic methods into organisational life.

By reflection, I refer to devoting time and "space" to understanding organisational experience. It involves thinking *about* one's work, not about *how* to do it. It is not about, for example, figuring out how much the health service should spend on new computers, or the right dosage for a patient, although the reflective stance might have an impact on how these tasks are undertaken.

My interest is in the processes of reflection *about* one's work, its efficacy and significance: registering what one observes of the organisation, the capacity to be informed by one's imagination and intuition, the opportunity to criticise constructively, and to influence the working environment. It is a second order activity: the effort to symbolise and think about the primary work activities of the group or organisation. In other words, to work in the mind with the organisation as a systemic process rather than with its transactions.

The systems psychodynamic tradition emphasises the role of reflection through its focus on emotional containment, social defence theory, learning from experience, the need for work group leadership over basic assumption functioning, the importance of the depressive position for effective managerial practice, and, more recently, the role of "negative capability" in fostering effective collaboration. Through reflection, and the capacity to contain the anxieties associated with the experiences, these lost capabilities can be regained or protected.

Why reflect?

In a general sense, the purpose of reflection is to enable people and their organisations to be more competent. Here, I want to suggest four distinct, yet related, sources for the need for reflection in organisations, based on an amalgam of the system psychodynamics tradition, my own experience consulting to organisations, and a broader understanding of the emerging post-industrial conditions within which our organisations must operate. Each purpose has implications for practice, explored in the sub-sections below.

Containing and modifying the impact of anxiety on work groups

Reflection on system dynamics addresses a dimension of organisational life that is hidden by operations that stress a false dichotomy between the individual and the organisation. This, of course, represents the fundamental and classic insights of the systems psychodynamic tradition. Following Bion's discoveries about how psychotic anxieties are managed in group contexts, Menzies (1960) and Jaques (1974) built conceptual lenses for rendering the impact of anxiety visible in the manifest functioning of organisations.

The essence of their discovery was to illustrate how an organisation's culture and structure evolve in part to absorb, and reinforce, the anxiety and defensive functioning of the people in them. Individuals externalise "those impulses and internal objects that would otherwise give rise to psychotic anxiety and [pool] them in the life of the organization" (Jaques, 1974, p. 16). In a similar vein, Menzies' nursing study show how these externalised anxieties become encoded in the very "building blocks", so to speak, of the organisation: their structures, practices, technologies, procedures, etc.

While the established "social defences" (Menzies, 1960) and stable projective configurations (Jaques, 1974) enable people to continue without being flooded by disabling anxiety, they also entail significant diminishment of their capabilities. Without access to important—albeit anxiety provoking—regions of their experience, people are unable to make reasoned judgements, thoughtful decisions, or intuitive links to important work issues.

Had the nurses in Menzies' study had alternative ways of handling the anxieties stimulated by the practice of nursing, and all that it entails of intimate contact with sick and dying patients, according to her hypothesis, they would have been able to enhance their sense of competence, the quality of patient care, and their sense of mature collaboration.

The implied "solution" is reflection: developing the kind of holding environments so that people can think about their experience and integrate the various bits of their experience into a comprehensive understanding of task, role, and system. Through integration, people can operate more centrally from the depressive position, which brings them into much fuller contact with themselves and their colleagues, and gives them access to a fuller range of their sophisticated capabilities, albeit with a more sober set of expectations.

Managing transition

Another stream of thought and development in the systems psycho-dynamic tradition is the focus on the role of reflection in relation to organisational transitions. The origins of the systems psychodynamic tradition are closely intertwined with the recognition that operating environments became fluid in the latter half of the twentieth century, requiring new ways to think about both the technical and social aspects of organisational life. Two works of Emery and Trist, "The causal texture of organizational environments" (1965) and *Towards a Social Ecology* (1973), illustrated how the effects of destabilised environments penetrated deeply into the reality of organisational life, for both the enterprise itself and the social and psychological experience of members.

There was also a growing appreciation of the loss and disruption to meaningful relationships that is entailed by the turbulent social, economic, and organisational context in which people found themselves. As the psychological challenges of active, ongoing adaptation to changing environments came to the fore, the meaning created by ongoing attachments and relationships came under constant threat and the experience of loss became commonplace.

As many have discussed, the psychological health and organisational capacity to adapt are affected by how these losses and disruptions are handled. When denied, the process of mourning cannot occur effectively and people will be unable to embrace the new order and emerging dynamic realities.

The impact of rapid environmental change can be devastating, leading to rapid deterioration of the social and organisational contexts and, in turn, the emergence of primitive defensive responses: heightened aggression, hostile splitting, and alienated withdrawal. Many of us who work in large corporate environments see the routinisation of these very destructive qualities (e.g., Sievers, 2002).

The work of Bridger (1980, 1987), Bar Eleli (1984), and Amado and Ambrose (2001) has systematically explored the role of reflection in enabling people and their organisations to manage what are now ongoing transitional states that reflect the turbulent environments of today's organisations. The only effective response is review and reflection, or, in the words of Bridger,

enabling people to change the way they think about the problems around them, to alter their perspectives, and to discover new
possibilities for action which can never occur to them as long as they
remain on the secure railtracks of their habitual mind-sets. (2001,
p. xvi)

Enabling members to develop sufficiently complex images of the organisation and its environment

Ashby's (1960) law of requisite variety examines why, if internal variety does not equal the external variety encountered by a system, the
penalty is failure to survive. The increased complexity of modern
organisation poses deep challenges for those trying to function within
them. For example, as Tom Gilmore has discussed, the number of
"stakeholders" that one must keep in mind has grown dramatically.
Similarly, the breakdown of simpler command structures in the face of
what Vaill (1982) calls the "constant whitewater" of modern organisations has led to a reliance of temporary task groups, multiple and
cross-cutting patterns of accountability, and an emphasis on negotiated rather than delegated authority.

The challenge is to draw new maps, create new measures, and
reinvent their organisations. Asking questions that drive them deeper:
what business are we in? What's our business model—are we competing in our product or on some unique way of adding value? What
should our organisation look like; what shape should it have, what
boundaries, how vertical, how horizontal? What are the skills we need
if we are competing on knowledge? How do we regard our clients: as
consumers, or something else?

Participating in such systems places a corresponding burden on
people. Reflection provides a means of enabling people to build an
understanding of their organisations and represents more fully the
complex dynamic forces with which they must cope. An internal
representation, or image, of the organisational context that ignores the
subtle interplay of the complex forces shaping all roles will inevitably
lead to ineffectiveness and conflict.

Facilitating knowledge work

While there has been some exploration in this area (Hirschhorn, 1990;
Pava, 1986), I think that the systems psychodynamic tradition has paid
too little attention to the impact of knowledge work and its emerging

predominance in contemporary organisations. The psychodynamic dimensions of knowledge work are profound.

Knowledge work is about conversation, and it emerges through relationships. Talking and listening are how knowledge workers learn, innovate, contribute, and change. Value is added through collaborative conversation.

Work, in this context, is intensely personal. Because it has to do first with ideas and knowledge, rather than products and services, work is experienced as beginning with the self. It is a fusion of intuition and experience, informed by the decoding of patterns. In every decision, every conversation, knowledge workers test some aspects of their own personal take on the world. And every decision is a prediction about the future, based on assumptions carried forward from the past—a past that is increasingly disconnected from the future

Increasingly, the leaders' job is to manage the "idea chamber" so that knowledge workers will risk trusting their own feelings. The prescience of the systemic thinking by A. K. Rice and others who saw managing as managing boundaries, not the people in them, is all the more impressive as it becomes clearer that managing knowledge work is about creating context. Managers do not manage knowledge workers, they manage context.

Where knowledge work prevails, managers are all faced with the problem of creating thoughtful conversation, including disagreements, and how to promote voluntary followership among knowledge workers. At one level, this raises the question of managing the "idea chamber" so that knowledge workers will risk trusting their own feelings. At another, it poses the challenge of creating a context in which people are able to learn publicly, risk exposure in the service of developing shared systemic understanding, and collaborate in such a way that vulnerability is neither hidden nor pathologised.

Social defences against the experience of reflection

Many new patterns of social defence have arisen since the classic explorations of Menzies and Jaques. To name two, Bain (2002) has recently identified "domain level" defences. These are patterns of defence pertaining to the particular practices that develop in specific industrial domains, such as education or health care. Another was identified in an earlier paper written by Gilmore and Krantz (1990) that shows how widely shared cultural fashions can serve socially defensive purposes, in this case the splitting of leadership and management.

To these, and others that have been discussed in the literature, I would like to add the following defensive patterns that I have encountered around the anxieties that are posed by the experience of reflection in contemporary organisations.

There is no time or space for reflection

The belief that activity and productivity are somehow equated leads to an implicit devaluing of reflection. I am often reminded of the concept of "negative capability" in leadership that has recently been discussed by French (2001).

I believe we need a corresponding concept, something like "negative space", which recognises and values the unspoken and unknown substrata that underlie organised activity. It is a kind of silhouette, a void that contains enormously important knowledge about the organisation (see Armstrong, 1997). But it can only be recognised when time devoted to seeing what emerges and how the preoccupations of people are linked.

The globalisation and technological acceleration of work life contributes to the robustness of this defensive posture. Especially, any time of reflection that requires working through, in particular organisational transitions, requires requisite time because deep changes entail working through issues at both the depressive and persecutory levels.

Splitting of reflection and action

Often, especially in commercial enterprises, reflection is regarded as weak ("touchy-feely") and associated with the superfluous (to real work) aspects of human resource departments. The gender connotations are obvious and pernicious. Yet, it also leads to a situation in which reflective work is devalued, reinforcing in turn rigid defences against novelty and the personal consequences of major change.

The oppression of technique

In the past twenty years, there has been a wide dissemination of the techniques of organisational development. There is often a defensive investment in the tool, techniques of organisational development, that then shields people from authentic reflection or engagement. It is *as if* the benefit derives from using particular social technologies rather than from whatever reflection and insight might emerge from their use. As they become ritualistic and characteristic of repetition in the psychodynamic sense, the analytic techniques destroy or bury the phenomena they are aimed at describing.

Converting insight into cliché

I am often struck by the way that thought is neutralised by the exchange of clichés about the dynamics of social systems. As with the social technologies of organisational development, the business press has popularised—and simplified—deeply important knowledge about the psycho-social realities of organisational life. When these important insights are converted into clichés, they become a kind of currency that is used to prevent discovery and thought. Refrains of "Oh, it's resistance to change", or "group think", or "loss from change" come to substitute for experience.

Markers of non-ordinariness

Of late, I have become increasingly sensitive to how I participate in "de-normalising" reflection by helping create contexts that inadvertently "mark" reflective work as not part of ordinary work. As with "quality circles", creating special structures around reflective work might bind the associated anxieties sufficiently to allow this work to occur, but at a cost. When reflection is defined as "other-than-ordinary", I think we participate in helping organisations keep reflective knowledge segmented and, to an extent, neutralised. To my mind, the challenge of reflection is how to integrate it into ordinary work—how to make it an authorised part of ordinary work.

Metaphor and reflection

Ultimately, I believe, all reflection involves the creation and elaboration of metaphor: evolving internalised images of the organisation, its tasks and stakeholders, our roles, and the emerging environmental forces. The foundations of systems psychodynamic thinking point to the notion that increased competence and vitality lie in those metaphors that contextualise experience, in contrast to those that fore-close linking or providing avenues for seeing the contextual roots of experience. Out of metaphors that allow for the contextualisation of experience arise the potential for the kind of negotiated understand-ing of task, purpose, and role that Shapiro and Carr (1991) discuss in their treatment of the dilemmas of finding one's meaningful authority in today's settings.

Health services case

I would like to offer a description of a recent experience with a health service that has taught me something about reflection and its place in organisational life (Krantz, 2009). This service was steeped in the traditions of reflective practice and its Executive Director (Mark) was deeply committed to enquiry about the impact of unconscious and tacit social dynamics on the functioning of the service. The organisa-tion provides health care, disability services, psychological coun-selling, and other related services to a large university.

I have consulted to this service and Mark for nearly six years, and, over time, we developed a particular approach to integrating retreats into their annual cycle of meetings (January and July each year). Each retreat lasted three days and tried to combine planning and review of ongoing operations with opportunities for reflection about the teams' dynamics, those of the health service more generally, and about how the emergent issues in the university and in the wider environment were affecting the service.

This past year, however, Mark felt he needed to cancel the January retreat because there were two vacancies just about to be filled in key positions on the management team. Mark was unhappy about miss-ing the retreat, but the timing of the new appointments in conjunction with the rhythms of the school year made it seem unwise.

We decided to try an experiment—convening what we called "mini-retreat". The plan was to devote thirty minutes of their weekly management team meetings to this reflective activity for eight weeks. For the first fifteen minutes, one person on the team discussed which of their priorities they felt they were making headway on, which had progressed the least, and what was their major "stealth" priority—the priority that had imposed itself on the manager due to unforeseen events. The second fifteen minutes was given over to reviewing an incident that occurred during the week, the outcome of which was either surprising or disappointing. Each person on the team offered one of these episodes for the team to think about for the second fifteen-minute period.

We were worried that there would not be enough time for meaningful conversation, but decided to go ahead on an experimental basis. We chose a sequence, interspersing people with more and less tenure at the health service.

The brief stories unfolded as follows:

1. The Director of Planning talked about how upset and surprised she had been during preparation discussions for a forthcoming labour strike. Everyone took it as obvious that her function was not a "critical activity" that required coverage. While it was obvious on the surface, she struggled with the experience of marginalisation and devaluation.

2. The new Medical Director spoke about his sense of isolation; he rarely works during the week with members of the team other than the Director of Operations, who is responsible for support functions. He mentioned that his office was near a "trash chute".

3. The new Director of Health Education and Outreach talked about a meeting during the week at which her staff expressed dismay at their feelings of marginality, saying that they thought the health care professions in the primary care area (doctors, nurses, and associated staff) did not even know what they did. She was taken aback by the intensity of feeling they expressed about their sense of legitimacy.

4. The Director of Disability Services talked about an interaction that left her feeling disadvantaged and resentful.

5. The Director of Psychological Services referred to his surprise at the comment made by another, new director on the team. When he asked how she felt a recent programme went, she said it had been a "waste of time". He was taken aback by the candid criticism and it led him to wonder about his own frankness and willingness to address failures openly.

6. The Director of Operations addressed a failed delegation. She had asked one of her assistant directors to address an issue, which he did in a way that made her uncomfortable.

7.   Finally Mark, the Executive Director, spoke of his shame and concern about having discovered a large budget discrepancy during the week.

In each case, the group grappled with the systemic meaning of the story presented, with differing degrees of comfort and insight. What was shocking was the pattern that emerged. Unconsciously, the sequence was divided along age lines: the first four were younger and the last three older. The consistent theme of the first sub-group was marginalisation, victimisation, and devaluation. The second group expressed, thematically, issues of failure and the exposure of incompetence. From a dynamic standpoint, the paranoid–schizoid dynamics were contained by the first group, the depressive themes in the second.

Bringing this reflective work closer to the "real time" functioning of the team and the service gave it a different quality. The seamless interweaving, or oscillation, between the thought work of the enterprise and reflection about it is, in my mind, an ideal that I have sometimes, but rarely, helped client organisations achieve. Usually, reflective work is held at some sort of "arm's length" to the ordinary, ongoing work of the organisation, which I have come, increasingly, to see as defensive in nature. While it might be enabling, it also tends to reinforce a subtle and, I believe, damaging notion that reflection is not part of ordinary work life.

The health service experience, if even by accident, was a reminder of the importance of continually testing the boundary between reflection and operations, and of the value of trying to bring them into a relationship of greater integration and permeability. The image I was left with was that of "moments of poetry" integrated into ongoing work.

Leadership as authorised curiosity

One question that this discussion brings to the fore concerns the role of leadership in fostering reflective practices. Metaphors that transform and enlarge our understanding are those that contain the potential for novelty, surprise, and discovery. Those that are fixed, unambiguous, and unchanging are characteristic of the concrete, paranoid–schizoid patterns of organisational life and inevitably destroy linking and thought. My sense is that organisations most traumatised by the impact of constant hyper-turbulent change are those that are least able to authorise the kind of reflective space that would allow for the emergence of transformative metaphor. Those that rigidly map one domain on to another without the possibility of ambiguity or novelty foreclose learning.

Leadership, in this vein, concerns the authorisation of curiosity and the deployment of resources—time and space—toward that end. The basic assumption counterpoint to curiosity is the defensive certainty that pertains to basic assumption states, which exist outside of time and context. While the emotionality associated with certainty is essential under some conditions, it is poisonous to reflective practice and efforts to develop mutually refined understandings of task, organisation, and context.

Reflections on socioanalytic methods

One disillusionment of my professional development is the recognition that it is not a imperative of (at least immediate) financial success that organisations are honest and open about themselves, though it still seems more necessary in systems that "process" people. Nevertheless, I think the data support the notion that reflective practice is enabling, creates substantial adaptive capability for organisations, and has a major impact on the psychic depletion or satisfaction of their members.

All systems, to a degree, are governed by membership in a conceptual system, a system which tends to remain opaque in depth by virtue of the fact that it provides the tools, rules, and the methods by which the system itself must be examined. Reflective space creates the opportunity for new thought, enrichment of the internal representation of the system within which people are functioning, and a clearer understanding of the factors that shape and influence their authorisation to work.

However, reflection on experience provokes anxieties that, in turn, calcify social defence systems. Fostering and sustaining reflective practice is an important contribution that leaders can make. The challenge, from my viewpoint, is to create feasible spaces in which reflection can occur and to find ways of authorising reflective practice so that it can be considered, and experienced as, an ordinary part of work life.

Socioanalytic reflection holds out the promise of being able to transform anxiety into knowledge and meaningful action; it provides an avenue for harnessing the intuitive substrata of experience and linking it to purposeful organisational behaviour. To provide the context in which people can "pull up anchor" and head in the right direction, in contrast to the vignette that introduced this chapter, is one of the greatest challenges for leadership today. Many of the familiar structures and practices that have historically contained anxiety are no longer feasible in today's fluctuating and turbulent organisational world. The capacity to reflect, however, and to illuminate the shadows that contain glimpses of the future, remains a tool of enormous potential.

References

Amado, G., & Ambrose, A. (2001). *The Transitional Approach to Change.* London: Karnac.

Armstrong, D. (1997). The 'institution in the mind': reflections on the relation of psycho-analysis to work with institutions. *Free Associations, 7*(9): 1–14.

Ashby, W. R. (1960). *Design for a Brain.* New York: Wiley.

Bain, A. (2002). Defenses against learning from experience. Unpublished manuscript.

Bridger, H. (1980). The kinds of organizational development required for working at the level of the whole organization considered as an open system. In: K. Trebesch (Ed.) *Organizational Development in Europe, Vol. 1A: Concepts.* Berne: Paul Haupt.

Bridger, H. (1987). To explore the unconscious dynamics of transition as it affects the interdependence of individual, group and organizational aims in paradigm change. Unpublished paper presented at the ISPSO symposium on "Integrating Unconscious Life in Organizations: Psychoanalytic Issues in Organizational Research and Consultation". Montreal.

Bridger, H. (2001). Foreword. In: G. Amado & A. Ambrose (Eds.), *The Transitional Approach to Change* (pp. xi–xiv). London: Karnac.

Eisold, K. (2010). *What You Don't Know You Know: Our Hidden Motives in Life, Business, and Everything Else.* London: Other Press.

Emery, F. E., & Trist, E. (1965). The causal texture of organizational environments. *Human Relations, 18*: 21–31.

Emery, F. E., & Trist, E. (1973). *Towards a Social Ecology.* London: Tavistock.

French, R. (2001). "Negative capability": managing the confusing uncertainties of change. *Journal of Organizational Change Management, 14*(5): 480–492.

Geertz, C. (1973). *The Interpretation of Cultures.* New York: Basic Books.

Gilmore, T., & Krantz, J. (1990). The splitting of leadership and management as a social defense. *Human Relations, 43*(2): 183–204.

Hirschhorn, L. (1990). Leaders and followers in a postindustrial age. *Journal of Applied Behavioral Science, 26*: 529–542.

Jaques, E. (1974). Social systems as a defence against persecutory and depressive anxiety. In: G. S. Gibbard, J. J. Hartman, & R. D. Mann (Eds.), *Analysis of Groups* (pp. 277–299). San Francisco, CA: Jossey-Bass.

Kahn, C. (1979). *The Art and Thought of Heraclitus.* Cambridge: Cambridge University Press.

Krantz, J. (2009). Unpublished manuscript.

Menzies, I. E. P. (1960). A case-study in the functioning of social systems as a defence against anxiety: a report on the study of the nursing service of a general hospital. *Human Relations, 13*: 95–121.

Pava, C. (1986). Redesigning sociotechnical systems design: concepts and methods for the 1990s. *Journal of Applied Behavioral Science, 22*(3): 201–221.

Schein, E. (1985). *Organizational Culture and Leadership.* San Francisco, CA: Jossey-Bass.

Shapiro, E., & Carr, W. (1991). *Lost in Familiar Places.* New Haven, CT: Yale University Press.

Sievers, B. (2002). Against all reason: trusting in trust. Presentation to the 19th Annual Meetings of the International Society for the Psychoanalytic Study of Organizations, Melbourne, Australia, 20th June.

Vaill, P. (1982). The purposing of high-performing systems. *Organizational Dynamics,* Autumn: 23–39.

PART II
METHODS

Observing anxiety: a psychoanalytic training method for understanding organisations

R. D. Hinshelwood

"[Esther Bick's] method can be said to have made a tremendous contribution to the naturalistic, reflexive approach of both clinical and research psychoanalysis to their field of enquiry"

(Briggs, 2001, p. 279)

T he aim of this chapter is to discuss certain aspects of the observation of organisations in terms of process material as reported by student observers, and the fruits of seminar discussion of their records. First, a short preamble will describe both the origins of the method, and also the way it has come, over the years, to be theorised.

Preamble

In the course of teaching trainee psychiatrists in the early 1980s, I wanted an exercise for the trainees to help them to understand the particular kind of psychoanalytic work which can access hidden and unarticulated psychic matters (Hinshelwood & Skogstad, 2000). I recalled that an important feature of my own training as a psycho-analyst was the mother–infant observation course, which helped to recognise the infant in the patients I would be seeing as a psycho-analyst. What, I wondered, would be comparable for psychiatrists to learn about? I reflected that they will eventually be part of a multi-disciplinary team and have a considerable amount of authority, being frequently seen as leaders of that team. Would it, therefore, be useful for them to have the opportunity to study the dynamics of teams and units in the hospital? If this proved possible, this could become a method for psychiatrists to become more aware of the hidden pres-sures on them (and others) in the organisational dynamics of the units they would eventually be working in. This observational exercise proved very popular, and was expanded with a more general aim of teaching people to have a wider perspective of the unarticulated pres-sures on themselves in any working situation.

Along the lines of infant observation, students are required to set up an observation in an organisation of their choice, for one hour, once a week, for three months; after each observation they would write process notes of everything remembered of the observation and then present their records to a seminar of the observers.

Currently, the course is run under the auspices of the Centre for Psychoanalytic Studies, University of Essex. For one term, the stu-dents attend theoretical seminars on psychoanalytic theorising and cases studies in groups and organisations. Concurrently, they attend a supervision seminar. This seminar runs for two terms; the first is preparatory for working on the negotiation and setting up of an entry into an organisation, and in the second term these seminar members present and discuss their records.

A few words on the method

This method is transferred from psychoanalytic baby observation, and is primarily a training exercise for students interested in organisations and group dynamics at work. It is worth distinguishing from what it is not. It is not a "fieldwork" type of observation, which is a more system-atic attempt to study a social grouping *in situ*. The psychoanalytic method of observing organisations does not attempt to cover the field of conscious reflection and understanding of the organisation by the members of it. It is intended as an access to hidden areas of the culture, or "atmosphere", of a working organisation, with a specific task.

The role does not include interviewing the subjects, or data collecting in a proactive way. Therefore, it contrasts with the method which seems to have been used by Isabel Menzies in her nursing study (1960). She was not informative at all about her method of collecting the data she used, but it seems to have been interviewing individuals and groups. The latter, the group interviews, might have been a forerunner of what we now call "focus groups". Her method was probably similar to, and standard for, Tavistock consultancies at the time, the method described by Jaques in his *The Changing Culture of a Factory* (1951). She used the material to formulate views and then replay these back with her subjects. It is a method that came to be called action research, and is a dialogic relationship between the researchers and the subjects. It has Habermasian resonances.

The organisational observation method is to be distinguished from this classical study of Menzies in various respects.

1.   First, it is not a consultation, and does not seek to "change" the organisation in any way, other than to accept that the impact of an observer does change the field, a change which it is part of the observation to understand.

2.   As a psychoanalytic observation, it attempts to deal with relatively invisible data, because it aims to add the dimension of unconscious phenomena to those already apparent. It is an adage in psychoanalysis that "If you ask a conscious question, you get a conscious answer". The data sought in this kind of observation are much more inferential, and come as much from the act of questioning or dialoguing during and in the observation as from the content of the dialogue. The act is a message in itself: process speaks as much as content does.

3.   Although this method has produced research results, especially in the baby observation work, it is intended primarily as a training exercise, to sensitise people to the culture and its hidden aspects within a place of work, notably where they might themselves be working. In one's own workplace, or a visitor in another, there is not the scope for conducting a series of questions or exploratory interviewing about the cultural attitudes and practices. The expectation is that the observation will provide the

student with practice in, and greater capacity for, thinking about what can be inferred. The aim is to refine a person's sensitivity to the *hidden* aspects of the organisation, its implicit unspoken attitudes, its forms of taken-for-granted practice, and the specific characteristics of the role relations. It attends to these aspects of the culture, which, precisely because they are hidden, cannot be enquired about.

The observation deals with a specific kind of "knowledge" about an organisation. Especially since the development of information technology (IT) systems in the past thirty years, knowledge has been increasingly seen as data such as that manipulated by computers, which are quantitative, cognitive, and articulated. The knowledge sought in these observational methods is different. It is hidden, apparently silent, unarticulated, and embodied in process as much as in enumerate and verbal data. It is knowledge which is, as it were, not yet knowledge, a pre-knowledge, knowledge yet to be, and, in significant measure, knowledge that resists becoming known. Bollas's term, the "unthought known" (1987), is apt for the raw material of a psychoanalytic or socioanalytic observation method.

In this sense, there is a specific psychoanalytic approach to this kind of level of dynamics. It entails developing a capacity to think about the experience while it is being experienced. It is a reflective practice, but specifically a reflection on the hidden and non-articulated suggestions of something to be revealed.

This can become mystical, but there is a capacity in all people to pick up the "vibrations", as it were. The observational method is not going to give people that sensitivity; it is part of human nature anyway. As Gardner (1993) claimed, psychoanalysis is "folk psychology", but elaborated and theorised, because human beings are innate psychologists and psychoanalysis builds on that. The observation course is an attempt to enhance and encourage, that innate capacity, and, while sensing those intuitions, to think about their meaning. That is what is psychoanalytic: the capacity to have an experience, and to think about it. It is a reflective practice tuned to the unexpressed. Psychoanalysis is not a mystique, it is a development of the capacities everyone has anyway. And, like everything else, practice, training, and the encouragement of supervision brings out what is already a potential.

Some theory

Although the structure of the observations, the observer role, and the general teaching intentions are similar to those of mother–infant observation, there are siginificant differences, and a degree of different theorising is necessary. In 1950, Trist was casting about for ways of understanding the linking of psychoanalytic understanding to individual unconscious experiencing of social activity; he turned to the idea of "culture" to denote ". . . comprehensive reference to the structure of social systems or internally to reach down to emotional phenomena at the deeper levels of the personality" (Trist, 1990, p. 540).

There are many definitions of "culture", so it is important to be clear that Trist's is a definition limited to the unconscious dimension, which rests on two pillars, the individual and the social. We must remain aware that unconscious attitudes and practices comprise a small segment of the whole field of cultural studies. Trist's idea of "culture" is, therefore, idiosyncratic, in order to create a "bridging concept", as he called it. Psychoanalytic or socioanalytic observation of organisations is aimed specifically at the meeting of the attitudes and practices of the social entity with the deeper layers of the personality.

I shall take it that Trist is addressing the cultural expression of unconscious phantasy. That is to say, unconscious phantasies couched in terms of a relationship of some kind with an object are motivating forces behind culturally shared attitudes to, and practices of, the work. In this case, the object of unconscious phantasy is the "organisation"— that view of the organisation which the individual has in mind. It is an internal object, in psychoanalytic terms, and is what Jaques (1955) described as the "phantasy social form and content of an institution" (p. 482), and is referred to today as the "organisation in the mind" (Armstrong, 2005), or the "workplace within" (Hirschhorn, 1990). Hence, the relation between the individual level and organisational level is mediated through this relation the individual has to his internal object, the organisation he has in mind.

If we accept that this does capture the necessary "bridging" between individual and organisation, we then hit a further problem. We have to account for how the unconscious phantasies in each individual conform in some way with those of others in the organisation.

This commonality of attitudes and practices is unproblematic for the conscious aspects of the culture, because they are simply agreed in relation to the task. But for the unconscious aspects, we need to understand how those cultural aspects are collectivised and "agreed". Freud was always impressed by what he called unconscious-to-unconscious communication, but what exactly is that communication which effects a dimension of the culture itself? At this point, I turn to the classical paper by Menzies (1960) on the nursing service. She operationalised the notion of "social defence systems" and, in particular, the notion that a common task in a working organisation will provoke a specific stress in the individuals. Thus, the unique stress of the common task has an impact on the same unconscious phantasy. So, it is the work which has an impact on, and collectively activates, the "deeper layers of the personality", their unconscious phantasies. In that way, there is likely to be collaboration at the unconscious level between the people engaged in the same task. Thus, a working organisation can be seen to have, potentially, an unconscious level to its culture that is genuinely collaborative across the workforce (although sub-cultures might, according to the way the primary task is broken down into component secondary tasks, form sub-groups or departments within the overall working enterprise). It might well be that a joint task that stimulates joint phantasies is one of the mechanisms by which the content of the associative unconscious described in Chapter One of this book operates. This theoretical model leads to focusing on the anxiety that drives the collective unconscious cultural attitudes and practices. Therefore, when we seek a psychoanalytic contribution to understanding the process records, the key is to find the point of stress, pain, agony, etc., and connect it with the working task from which the commonality of the stress arises.

Experiencing the "organisation"

To experience an organisation implies an experience of oneself *in* the organisation. Walking off the street into a building is a personal experience, whatever the nature of the work going on in the building. At the very least, it is a different physical environment. The street space might be cold and wet and the building is then protective. Some buildings are open-air, like a football stadium, but, despite experiencing the same physical conditions as outside, it is bounded for a focused activity to take place—football. Space, task, and ambient conditions are so familiar we hardly register these experiences consciously, and especially if the building is one that we are accustomed to. The phenomenon of being familiar is very strong and can numb the experience. Part of the role of observer is to rediscover the newness of the experience, to set aside familiarity.

Some organisations set great store by the first impact of coming into the organisation's space, its building. Many restaurants, for instance, make a lot of effort to provide a specific experience immediately on entering. Expensive ones might create a decor that resembles a homely scene; more inexpensive ones—I think of the Little Chef chain, for instance—might use bright neon lighting and easy-wipe tablecloths to emphasise cleanliness and hygiene. And the first contact with a waiter sets the human context. Consider entering a large supermarket, and a small, specialist delicatessen shop. The different immediate experiences conjure up quite different expectations. Some buildings express a very different kind of organisation; for instance, the walls of a hospital outpatient department are often covered with public notices and information. The sense one gets is an unplanned efficiency, rather busy and maybe impersonal, suggesting no overall ownership of the space by anyone in particular.

I want now to turn to some of the observers' experiences that are more memorable from across the years. These are selected on the basis of their vividness in my recall, though I aim to give them some coherence, but, as it were, starting from the beginning, I will work through certain aspects:

- the impact of the working task;
- finding a "role";
- cultural schisms;
- unconscious phantasy;
- the place of subjectivity;
- unconscious-to-unconscious communication.

The impact of the task

First impressions of an organisation, like those of an encounter with another person, can be very powerful and revealing; very often the very first encounter holds crucial information about the organisation and the work it does. It might be the first contact for the observer, but the organisation has already developed an interface with the outside world. So, then, the contact the observer makes is an illustration of the specific kind of relations the organisation has with its public environment.

One observer wanted to do their project in a London design consultants in the City. The impact of entering the building was breathtaking, with a vast atrium filled by an enormous hanging sculpture of glass. The effect was highly calculated, and obviously intended to advertise the quality of the design service on offer.

Equally "calculated" is the experience of entering a prison, which may be a time-consuming and laborious process involving locked doors, an ostentatious use of keys, and often an accompanying chaperone who takes a long time to appear from other duties in a distant part of the organisation. In both these examples, the way the observation task is conceived is powerfully expressed in the impact it makes on a person's initial contact. An immediate first impression is a powerful experience. It is not arbitrary; the impact comes directly from the interpretation of the task.

Another observer decided to conduct his project in a local authority information centre in a High Street shop. There he was accepted without question. The openness of the organisation to observation was commensurate with the style of the organisation's task—to accept all walk-in enquirers and provide a free service. The impact and the task can be seen to be directly connected.

Rather differently, another observer decided to conduct their project in the offices of a charity concerned with placing children for adoption. The access to these offices on the second floor of a modern office block was by a lift and a door into a reception area. The door was kept locked and could be buzzed open by the receptionist. Repeatedly, during the period of the observations, there were difficulties for people to gain access through the door to the reception where the observer stationed himself. One of the problems was that the receptionist had a lot of trouble seeing through the glass door to ascertain who wanted to enter. The impression was of a service difficult to access, and one that had difficulty in assessing who to access. Again, it is possible to predict that this impact reflected the difficult work of the service in finding adoptive parents.

I am arguing that a person, in fact any person, will have a specific experience of an organisation simply when walking into the organisation's space. An observer is required to take note of that experience. He feels the "atmosphere" as he makes the transition into the space or building. Although we get only a sample, these observations can give arresting information.

"Finding" a role

Now, about the observer role, this is not simple. Being an observer is a powerful experience in its own right. It is a strange role, often stripped of ordinary social responses. It is uncomfortable to confound social expectations. However, the organisation frequently has difficulty in understanding the observing role, and will nudge the observer into some role more familiar and expected for the organisation. Exactly what role the observer finds himself in gives an indication of the nature of the organisation.

One observer, recording weekly sessions in the waiting room of a social services agency, noticed one week that there was a new atmosphere. There was a more serious tone to people's voices, and, later, one of the office staff came to sit next to the observer to confide that the son of one of the staff had had a serious motorcycle accident. This confidence conveyed a belief that bad news was something that everyone should be aware of, as it was important that the observer should not say anything inappropriate to the affected person. As the observer had always kept very much to role and had never had personal contact or conversations with staff, this was an unexpected occurrence that seemed to say something about the organisation's attitude to making sure there was a seemly seriousness and consideration to bad news. As an agency working with poor people in difficulties in various ways, the attitudes to the personally harrowing nature of the work were very apparent in this observer contact. The observer was drawn closely into the organisation as a person who might be another member of staff, and who would need to know the news.

Observers frequently become aware of being placed in a role other than the one negotiated. Indeed, it is very common and almost ubiquitous to involve the observer in roles familiar to the organisation. Students practising observation for the first time find they do not get much help from the organisation and feel very uncomfortable resisting the pressures, while also feeling uncomfortable about failing at the observer role. It might take some while for them to recognise that the way they "fail" is very informative for them.

For instance, in a voluntary sector home for community care assessment of people discharged from mental hospital, the observer found themselves largely left alone, sitting vacantly against a wall, and only interacting to accept or refuse cups of tea and plates of food in advance of the house meal. There seemed to be assumptions in the social attitudes that placed the observer in a role reminiscent of one of the transitory inmates: people, it seemed, who need basic bodily nurture. The organisation tends to place the observer in one of the roles existing in the organisation—staff, client, member of the public.

One young doctor decided, bravely, to do his observation in a locked, male ward of a mental hospital. He sat in the day space, while the staff clustered together inside the nursing station, seemingly as a protection from the threatening and uninterrupted mayhem in the rest of the ward. The atmosphere of fear was permanently palpable, and probably affected confined patients as well as staff. The observation was an extremely inclement experience, not helped particularly by frequent approaches by patients, and sometimes nursing staff, asking if he was a patient or a doctor. Although his role was not a doctor, he increasingly felt something *was* expected of him *as a doctor*. Late in the period of observation, he observed the arrival of a doctor, which drew the attention of everyone. The wild activity diminished, as, it seemed, he might bring news of the fate of patients: who might move out of the ward, for instance. The persistent pressure aimed to reassign his role to that of a needed doctor, because of the desperate emotional conditions of the setting. In fact, he was particularly impressed to realise just what the doctor meant on this ward, and the effect it had on the inmates' behaviour.

Another role reassignment comes from the fact the observer is involved in his own learning. Many organisations have trainee roles, so the observer might be subjected to impromptu tutorials about the work of the unit, or the specific things of interest in the work that have been happening today.

Similarly, many organisations know something, or have heard something, about business consultants who come into an organisation to help put it right, and the observer's role is sometimes seen as a consultant, so the student's interest in the organisation is an interest in *what is wrong*. When members of the organisation see themselves scrutinised for what is wrong, it might indicate the organisation's concern that something is wrong. As no organisation runs perfectly, it is not uncommon that the observer is seen in a superego role. New observers are often sensitive to being seen as critical, and it might link with the observer's own sense of inadequacy in their task, and of being under scrutiny by their supervision group, or by their organisation. Perhaps observers will always struggle to avoid criticising what they observe—sometimes this is difficult in failing organisations. For instance, care organisations commonly appear depersonalising and uncaring, in the manner described in Menzies' nursing study (1960). Given the propensity for everyone to have an active superego, all parties, the observer, the observed, and the seminar group, will find themselves prone to criticising each other and themselves. However, one variant of this is an organisation which welcomes the observer almost joyfully, in a way that suggests the organisation believes it has been selected for its special excellence. This is usually an indication of a high morale organisation. Alternatively, some demoralised organisations feel the presence of the observer as a great reassurance that someone is taking an interest in them, and no longer feel as neglected or disreputable as they customarily do.

Cultural schism

Some organisations have complex or multiple tasks, and it is difficult to span the full dimensions of the work. That difficulty could then be eased by separating the task into pieces along the dividing line. One example is that reported by Miller and Gwynne (1972) in their work with the Cheshire Homes for severely and permanently disabled people. I will not redescribe that separation of the culture into two different kinds that occurred in different homes, but will simply mention the separation of cultures that occurs in different departments or divisions of the organisation which are devoted to different sub-tasks, such as marketing *vs.* research and development, which have quite different stresses that feed through into palpably different cultures.

In my supervision, I came across the following occurrence. One observer did his project in a health unit in which medical research was being undertaken into a condition the unit specialised in. He found that the sense of surveillance was very pervasive, and challenging for the staff. Patients were often seen ambiguously as both persons suffering an illness and subjects of a rigorous experiment. The observer (not medically trained) was often subjected to careful descriptions of patients and the illness, but he felt it was a painful situation where his own learning was under scrutiny, and painful especially because he had no knowledge of, or, indeed, particular interest in, the condition under study, and frequently failed to understand the explanations he was given. These complex accounts seemed to satisfy the member of staff by believing he helped the observer's project. The observer was, thus, recruited to the staff as a researcher. Then, in contrast to this research focus, staff members often went into cubicles for intimate and personal discussions about the patient's lives, which, however, were perfectly audible because the cubicles were separated only by a curtain rather than a door. This seemed a significant signifier of the cultural attitudes, in which the research data were flimsily separated from the personal interaction. Although the physical boundary, the curtain, was actually ineffectual in maintaining privacy for what was personal, in fact it was effective culturally; it allowed separate social attitudes to accumulate in different places, at different times, and in different role interactions. Inside the cubicle, the personal suffering was important; outside, as in the discussions with the observer, the data were important.

The separation of desires and duties

A somewhat similar curious example of a cultural divide occurred in the observation of a soft drinks factory. The observer sat in on a production meeting. At this weekly meeting, the heads of half-a-dozen departments reported their performances in relation to targets for the week. The meeting was held in two parts: for the first thirty minutes, the members moved around the room informally, eating lunch provided by the company, including soft drinks manufactured by the company. At a signal from the production manager, the members sat around the meeting table away from the lunch, and began the formal process of reporting production and comparing with their targets, with a good deal of implicit competition, winning and losing. The division of the meeting into a formal and an informal part implied a division in the cultural attitudes towards the organisation's task. The informal lunch seemed connected to basic bodily sustenance, which the company's product satisfied. Thus, the oral nature of the company's primary task had to be cleared away before the sophisticated management task could proceed.

Unconscious phantasy

This illustration leads to the discussion of an important issue, that of unconscious phantasy. Personal, oral satisfactions in the work situation bring us to the awareness of unconscious phantasy. The place of this primitive, more bodily realm of experiencing seems to require separation from sophisticated work. Such impulses might be captured in the words, "I want to take this organisation into me, as mine" (Freud, 1925h); or even, "I want to scoop everything I can out of the organisation" (Klein, 1975). These words express unconscious wishes and experiences. In their bodily primitiveness, such impulses express primary process of the infant and contrast with the rational "secondary process" of management activity. This separation of basic satisfactions from work was also observed in the formal meeting itself. The meeting was conducted in a quite methodical and tedious way, reporting dull production figures around the table. However, at the same time, other manifestations occurred. On one occasion, a man played with a ruler and a screwed up ball of paper, which he accidentally managed to flick across the table, hitting another member. This appeared to express the otherwise hidden competition between section managers, kept in check by the dull management meeting. Management is, by its nature, competitive, and this meeting, which pitted different departments against each other, was the arena for a rivalry that never became explicit. Although flicking the ball of paper appeared accidental, it seemed emblematic of an action that could not be overtly expressed.

The observer noticed, too, that glances frequently crossed between male and female members of the meeting with apparently playful suggestiveness. In this subdued vein, quite definite impulses of phallic conquest and narcissism gained expression.

It seemed that two levels of interaction were going on together: both the dull formal exchange of information, and also the more lively manifestations of basic oral and genital impulses. The undercurrent of human impulses remains alive beneath the overt level and is held there to avoid serious interference in the primary task. The workforce of a company promoting basic bodily satisfactions is likely to be perfused by impulses of this type. So, the separation of the meeting into two halves might well have helped to contain the undercurrents of unconscious phantasies we might expect to be stimulated by the oral task of the organisation, though clearly it did not completely succeed in this separation. One consequence was the particularly lifeless and impersonal form of the management activity when the lively unconscious phantasies had been so carefully corralled into the first half-hour.

The stimulation of basic needs, pleasures, and terrors is not uncommon in a working organisation with a serious purpose. The way that the objective situation of the organisation's task has an impact on the underlying primitive layers of the personality was noted by Menzies (1960): "The objective situation confronting the nurse bears a striking resemblance to the phantasy situations that exist in every individual in the deepest and most primitive levels of the mind" (p. 46).

That deeper layers of the mind under the impact of a common stimulus promote common aspects of the culture, its attitudes and practices, exemplifies the collectivisation theorised in the introduction to this chapter. In the case of the soft drinks factory, the objective situation is not as desperate as the life and death issues experienced by Menzies' nurses. Nevertheless, there are small occurrences that betray the unconscious phantasies of oral satisfactions, and also those of anal competition and genital conquest. The "defensive techniques", as Menzies (1960) called them, in the practice of nursing, can be expressed in the terms of the unconscious phantasies. The apparent splitting up of the nurse–patient relationship, which forms a protective denial, can be expressed in the nurses' words as, "If I get close to this patient, I am likely to get overanxious about their pain and their survival; therefore I must numb my feelings when working on their body, as if it were inanimate" (see Hinshelwood & Skogstad, 2000). This brings together the deeply personal phantasies and the socially shared attitudes.

The place of subjectivity

These observations have a particularly subjective quality, and, like a
psychoanalysis, the intention is to focus precisely on subjectivity.
Moreover, the instrument for observation is also subjective, the subjective mind of the observer. This deeply subjective level of experience
might not be accessible by any other means than using the subjectivity of the observer. However, the penalty for this reliance on the
subjective is that conclusions from these observations can often be
condemned as *subjective*, and, thus, discounted. One standard response to the use of subjective data is to try to exclude subjective biases
by using sampling methods that allow a generalisation based on
multiple persons or observations. In the research, a generalisation is
effected not by the observer, but by a collectivisation across the pool
of members acting within the field of observation. Although there may
be some validity in this suspicion, it is not so simple. Just as the
members of the organisation have an unconscious that is fully active
at work, so, too, does the observer. The stresses of *his* work also lead
him to unconscious reactions to his practice. Those reactions, however,
are significant. It is precisely the distortions in the write-up of the
process records that signify something of the unconscious stirring. The
distortions are likely to be at the points of maximum emotional stress.

   For instance, in one observation of a long-stay mental hospital
ward, the observer's records dwelt on a specific trivial incident, the
visit of the hospital chaplain. In fact, the incident lasted less than five
minutes, but took up twenty per cent of the records. This might be
criticised as a subjective bias, with unreliable notes. However, it is
possible to look at this differently. The distortion has a cause, and the
emphasis arises from the sensitivity of the observer in the setting. The
significant incident in focus was the chaplain's visit. It was brief, and
he spent almost no time at all talking to the very chronic patients
sitting silently around the walls; instead, he devoted his attention to a
plant in a small pot, which appeared unwatered and dead. He had, it
seems, given the plant to the ward and now it had died. The observer's unconscious distortion seemed, therefore, to pick out a vivid
iconic metaphor of the deadness of the life in the ward. The observer
was unwittingly expressing the observation of this deadness. In this
sense, her subjective distortion betrayed the painful fact of *patients* left
as dead in this chronic ward.

In the seminar supervising these observations, hesitancies, gaps, slips, etc., in the records are all easily noticeable and available for discussion. One observer found it very difficult to produce detailed process records, and tended to give themes about what went on. The immediate impression was that the observer did not understand the task, and he and his colleagues in the seminar discussed what was necessary from him; he repeatedly avowed that he did understand. On the next occasion, he produced the same inadequate presentation. Being from another culture with only moderately good English, the temptation was to put the problem down to an understandable cultural and linguistic one. However, on this second occasion, the rather thin discussion improved when one of the seminar group asked him how he actually felt while in the organisation. This observer had decided to observe the waiting room of a fracture clinic where a medical friend of his worked. This personal link with the organisation made him feel he was somewhat different from the other people, the patients he was sitting with in the waiting room. In answer to the direct question about his feelings, he replied reassuringly that he felt all right, but it transpired that he felt far from all right. He felt inadequate, and that, he admitted, was because everyone in the room spoke so quietly he could rarely understood what they said (no doubt compounded by his less than perfect command of English). His feeling of lostness and bewilderment was clearly painful for this man who had sought a special place endorsed by his link with a medical authority in the clinic.

The questioner then persisted, and pointed out that it was not words but feelings he was expected to report, and encouraged the observer to tell us what he felt. He then produced a most fascinating series of images of people arriving supported by all manner of sticks, crutches, wheelchairs and encumbered by large quantities of Plaster of Paris attached to every part of the body. He described with a similar zany humour how the receptionists for the clinic appeared to be almost totally non-verbal, communicating with minimalist monosyllables and grunts that the newcomers should sit and wait their turn, leaving them, in effect, to feel forgotten and increasingly anxious that they were non-persons completely alone with pain and disabilities. There was clearly some relief in being able to describe this, and mediate the awfulness with his engaging humour. It was then possible to see how the thin and uninformative process records were not just inadequate because of the observer's limited English and under-standing of the observing task, they were actually a very eloquent expression of the patients' experiences of being lost in a bewildering place that made no effort to address the individual's plight. Following this seminar, the observer's notes did improve remarkably.

This observer had a set way of viewing his task as an observer, and this might well have been determined in part by his cultural origins, which gave different priorities to words over feelings. However, what was in the observer was activated in a way that gave special expres-sion to something actually there in the culture of the organisation. There is a fit between something in the observer's sensitivity and something in the organisation that brings out that aspect of the observer. Subjective distortions can, therefore, be key to an aspect of particular significance identified unconsciously by the observer. We do not have to intrude into the individual observer's own baggage in order to be able to get out of the subjective biases a particularly pointed emphasis on a feature of the organisation. There is, as Freud would have said, that curious unconscious-to-unconscious communi-cation, and we are interested in the subjectivity of the transmitting subjects (those who are observed) and not in the receiver (the observer).

Unconscious-to-unconscious communication

The next example is of this unconscious-to-unconscious sensitivity. The observer was a student at a university, and she conducted an observation in the office of the Students' Union, which includes a reception desk manned by students on a rota basis, and a small office with a manager and two typists. In one observation session, the observer stressed the orderliness of the space and of the occurrences that went on. She was aware of the way the paid and permanent Union staff related to the student volunteer, and, indeed, the way the manager related to the two secretaries. Some seminar discussion focused on these relations between the categories of people, where students seemed to carry the role of irresponsibility and potential disorder.

The process record continued with the observer saying that her mind wandered, and it was nothing to do with the observation. Then she had some speculations about the different character of the atmosphere when the manager was away. At the end of the presentation of the record, the observer was asked about the distraction. She said it was nothing, just a film she had seen recently. When asked about the film, she said it was called *The Other Boleyn Girl*, and we clarified that this was about Henry VIII's choice of Anne over her older sister. The seminar could then see that this distraction was not "nothing"; in fact, it expressed the observer's sensitivity to students being looked down upon, not being the chosen ones. Precisely because the observer was a student, she was sensitive to the lowly place of students in the office of the Students' Union, a somewhat surprising aspect of the culture, but one confirmed from other elements of the observations.

The point is that the student could present an apparently irrelevant substitute account of rivalry and favouritism, but fictionally in a film. It is like a dream substitution of a symbol. One can say that this observer's unconscious was being an astute observer, but it needed some perceptive work on the part of the seminar for its message to be read. This occurs ordinarily in the seminars, and indicates the ability of psychoanalytically unsophisticated observers to pick up aspects of the culture that appear quite out of reach.

Conclusions

There are a few points to be made in conclusion. This is a method that is not encumbered by the responsibilities of consultancy and the expectation of change and benefit to the organisation. This is for the observer alone to learn and, perhaps, develop in himself. Pressures arising from the expectations of a consultancy do not interfere with the sensitivity of the observer. In some sense, other pressures might do, especially for the novice, including, for instance, the guilt of apparently "getting something for nothing". The precise way in which the pressures on someone in the strange role of observer may be specific for the organisation, and then potentially a part of the observer's sensitivity, so long as he has the space to reflect on it.

This method of observation attempts to contribute a dimension to organisations not accessible by other non-psychoanalytic methods. Psychoanalysis is not a "theory of everything", and socioanalytic observation should restrict itself to the unconscious dimension;

conscious collaboration and the practices involved in the conscious pursuit of the task are the field of the more usual theory and practice of organisations.

Again, in contrast to consultancy and research, this method of observation aims to sensitise subjects to the emotional and unconscious dynamics of the objective field. The purpose is to help people orientate themselves in their own working situation, not for purposes of change, but for raising consciousness about the role, role relationships, and role pressures someone occupies at work. It aims to help people refrain from simply criticising and dismissing the apparent absurdities that all organisations are permeated by. Instead of criticising, it is to encourage people to think about *explanations* of the occurrences in which they and other well-meaning people feel trapped. To this end, there is no requirement that people should observe outside their own type of organisation, as other comparable methods do, and if observers do choose organisations divergent from their own, there always has to be some assessment of what is transferable knowledge from the place of observation to the place of work. It is true that in organisations similar to the work one, observers might take their own baggage from work to the observed organisation; however, that can function to put their own baggage, acquired in their work, under scrutiny (as, for example, the doctor in the "disturbed ward").

The method, following Bick (see Briggs, 2001), is to address the "fine-grain" of the process record, and is, thus, an unusual method that attempts to stick close to the subjective experience of the observer and also to those of the subjects under observation. It is not primarily intended to reach generalisations about which some objective truth might be claimed. It is, thus, much more like the psychoanalytic method itself: something happened on this occasion among these people, and can be understood in this instance to be possibly a result of X or Y. It is not a process of verifiability, objectivity, and truth. It is about a subjective sensitivity and developing a capacity to understand where one is situated dynamically within a social context. Despite the degree of sophistication needed in this, it is not book learning, and the evidence of the observations conducted over twenty-five years; the task is to develop a sensitivity which already exists in people to assess their own subjective field. It is in the nature of human beings to have this sensitivity, though it is often overlooked in the development of other, cognitive capacities. This method is, therefore, attempting to redress the balance rather than to teach something quite novel. Therefore, many observers who have been through this course have been psychoanalytic novices, and quite unsophisticated psychologically.

References

Armstrong, D. (2005). *Organisation in the Mind*. London: Karnac.
Bollas, C. (1987). *The Shadow of the Object: Psychoanalysis of the Unthought Known*. London: Free Associations.
Briggs, A. (2001). *Surviving Space*. London: Karnac.
Freud, S. (1925h). Negation. *S.E.*, *19*: 235–239. London: Hogarth.
Hinshelwood, R. D., & Skogstad, W. (Eds.) (2000). *Observing Organisations*. London: Routledge.
Hirschhorn, L. (1990). *The Workplace Within: Psychodynamics of Organizational Life*. Cambridge, MA: MIT Press.
Gardner, S. (1993). *Irrationality and the Philosophy of Psychoanalysis*. Cambridge: Cambridge University Press.
Jaques, E. (1951). *The Changing Culture of a Factory*. London: Tavistock.
Jaques, E. (1955). Social systems as a defence against persecutory and depressive anxiety. In: M. Klein, P. Heimann, & R. Money-Kyrle (Eds.), *New Directions in PsychoAnalysis* (pp. 478–498). London: Tavistock.
Klein, M. (1975). *Envy and Gratitude and Other Works 1946–1963*, M. M. R. Khan (Ed.). London: Hogarth.
Menzies, I. E. P. (1960). A case-study on the functioning of social systems as a defence against anxiety: a report on a study of the nursing service of a general hospital. *Human Relations 13*: 95–121. Reprinted in: I. E. P. Menzies Lyth, *Containing Anxiety in Institutions*. London: Free Association Books, 1988, and in: E. Trist & H. Murray (Eds.), *The Social Engagement of Social Science*. London: Free Association Books, 1990.
Miller, E., & Gwynne, G. (1972). *A Life Apart*. London: Tavistock.
Trist, E. (1990). Culture as a psychosocial process. In: E. Trist & H. Murray (Eds.), *The Social Engagement of Social Science, Volume 1: The Socio-Psychological Perspective* (pp. 539–545). London: Free Association Books.

CHAPTER FOUR

The use of drawing as a tool in socioanalytic exploration

Brigid Nossal

Introduction

D rawing is a powerful tool in the work of socioanalytic exploration. Its power resides in its capacity both to give simple
expression to complex feelings and ideas about organisational life, and to provide a vehicle for change and adaptation for the
individual and the group during the sharing and exploration of what
the drawing reveals.

This chapter presents the what, how, and why of drawing as an
important tool in socioanalytic exploration with clients or research
partners in organisations. It explores research with socioanalytic practitioners (Nossal, 2010) and case example material from organisational
consulting assignments. Its intention is to serve as a guide to practice.

A case is made for the following key ideas:

• drawing provides an enormous amount of rich data about both
  the conscious and unconscious experiences that people have of
  an organisation;
• through the act of drawing, and then sharing what is revealed by
  the drawing, participants are provided with a means to develop

their capacity to think creatively and openly about their work in the organisation. This is helpful to the consultant in developing the appropriate "container" and context for socioanalytic exploration;

- the planning for, and introduction to, the task and the way in which drawings are explored, either with individuals or groups in organisations, have a significant impact on both the data that is generated and the opportunity for growth that is created through the dialogue;
- the way in which the drawing activity is held in mind by the socioanalyst is significant for the kind of containment for the task that will be provided;
- last, but not least, drawing can be fun and exciting and it provides a novel means of engagement with people in organisations.

One challenge for the socioanalyst when working with people in organisations is to create the space or the right "container" in which to engage them in exploring emotional and, perhaps, unconscious experiences. While as consultants or research socioanalysts, we may undertake training programmes in this methodology and work hard and continuously at developing a "mind" for the work, the question arises, how is the *client* to begin to develop, through experience, a like "mind" for their own learning and exploration in their work? What is meant here by "mind for the work" is captured in Bion's entreaty that, when working with patients, the analyst should attempt to be without memory, desire, or understanding and to adopt a state of "reverie" (Bion, 1970). The same is true for the socioanalyst working with clients. That is, one needs to be able to clear one's mind of preconceptions and premature conjecture or conclusions and allow the kind of reflection that will enable the emotional reality of the situation under investigation to emerge (see also Long, 2001 on the "state-of-mind" for this work.). Part of the role of the socioanalyst is to stimulate this capacity for thinking in the client and, in this way, to provide an opportunity for self-development and an improved capacity for creativity in their work. This was the starting point for the research that is reported here. It seems that drawing is a very useful and powerful tool for enabling both the individual and the group to enter a "thinking" space where there is openness to sharing and exploring in new ways.

About drawing

Drawing as a practice in socioanalysis is thought to have been used first by consultants at the Tavistock Institute in London in the 1970s during an action research project into day nursery care. Some of the thinking that informs the use of drawing in socioanalytic exploration has roots in psychoanalytic practice in the treatment of individual patients. Jung was a pioneer in this field, with his emphasis on the importance of symbols. "Jung saw value in drawings containing symbols from the unconscious that could work as a healing agent" (Furth, 1988, p. 1). In the literature of psychoanalytic practice, drawing is referred to as a potent and effective analytic tool. Kübler-Ross writes, "Like dream language, the language of pictures is the language of the unconscious, and it speaks when the conscious voice fails" (1988, p. x).

This is a view that is echoed by many socioanalytic practitioners. Another Jungian analyst (Brutsche, 1988) says that the interpretation of a drawing "allows (the patient) to experience that, deep inside, his unconscious is allowing for a surprisingly accurate expression of his emotional state of mind . . ." (p. xii).

In the field of socioanalysis there has been much debate about what usefully can be translated from psychoanalytic practice with an individual to the work of a socioanalytic consultant in an organisation (Armstrong, 1995). It is not my intention here to further this debate. From discussions with socioanalytic practitioners and from my own experience, there is enough anecdotal evidence to suggest that something of the way in which drawing is used and thought about in the psychoanalytic domain also has relevance and application in socioanalytic consulting to organisations. It is a hypothesis in this book that the associative unconscious is "tapped" in both contexts.

What those in other disciplines have to say about the use of drawing

Socioanalysts do not have a monopoly on the use of drawings in organisational consulting. Cognitive psychologists and other organisational researchers have also discovered its virtues. Meyer (1991) has produced some interesting work in this field. He explores drawing from the perspective of cognitive psychology. He presents a strong argument for the use of drawing as a tool in organisational research. What is explored here is the limitation of continually relying upon responses and data from people in organisations that are expressed either in writing or verbally. He says, ". . . in gathering data, we almost always limit our subjects to counting, talking, and writing" (p. 219).

Meyer does not argue, as a socioanalyst might, that what is missed is an opportunity for a dialogue with the unconscious, but, rather, that there is good research data to indicate that we also know *consciously* more than we can tell.

> Pictures and graphics are seen as affording a means of communicating information about multi-dimensional organisational attributes with clarity and precision . . . informants often possess more copious and meaningful information than they can communicate verbally. (Meyer, 1991, p. 220)

He goes on to say that the brain is able both to store and give expression to far more complex data in a visual form, such as a picture, than it is able to do verbally. Meyer argues that

> organisational researchers try to devise instruments that will elicit verbal data conforming to a limited set of coherent categories . . . often, especially in research taking the entire organisation as an analytical unit, the phenomena of interest are fuzzy multidimensional constructs. In such cases, the coherence of respondents' verbal reports may be specious. (p. 221)

Meyer contends that "people possess more complex, subtle, and useful cognitive maps of their organisations than they can verbalise" (p. 231). Finally, he concludes, "Visual data seem especially worthwhile in efforts to move beyond mechanical and biological models of organisations to view them as systems for creating meaning" (p. 232).

While Meyer is not referring here to drawing as a means to accessing the unconscious in organisations, there is some synergy with the way socioanalysts also think of drawing as a way of communicating more than can be discerned from what can be consciously observed and verbally reported about the mechanical and biological dimensions of organisational life.

A number of other writers similarly advocate the use of drawing as a useful tool in working with people in organisations. Morgan describes using existing pictures and metaphors to elicit more detailed exploration of organisational issues. He writes,

> ... modes of visual imaging can break the constraints of an organiza-
> tion's conventional discourse and create a new space or new ground
> on which new developments can be built. Images speak far louder
> than words, concepts and theories about organizations could ever do.
> (Morgan, 1993, p. 233)

What he observed were "regular people using basic insights and imagery to communicate what they felt were fundamental truths about the state of their organization and its possibilities" (Morgan, 1993, p. 233).

Two other researchers, Nossiter and Biberman (1993), asked people to draw the picture in their mind of the organisation and then to describe in writing what they had drawn. They compared the responses of these people to answers from those who only answered a questionnaire. In this instance, there was no engagement between the client and the consultant other than to receive the instructions by mail. They concluded that not only was the "data" of a drawing richer and more detailed than those who answered a questionnaire, but also "respondents reported they enjoyed completing it". They reported that they believed "the more unconscious and less rational aspects of corporate culture" emerged. "The methodology focuses attention on the most salient idea or perception, discouraging the use of trite phrases and/or half truths" (Nossiter & Biberman, 1993, p. 15).

It is interesting that in the work of consultants and researchers outside of the socioanalytic domain there were so many echoes and resonances with what practitioners *in* the field have to say about the use of drawing as a tool. This is presented in detail below.

About the use of drawing by socioanalytic practitioners

Earlier research into the use of drawing in socioanalytic exploration (Nossal, 2010) reported that consultants and researchers applaud the utility and pleasure of using the tool. What is presented in this section is a summarised version of the findings under the headings of the questions asked.

What has been discovered from using drawings as a tool?

It captures the imagination and enlivens the spirit for the work. "[Drawings] make manifest . . . unconscious, preconscious and therefore previously unexamined attitudes, beliefs, feelings and fantasies" (Gould, 1987).

Drawings enable a very powerful and instantly different way for the group to relate to each other, often giving voice to the things that previously could not be named.

Taken together, what the reported ideas about drawings convey is that it is not just the content (the issues aired, the feelings expressed, the themes identified) that is given expression. The drawings also enable an exchange to take place between people in which important links are formed, old patterns in the dynamics are challenged and sometimes change.

What is proposed is that drawings, unlike many verbal responses, provide access to unconscious material and make it available for exploration. It is this ability to give expression to what was perhaps "known" but not yet thought (Bollas, 1987), or previously verbalised, that provides for the occasion of healing and learning for both the individual and the group. What is also worth emphasising is that often, through drawings, expression is given to thoughts and feelings that are more widely felt than just by the individual who drew the picture. In this way, an enormous amount of shared experience can be explored in a relatively short time, perhaps indicating "access" to the associative unconscious.

What are the applications in socioanalytic work for the use of drawing?

The range of applications for the use of drawing in socioanalytic work is very broad. Some examples follow.

- In the diagnostic phase of an organisational consultancy, in both individual interviews and group workshops.
- Drawings can be used as a means of communicating with the steering group in a consulting project about key issues emerging out of group work.
- Drawings can be used as a permanent record of a point in time in a project; they can be revisited again some time after the event as a means of reflecting on change and progress.

- In organisational role analysis, drawings can be used to open and deepen the exploration.
- The invitation to a client to draw a picture including the consultant/researcher might help to reveal what is being projected into these roles in accessible ways.

The invitation to draw a picture that portrays experience can be used as a diagnostic tool that, in the process, also serves as an intervention. Both the consultant and the client or client group have access to what the drawing reveals and this in itself can open the way to new insights and choices.

When do you introduce drawing as an activity with a client?

There was a diverse range of views about the timing of when a drawing might be introduced. Some consultants felt quite strongly that drawings are not something that you introduce up-front with a client, as expressed here:

> Don't spring drawings on people.

> Don't use drawings in the very first session of an organisational role analysis (ORA)—people can reveal/expose too much of themselves which can create too much anxiety and people may be left with more than can be worked through in the session.

> I only use drawings now with one-to-one client consultations when it is difficult to reach a deeper associative level of thinking. Sometimes there is something beginning to emerge, but we can't put a finger on it—when the client does a drawing, it often comes out in the imagery.

Others expressed a completely different view about when to introduce drawing:

> Drawings are the very first thing we do with a group of people.

> I use drawings as a way of beginning the ORA discussion.

> Drawings are a very helpful way to begin an unstructured interview in the diagnostic phase of a project. It's a good way to move very quickly to the important issues in the organisation and it frees people up to be quite open.

In my practice, over many years now, clients are often asked to do drawings at the beginning of a focus group or an interview during the early diagnostic phase of a project, or at the very beginning of a group workshop with the aim of developing shared hypotheses about the current state of the culture of an organisation. On all these occasions, while there is an aspect of "springing" the activity on people in the hope of eliciting spontaneous rather than studied responses, the experience has been positive. The drawings that emerge are invariably helpful to the process of generating rich and open discussion. There is something in this process that works to make the process of data creation more of a shared enterprise between the consultant and the client (and between clients) as all parties become co-explorers in associating and making sense of the drawings.

The opposing views of practitioners about the merits and pitfalls of the timing of the introduction of drawing into an engagement might stem from different ways of thinking about the field under investigation. That is, when investigating organisational culture, it is the system of the organisation (its people and context) and not the individual (and his/her intrapsychic) that is the "container" for thinking about the drawing. Similar to the way dreams are discussed in social dreaming (see Chapter Six of this book), one might say that it is the drawing and not the artist that becomes the vehicle for exploration. It is beholden upon the consultant to ensure that there is clarity on this point and to intervene to prevent group members from drawing conclusions about the artist in the process.

These distinctions are less clear when it comes to using drawings in organisational role analysis (ORA) with individual clients (Newton, Long, & Sievers, 2006). The interplay between the "internal organisation" (the personal and the intrapsychic) and the "external employer organisation" through the exploration of role becomes part of the field under investigation. Again, consultants differ in their decisions about the timing of using drawing in ORA. Some suggest that by using a drawing early in the work, it is possible to move more quickly to a deep level of exploration. My own preference is to build a trusting working relationship first and possibly only introduce drawing in the event that it is difficult for the work to progress. The use of drawing as a tool in ORA reliably opens up the space for more profound work (Harding & Nossal, 2008). How far into the territory of "the personal" a role analyst and analysand delve is likely to be determined by a number of factors, for example:

- the training and competence of the consultant to manage and appropriately contain what might surface unexpectedly about the individual through the exploration of a role drawing;
- the consultant is led by the client; the territory for investigation is constantly renegotiated and tested as the exploration progresses. The consultant needs to be attuned to the anxiety levels of the client in order to make an assessment of how far to go with offering associations to the drawing;
- the contract for the field of investigation is negotiated at the outset: exploration of role is the primary task of an ORA (Newton, Long, & Sievers, 2006). While the exploration might wander into the territory of the personal, it always comes back to how it helps to illuminate something about the experience in role.

The conclusion about *when* is the appropriate time to introduce drawing is non-definitive. As I have sought to show, a number of factors warrant consideration and one of them is the preference of the consultant.

How do you introduce and set up the use of drawing with clients?

The way in which the drawing activity is set up has implications for the atmosphere for the work that is created and the kind of material that is generated for exploration. For example, since people are able to give quite precise expression to their internal world through drawing, thinking through the task of the drawing is important: what is the territory or issue to be explored and in what way is it going to be managed and contained? It is likely that you will elicit the drawing that you ask for, so be sure to ask for what you want.

While both Vince (1995) and Gould (1987) describe giving relatively detailed instructions in presenting the drawing task to clients, other consultants vary in terms of how much explanation they go into about the activity. My experience is that people seem happy to proceed with the task with very little in the way of a theoretical framework or rationale for the activity. Some of the things that are worth taking into consideration when planning are listed below.

- It is important to avoid being too literal in the instructions you give because this will limit that to which expression can be given.

- Typically, the individual is invited to "draw a picture of your experience of the organisation" or "draw a picture of your experience of your role". Depending on the focus of the investigation, it might also be appropriate to frame it as "draw a picture of your experience of working in this team", or "draw a picture of the experience of intergroup dynamics in this organisation".
- In the instructions, people are invited to use their imagination, to use colour, to use metaphor, to draw a "picture" and to avoid using words or charts.
- It is important to explain that the drawings are not a test of artistic ability and, if appropriate, to show some examples of typical drawings that use stick figures and quite child-like imagery.
- Give a brief rationale for the use of drawing and explain that what will be generated is a richness of information that does not come from just talking. Through drawing, the right side of the brain is accessed, and this can allow for more spontaneity. As part of this, it may be appropriate to acknowledge that the activity might feel a bit uncomfortable at first because it is a way of communicating thoughts and feelings that is unfamiliar. But something useful always comes out of it.
- It is important that the playfulness inherent in the activity is allowed to be present by encouraging people to have fun with the activity.
- I always use good quality paper and pens or crayons. Some people provide lots of materials, including glitter glue, cut outs, stamps, and stickers.

Practitioners will find their own way of working with the introduction of the drawing task.

How do you explore the drawings with clients?

Again, there are some important differences of opinion about the way in which, once completed, the drawings are explored, especially in the group setting. There follows a number of responses from consultants.

> One of the lessons that I have learned is to allow as much time as possible for the exploration of the drawings. This part of it should not be rushed. There needs to be time to work with all of the drawings and time to discuss and work through what emerges from them.

I invite the group to associate to the drawing first and encourage them to be as wild and free as they like in this process. The individual then talks about what they drew and makes his/her own associations. We then put all the drawings up on the wall and look for the common themes and things that may be missing.

The focus for the exploration of the drawing is important. It needs to be clear in the consultant's mind that these drawings are not there as an indication of the state of mind of the individual, but rather as a means of exploring the "state of mind" of the organisation.

In the following responses, quite a different approach is reflected:

Show respect for the individual's drawing by looking at only one drawing at a time and inviting the artist to explore the drawing first before others make their associations.

Pay very great attention to the issue of containment when exploring the drawings. Sometimes the drawings expose the unconscious in unexpected and painful ways and the consultant needs to contain this experience.

It is always important to consider who is doing the interpretation. Different feelings and interpretations of drawings need to be shared and compared in order to provide a range of possible perspectives. Ideally, interpretation and sense-making in drawings is done initially by the individual who drew the picture, then collaboratively in the whole team (Vince, 1995, p. 13)

While it was not discussed in the interviews, it did appear in the literature that, in the exploration of drawings, it is important for the consultant to attempt to be aware of what they might themselves project on to the drawings, especially when working in a one-to-one context.

The material coming from drawings can be very rich and detailed. Strong feelings can be given expression and the unexpected can often emerge from drawings. What is reflected in the responses above is a tension between acknowledging what of the individual is given expression in the drawing and, at the same time, making the data about the conscious and unconscious world of the organisational system available for exploration. The more freely a group is allowed to associate to a drawing, the more opportunity there is for creative thinking to emerge. It is the consultant's responsibility to ensure that the task is presented and contained in such a way that the purpose is clearly to explore and work with the organisational system and not the individual's personality or "pathology". This being said, the work does not preclude the exploration of possible "pathology" adhering to work roles or even groups and organisations, through the history of the role, group, or organisation and that which might have been "left" behind by previous incumbents or unresolved issues (Chapman & Long, 2009). In this way, the drawing becomes a "vehicle" for the exploration of organisational issues and this is where the focus remains.

Quite often and quite unexpectedly for the client, the picture of the organisation that emerges gives expression to a lot of pain, frustration, and a sense of powerlessness. It is the task of the consultant to ensure that this is handled in a sensitive, containing, and enabling way. Some examples are provided in the following section.

Examples of the use of drawing in consulting to organisations

The following drawings and descriptions offer some case example material that seek to demonstrate, in the applied context, the utility and power of what the exploration of drawings can reveal.

The use of drawing in ORA

Case example 1

Figure 4.1 shows a drawing that was made during an ORA consultation with a nurse unit manager of a small hospital. The invitation was to draw a role biography (see Chapter Eleven). Up until this point in the work (about the fourth session), both client and consultant were struggling to make progress in exploring what was offered by the client as the "presenting issue". She recently had to performance-manage a very difficult member of her team. This finally resulted in the staff member leaving the organisation. The client described herself as ordinarily strong and confident in her management role. But in this instance, she had felt so manipulated and undermined by this

Figure 1.   Nurse unit manager role biography.

member of staff that she had lost much of her confidence in her management capabilities. She sought to understand what had happened that could "unravel" her in this way in order that it might never happen again.

What was immediately striking about the drawing was that it was drawn in monochrome blue. It seemed neat, clean, and orderly. The orderliness stood in stark contrast to the literal nature of her work (an operating theatre full of blood and body parts), her role history (which had been punctuated with some extraordinary and dramatic events), and the recent torrid experience of managing difficult staff members that had been described. One of the associations to the picture was that this was the "sanitised" version of the role that somehow hid the "messy" and difficult realities. While this "sanitising" provided a good defence against anxiety, it also made what was hidden behind it unavailable for thinking. This, in turn, prevented her from gaining any insight into what had so undermined her confidence in the wake of recent events. By using the drawing as an associative resource, I asked her to look at the role biography that she had drawn and see if she could identify any point in the narrative of her work or life roles where she had experienced similar feelings or difficulties in the past. While I could not have known, this proved to be the key to unlocking the source of her disturbance.

In fact, she was able to identify precisely the point in the picture (and her past) when she had had experiences of feeling similarly undermined and afraid. This led us into a rich and in-depth exploration of the ways in which these past experiences, at an unconscious level, continued to have an influence in how she experienced her role. Strong feelings from an earlier time in her life had been powerfully reinvoked by recent events. Once the originating cause of the disturbance was brought to the surface by associating to the drawing, it was available to be thought about and worked with.

Using the drawing as a tool for exploration, we were able to uncover, in a relatively short period of time (about four additional fortnightly sessions), some very deep and previously hidden internal dynamics that had been getting in the way of this manager accessing all of her resources for the role. As the consultant, I allowed her to lead the exploration; trying to stay carefully attuned to how much she was comfortable with revealing and exploring. In this respect, this client was extraordinarily humble, brave, and adventurous.

Case example 2

The drawing depicted in Figure 4.2 was created by a young senior manager, Peter (not his real name), in a university-based service provider office, who was presented with the challenge of leading his staff through a service and work culture renewal process. He had been promoted to the role of director ahead of some of his older colleagues who had been in the service a long time and who had also applied for the job. His staff described themselves as over-worked, stressed, and feeling pushed by their internal clients into the less interesting, process-driven work that was really the task of clients.

Peter can be seen in two places in this drawing: as the middle person in the group of three and as the figure floating above the two groups. Earlier in the consultation, the consultants working with the organisation had learnt that the three managers who went for the senior management role had made a "pact" that whatever the results, the three of them would manage as a threesome. The model was unworkable and made it nearly impossible for Peter to assert his authority and take

Figure 4.2.   Peter's experience of role.

up the kind of strong, directive leadership that would be necessary to bring about change. Staff members (including the other two managers) were sticking resolutely to old ways of doing things, but continuing to complain about the current state as unworkable.

Through our associations to it, what the drawing reveals is that, at the outset, Peter did not have a lot of confidence in his capacity to lead the change. It was as if he would have to be a "super-hero" to do so. The figure floating in space (while intended to depict Peter as further along the path to change) appears to be held up by a rather flimsy-looking gas balloon that might or might not drift to the "island getaway" in the upper right corner of the page. The arrow depicts the direction that they should be heading (towards a brighter, less stressful future), but everyone, including Peter, has their backs to it as if looking towards the past, and this is felt to be solid ground. This island destination is in a cloud that might also drift away. Our association to this was to the seeming difficulty in believing that it would be possible to bring about real change—it seemed like an impossible goal at this point.

The other thought bubbles, as described by Peter, represented the mixed feelings in the group and these symbols are replicated in his own thought-bubble as acknowledgement of what he has to contain as their manager, as well as some of his own feelings of ambivalence. The detail that Peter had been less aware of, but that nevertheless proved important, was the fact that all the figures lacked any facial features such as eyes and mouths. This led to an exploration of how relatively voiceless Peter and members of the group felt in the context of the broader system. They were severely under-staffed, owing to a large increase in their workload, but their suffering seemed invisible to those who could act to authorise the employment of more staff.

The drawing proved a helpful way of creating an appropriate thinking space for the work. In his words:

> From my perspective it was a really important first step. I don't think that I am necessarily or automatically an open person, so the drawing gave us both some things to think about at the very beginning. I think it also high-lighted to me that I was feeling isolated in the role and helped me recog-nise that this was an issue for further discussion—it stopped the feelings of isolation being an additional hurdle.

As we explored what was depicted in the drawing, much infor-mation about both the literal and emotional aspects of how the role was experienced were given expression in a short space of time. It was as if the territory for the work of the ORA was visually mapped out. Over time, we would often refer back to aspects of the drawing as a kind of "touchstone", or reference point for how things had either changed or stayed the same.

Drawing as a tool in culture diagnosis

As described above, drawings provide material for a co-created understanding of role experience (both conscious and unconscious) and this can be used diagnostically by the pair. Drawings can also provide a lot of data about the perceived culture of an organisation when used as part of a diagnostic process. The following case exam-ple offers an illustration of this.

Case example 3

The client organisation was a sub-section of a large government department. The project was initiated by the newly appointed director, who sought leadership development and culture change both for his executive team and the senior management group. He had inherited what he described as a culture where senior people expected to be told what to do. His predecessor was described as a "benevolent dictator" with a "command and control" style of management. He was also very concerned about the fact that the teams, with interdependent tasks and responsibilities, worked as if in "silos".

We began the process with what we describe as an organisational culture diagnosis—an in-depth examination of the work culture. We held individual interviews with the seven members of the senior leadership team and small focus discussion groups with the next layer of management in their functional units (a total of twenty-four people took part). Everyone drew a picture as part of this process. The invitation was to "draw a picture of your experience of working in Department XX and put yourself in it". In the interviews, the request for the drawing came at the end, whereas in the focus groups we began with the drawing activity and the drawings became the starting point for the discussion. In the focus groups, each drawing was considered in turn. First, the artist was invited to explain what they had drawn and then the group as a whole was invited to associate freely to what they could see in the drawings. These associations were captured on an electronic whiteboard. Some examples of the drawings and the associations to them are presented below.

Figure 4.3 is a "Mr Men" drawing, while Figure 4.4 depicts a feudal scene.

Mr Messy is in control, not you!

All the managers are playing very different instruments, but none is looking at the conductor.

There are different strengths in the organisation, but how do you conduct them?

The artist [in bottom left hand corner] looks very small and powerless.

Some of the associations to Figure 4.4 were:

Each of the areas is fenced off from the others. Occasionally a sheep jumps the fence. There is a bridge to a brighter future, but no gate to go through.

Figure 4.3.   Mr Men drawing.

Figure 4.   Feudal scene.

The castle looks like a fortress built to protect us from outside attacks from our stakeholders.

The "shepherd"—the Director—looks like a wicked wizard.

Figure 4.5 shows a chariot rider confronting the barrier of a brick wall.

We're constantly fighting a battle—with no one in particular—a combination of all the groups.

We're trying to sell a message, but we hit a brick wall.

We're fighting to get people to work with us—inside and outside.

The brick wall is the rules we hide behind.

Figure 4.6. represents the feeling of being stuck in the middle.

We're stuck in the middle between two groups who don't understand each other.

There are a lot of unhappy people and we're holding people back.

The groups are divided; you need very long arms to try to connect them.

Figure 4.5.   Chariot rider facing brick wall.

Figure 4.6.   Stuck in the middle.

Some obvious common threads in the drawings are the divisions between teams and elements of threat, hostility, or chaos. After the discussions with the groups, the consultants collated and analysed all the associations to the drawings (including our own) from both the interviews and the focus groups and looked for discernible themes in the data that had been created. These became the basis for a working note: a summary of the themes and some working hypotheses about the current work culture.

The next step in the process was to bring all the project participants together for a one-day workshop to explore the findings. Rather than simply present our working note at the beginning of the day, we began by creating a gallery of all the drawings (with permission from the participants—thirty-one in total). Participants were invited to view them and in small groups discuss their associations and what, if any, themes they could discern. For example, were there any recurring images or patterns? Were there any surprises? What overall impressions were they left with? What working hypotheses might they form about the current work culture?

Our experience has been that by working in this way, we are not privileging the consultants' interpretations over those of the clients. Rather, the hope is that both the consultants' and the clients' work culture diagnoses will be consistent, or if they are different, this also becomes a basis for an interesting discussion of things that might be observed by the consultants that might be more difficult to see by the clients. In general, by the time we come to presenting our working note, it merely serves to reinforce what they have already discovered as a group about their current work culture. The working hypotheses that we then offer about more hidden (maybe unconscious) aspects of the culture can be more readily engaged with. These hypotheses are just a small step beyond their own diagnosis and might or might not provide a deeper layer of insight. Once this kind of shared under-standing of the current state of the work culture has been created, both consultants and clients are in a good position to think about appro-priate next steps.

The drawings provided the group with a very powerful visual representation of their shared experiences of the organisation. It was as if the drawings, with their primitive, yet inescapable clarity of expression, helped to open our clients' minds to the issues in a way that the spoken or written word is so often not able to do. It is not just the person drawing who is enabled to find expression, but also those who view the drawing, who, in what they see, connect readily to their own experiences and those of others. As one participant said,

"It was a bit weird at first, but I found it a lot easier to draw a picture and then talk about it, particularly since my opinion was not one that I would come out and just say in an open forum like that."

These examples also illustrate clearly some of the depth of feeling that can emerge from the work with drawings. This way the work can help individuals and groups to gain a shared and in-depth perspec-tive about the work culture. They can then use this to decide what they would like to change and to refocus their attention and energy on the primary task of the organisation.

Concluding remarks

Through working with drawings, something shifts in the way people work together to develop understanding, to make meaning, and to learn. This shift can take place within the individual as well as in the group, and I believe that sometimes this occurs in the realm beyond what we can consciously name. All we know is that things have changed in some subtle, yet quite profound way. This puts me in mind of something Armstrong wrote. He seemed to suggest that the work group might become an "arena for transformation" when it engages in its capacity for "serious play". "Or in those moments in a group . . . when people are able to associate to others' material without an irritable preoccupation with ownership and without recourse to a prescriptive idea of 'relevance'" (Armstrong, 1992). For me, this connects to the very heart of what it is to work in a socioanalytic way. There is something in the inherently playful and sensual nature of drawing that helps to create a working space where there is the freedom to engage with the real experience of people in organisations. Drawings seem to enhance people's capacity to think creatively together. It provides a opportunity to "breathe new life" or "fresh air" into a space that might have become saturated in such a way that people feel stifled or so anxious that they are no longer able to think. Sadly, this saturated space is the one in which many people in contemporary organisations work.

If we are prepared to accept the proposition that drawings not only speak the language of the unconscious and create an "arena for transformation", but also speak of more than can be described or captured verbally, it has to be acknowledged that what we have is a very powerful and simple tool that can assist us in the work of creating the opportunity for individuals and groups to increase their capacity for creative work on their primary task.

References

Armstrong, D. (1992). Names, thoughts and lies: the relevance of Bion's later writing for understanding experiences in groups. *Free Associations*, 3(26): 261–282.

Armstrong, D. (1995). The analytic object in organizational work. Paper presented to the ISPSO Symposium, London.

Bion, W. R. (1970). *Attention and Interpretation: A Scientific Approach to Insight in Psycho-Analysis and Groups*. London: Tavistock.

Bollas, C. (1987). *The Shadow of the Object: Psychoanalysis of the Unthought Known*. London: Free Association Books.

Brutsche, P. (1988). Preface. In: G. Furth, *The Secret World of Drawings: A Jungian Approach to Healing through Art* (pp. xi–xii). Boston, MA: Sigo Press.

Chapman, J., & Long, S. (2009). Role contamination: is the poison in the person or in the bottle. *Socio-Analysis: the Journal of the Australian Institute of Socio-Analysis, 11*: 53–66.

Furth, G. (1988). *The Secret World of Drawings: A Jungian Approach to Healing through Art.* Boston, MA: Sigo Press.

Gould, L. J. (1987). A methodology for assesssing internal working models of the organisation: applications to management and organisational development programs. Paper presented to the Annual Meeting of the International Society for the Psychoanalytic Study of Organisations, New York.

Harding, W., & Nossal, B. (2008). The opening-up of a different space: ORA from the client perspective. *Socio-Analysis: the Journal of the Australian Institute of Socio-Analysis, 10*: 51–64.

Kübler-Ross, E. (1988). Foreword. In: Furth, G. *The Secret World of Drawings: A Jungian Approach to Healing through Art* (pp. ix–x). Boston, MA: Sigo Press.

Long, S. (2001). Working with organizations: the contribution of the psychoanalytic discourse. *Organisational and Social Dynamics, 2*: 174–198.

Meyer, A. (1991). Visual data in organizational research. *Organization Science, 2*(2): 218–236.

Morgan, G. (1993). *Imaginization: The Art of Creative Management.* Newbury Park, CA: Sage.

Newton, J., Long, S., & Sievers, B. (2006). *Coaching in Depth: The Organisational Role Analysis Method.* London: Karnac.

Nossal, B. (2010). The use of drawing in socio-analytic exploration. *Socio-Analysis: the Journal of the Australian Institute of Socio-Analysis, 12*: 77–92.

Nossiter, V., & Biberman, G. (1993). Projective drawings and metaphor: analysis of organisational culture. *Journal of Managerial Psychology, 5*(3): 13–16.

Vince, R. (1995). Working with emotions in the change process: using drawings for team diagnosis and development. *Organisations and People, 2*(1): 11–17.

CHAPTER FIVE

Socioanalytic interviewing

Susan Long and Wendy Harding

Introduction

T his chapter will explore issues in conducting interviews for socioanalytically orientated research and consultancy. This broadly includes two interrelated areas.

1.   The systemic processes within a group, organisation, or society. Such systemic processes become evidenced through the experiences and behaviours of individuals and their interactions. As said in Chapter One of this book, "a metaphor is that of a jigsaw puzzle where each individual part is shaped very differently, yet the picture as a whole has its own unique integrity". Consequently, with this in mind, individual interviews are considered by us as exploring the uniqueness of the individual while attempting to gain a picture of the whole.

2.   The in-depth discovery of unconscious processes that affect the group, organisation, or society. Such unconscious processes might be evidenced in individuals (as in narcissistic leaders, e.g., Kets de Vries, 1996), although in socioanalysis we are interested in how these processes are shared in, for instance, basic

assumption behaviour (Bion, 1961), social defences (Menzies Lyth, 1988, 1989), and other structural and cultural phenomena.

Given this formulation, while a socioanalytic research interview may include traditional questionnaire or short answer type formats giving rise to quantitative data that can then be examined for patterns and implications beyond the surface of the data (see, for example, the research appendix in Long, 1992, where a multi-dimensional scaling analysis is done on data generated through a grid of interpersonal ratings), such research is generally complementary to socioanalytic research. Our main focus here will be to examine qualitative in-depth interviews.

While qualitative research interviews are generally regarded in the research literature as having the objective of collecting thick, descriptive data (Geertz, 2008), that is, descriptions of interviewees' experiences (Rubin & Rubin, 1995; Spradley, 1979), the socioanalytic research interview utilises, yet goes beyond, an existential or phenomenological approach. We hypothesise unconscious dynamics at a systemic level that influence direct experience. Just as for Freud dreams, symptoms, parapraxis, and jokes all contain the hints of unconscious thoughts and suppressed feelings, so the direct experiences of individuals contain the hints of unconscious systemic dynamics. (See Hollway & Jefferson, 2000 for a discussion of research interviews reaching beyond the surface.) In our discussion, we emphasise that the socioanalytic research interview is just one part of a broader research exploration. The researcher is interested in understanding the dynamics that support and obscure social and organisational structures and cultures. The interview is one avenue into such an understanding.

Socioanalytic interviewing aims to enable the exploration of both conscious and unconscious organisational phenomenon to expand the understanding of the organisation for the interviewer and interviewee. Usually, this is to come to an understanding of particular organisational problems that maybe related to the whole organisation or a subcomponent of the organisation. Interviews may comprise the extent of the methods undertaken in organisation research or consultancy or they might be one of a number of methods. Very often interviews are involved in the first phase of organisational research or culture analysis where the researcher or consultant is learning about the organisation. However, the socioanalytic interview is designed not only for the interviewer to "collect" data because there is the intent also for the interview to be a potential space for the interviewee to explore their own thoughts and feelings about the organisation and the issue(s) under question. The opportunity for organisation members to be heard and supported in exploring their organisational experience is often felt by interviewees as a rare and valuable experience and can lead to insights about the system that take the interviewee by surprise. The socioanalytic interview is not a passive space, but one that has potential to dynamically contribute to the development of the system as part of action research or consultancy.

Conceptual context for socioanalytic interviews

A socioanalytic perspective is located in the conjunction of its systems and psychoanalytic dimensions. The systems dimension speaks to the structural features of the organisation. It articulates interdependent relations between system elements and the system as a whole, and the system and its environment. "Systems thinking" provides a framework for understanding the way in which the positioning of system elements support or obstruct the survival of the system (Angyal, 1978; Katz & Kahn, 1978).

The systems dimension articulates system parts not significantly connected with each other except with reference to the whole (Angyal, 1978). This rejects the idea that to understand an organism or a social system it is necessary simply to understand causal relations between its parts. All system elements are linked through a superordinate factor, which is the system (Gould, 2001). This interdependence of system elements orientates socioanalytic interviews towards seeking each person's experience as a set of representative dynamics that contain meaning about the whole system, leading us to understand behaviour of group members not as idiosyncratic to the individual, but, at least in part, resulting from interaction between the individual and the organisation (Wells, 1980). Stacey describes this:

> The system is then thought of as a bounded entity consisting of individuals who are its parts. The system is formed by the interaction of the individuals and exists at a higher level than the individual following laws of its own, which might be thought of as emergent properties. (Stacey, 2003, p. 327)

The psychoanalytic dimension adds depth to understanding system interactions through incorporating a conscious and an unconscious rationale for system behaviour. By inclusion of the unconscious in thinking about the organisation, enquiry extends into hidden motivations that profoundly influence the organisation's capacity to work to task (De Board, 1990; Gould 2001; Miller & Rice, 1975). In particular, our attention in thinking this way is drawn towards the ways that organisational structures and cultures are affected by unconscious system defences against primitive anxiety, anxiety related to the emotional labour of the work and to small and large group dynamics (Hirschhorn, 1988; Jaques, 1955; Long, 1992; Menzies Lyth, 1988, 1989).

These two dimensions, systems and psychoanalytic, interact to create an enquiry space different from, but informed by, both conceptual frames. The conceptual frame supports deep enquiry about the meaning of phenomena in the organisation. As examples: what feelings does the organisation evoke in group members? What does the experience of the interviewee symbolise and express for the organisation? How does it serve the organisation for this member/subgroup to take on these feelings or roles? How is each of these aspects manifest in the structure and culture of the organisation (Wells, 1980)?

In this context, the interview becomes a place where we seek to discern from data across interviews a whole picture of the organisation and its parts; rather than compare each interview primarily for the extent of replication from one interview to another. The socioanalytic interviewer accepts and values that different parts of the system contain quite different experiences of the organisation, each valuable to the understanding of the organisation as a whole.

To create interview settings that are conducive to this type of enquiry requires careful attention to interview design, interview structure, the respective roles of the interviewer and interviewee, and to content.

Interview design

The role of interviewer includes managing the boundaries of the task, time, territory, and research/consulting ethics. The socioanalytic researcher or consultant (perhaps as part of a team) will have initially designed their research purpose through the development of a research or consultancy rationale. This might have been done in conjunction with their research partner (in collaborative action research) or their client (in consultancy). The research design will then be developed, including tasks for the research. The purpose and tasks of the research—further developed through the interview process—frame the management of the research boundaries.

For the interviewer, there is great responsibility to create a thought-through and safe environment so that both the interviewer and interviewee can authentically enter the space. This is usually regarded as providing a "contained" space, where the thoughts and emotions of the players are respected and optimal conditions for the development of trust are provided (see Bion, 1970 for ideas about the container and the contained). The idea of containment implies that the interviewee is "held in mind". Another description is that of a safe "holding environment", so named as to reflect the safe physical and emotional holding of an infant by a caring parent (Winnicott, 1971). This description fits with the implicit differences of power where the interviewer is regarded as "in charge" of the task, at least initially. Keeping to agreed tasks and time and providing or negotiating a space free from intrusion helps to build a sense of safety.

Management of ethical considerations is also important. While funded or university supported research usually is subject to specific ethical regulation, as may be research done in government organisations, consultancy relies primarily on the professional integrity of the consultant. Apart from general law, there is no formal regulation of ethical standards. The discrepancy is wide between how interview data is handled or how interview subjects are selected in research and consultancy. Despite the potential problems of restrictive or over-regulated research, socioanalytic consultants could learn much from research ethics processes when conducting discussions, observations, and interviews as part of their work. The research ethics process generally asks that all interviewees be recruited voluntarily, that they be given a plain English statement of the purpose and nature of the research, that they can withdraw themselves or their data at any time, that children under eighteen have the consent of a parent, that there is a complaints process available, and that interviewees are asked to sign a consent form. The latter provides a safety net for both interviewees and interviewers.

With or without such a formal process, it is important to design the interview in four main parts. We describe here these parts of the process for socioanalytic research. The first three all set the scene and prepare for a space where a free-flowing conversation can take place.

Initial contact

The initial contact involves negotiating the interview with the interviewee. This might be done through a third person (manager, associate, colleague); however, it is preferable to have some personal contact before the interview to explain the purpose and gain authority to conduct the interview. Gaining authority from the interviewee as well as from the organisation allows the interviewer the authority to pursue the task of the interview and helps the interviewer into their role from the beginning. In arranging the interview, make sure you have a clear agreement about the interview. See this initial negotiation as a source of data.

Boundaries are important and should be clearly and mutually agreed before the interview. They include:

- purpose of the interview;
- general range of issues, etc., to be covered;
- approximate length of time;
- the setting;
- whether notes will be taken or the interview taped (and why);
- for what purpose the data will be used;
- whether the interviewee is to be given a transcript or not for checking (and why);
- what will happen to the notes or tape;
- if and how the identity of the interviewee will be protected in the final data/report or thesis.

Beginning the interview

The interview should ideally begin with introductions, restating the purpose of the interview and iterating the conditions under which information gained will be handled. Is the interview confidential? Is it anonymous? Will quotes be used? Is a tape recorder utilised and permission gained? How will the data be stored? While it is important to let the interviewee know about, and consent to, these details, it is important to maintain a balance between gaining agreement, giving information, and not overstating these issues in such a way that a paranoid and suspicious atmosphere is engendered. We try to be as matter of fact as possible and have most of these details dealt with in the initial contact. Often, we have the chance to interview in pairs, explaining that one of us will sit in the background taking notes while the other will conduct the interview. The person taking notes only intervenes when it seems to them something has been missed. This division of labour allows for the interviewer to concentrate on the interview and the relationship with the interviewee.

Shape of the interview

It is helpful for the interviewer to briefly outline the shape of the interview. For example we might say, "First I will gain some background data just to locate you in the organisation, how long you have been here, and what roles you have taken. Some personal details will also be helpful when we are looking at overall patterns. Then I will ask some questions related to the main purpose of the research. These will be open-ended and please feel free to elaborate or add anything that you think is important. Finally, I would like just a little time to review the interview process with you." For research, we often need the demographic background data in order to look at how various themes in the data emerge from different roles, genders, age groups, employees who have been with the organisation for many years *vs.* newcomers, and so on. We explain this to our interviewees. The review at the end of the interview is very helpful. It provides a space for the interviewee to debrief, and often new material is offered in what seems a less formal space. The interview material is there as a "third" position that can be discussed less self-consciously.

Conduct of the interview

We then conduct the interview as explained. We let the interviewee know that if something is missed, we may return to it. We try not to set ourselves up as experts who make no mistakes. If we forget something, we are natural about returning to a point we wish to follow up. We explore the areas that we have indicated and allow for the interview to diverge into areas that the interviewee brings forward. We follow through with secondary questions that explore the interviewees' meanings. Finally, we thank the interviewee for their participation. We let them know that should anything further come to mind, they can contact us.

Creation of interview data. What to look for:
a potential space for thinking the unthought known

In traditional social science interviews, the interview is a space where the interviewee is invited to express their experience and the interviewer pays attention to content and emotional texture, sometimes including the body language of the interviewee. Socioanalytic interviewing expands this to include attention to signs of unconscious phenomena that lie below awareness in the organisation but that critically affect it.

Schein (1984, p. 3) calls these elements "underlying assumptions". He contends that these are the deepest and most embedded elements of organisation and have arisen out of problem solving (or, more accurately, not problem solving) characterised by avoidance of anxiety. He argues that they are the deepest and most difficult to shift because to revisit these elements means that the original intolerable anxiety will resurface.

In organisations, underlying assumptions manifest in particular system properties and relations between those properties. One such relation is the management of anxiety through splitting and projection, one element of the split being imbued with the "good" and the other the "bad". Splitting and projection are widespread human ways of avoiding anxiety, of not problem solving at all system levels. Inevitably, organisational structure and culture is made up of many examples of this type of system defence mechanism. One fairly simplistic example found in university settings is reflected in the common dynamic of lower level administrative staff being blamed for many things where responsibility would more aptly be directed towards teaching staff; it is too risky and anxiety producing for students to direct blame towards those who might be assessing their exam papers. The teaching staffs are then free to be idolised, the opposite "good" polarity of the split. Often, the dynamic is enacted with the "bad" other becoming (at least in part) the character of the projection: for example, in this case, withdrawn, rigid, and intractable, obstructing the delivery of the work.

Defences are not destructive *per se*; they enable survival. The socioanalyst is interested in thinking about whether or not a particular collective defence is helpful to the work of the organisation.

Access to unconscious phenomenon in organisations may be found in the content of the interview and in the interviewer's and interviewee's experience in the interview. The following touches on how to recognise some of the projective organisational phenomena within the interview.

Unconscious material in the content of the interview

System defences are commonly employed unconscious processes to rid systems (individual, interpersonal, subgroup, organisation as a whole) of intolerable feelings so that the system can survive. Primitive defences range in strength and endurance through basic assumptions, covert coalitions, and organisational rituals (Hirschhorn, 1988); however, all have some similar properties. These include immediate and unconscious occurrence, and thoughtlessness about consequences; they feel intractable; they are not rational, but instead are an emotional response to the fear of dissolution that primitive anxiety mobilises.

Hints of defensive mechanisms might be found in the content and behaviour in interviews. For example, does what is being said have an unthought-through quality? In delving into the content, do you experience a blank wall? Is thought possible? When and when not? Are there slips being made? Is there incongruence between affect and the nature of the content? Is the interviewee late or wanting to leave early consistently (in multiple interviews)? Considering when these things occur, what they might be about, and what was being talked about previously can help you to understand what might be being unconsciously communicated to you by the interviewee about the organisation.

The idea of unconscious communication can be taken further to include the experience in the interviewer role: for example, how are you being made to feel? Are you able to stay in the interviewer role or do you feel you are being pulled and pushed into other roles? How difficult is it for you to keep to the time, territory, and task of the interview? Are you having your own defences mobilised, and if so, in what ways? The following explores this aspect further.

Unconscious material in the interviewer's experience as potential data

Socioanalytic interviews provide the potential for discovering and legitimising, as data, unconscious organisational and broader social elements through paying attention to the experience of the interviewee in the interview and later in thinking about the interview experience. It is presumed when working socioanalytically that, at times, the organisation's projective material located in the interviewee will be enacted in the interview with aspects projected on to the interviewer and the interview setting. Through transferences and projections, the interviewer often comes to think and feel in ways that originate in the organisational system studied. Examining what feelings and thoughts are solely yours (the interviewer) and what might belong to the interviewees/organisations can provide data unable to be discovered in any other way.

Even more correctly, we might say that the research/consulting project is itself a new and temporary system with its own dynamics emergent from both the interviewer and interviewee's "home" systems. Exploring when and where the dynamics from either "home" system enter the temporary research system is critical.

Thinking about projective material is difficult because being caught in the experience is an unconscious, in the moment event. Coming to know that you were the recipient of projection and what that projection might represent is mostly retrospective. Ways to support bringing those experiences to awareness are critical aspects of research design. It is necessary to have a transitional or "third" object to enable this, be it through dialogue with an interview partner or research support team, through writing, or through developing internal cognitive and emotional capacity to expect, experience, and think through the projective material very carefully.

The importance of being open to being "caught" in this way in the interview setting cannot be stressed too greatly, as this is to be potentially in touch with deep organisational elements difficult to be found in any other tradition of interviewing (Mersky, 2001). While it might be difficult to experience what the system has found intolerable, it is to be welcomed in the socioanalytic interview.

The interview allows you to "create" data as part of your research. This means that data are not "found" somehow outside the working relationship of the interview, but are remembered, reworked, conceptualized, and experienced inside that relationship.

The research interview is best seen as a mutual process of exploration, where interviewer and interviewee take up different roles in the exploration of an issue, topic, or situation. It should not be simply the interrogation of one by the other. If your interviewee knows the purpose of the interview, he or she can join with you in an exploration. This creates the "third space". Hollway and Jefferson (2000) warn us that in socioanalytic research the research subjects are "defended" and might resist finding the truth in their experience. None the less, we can reduce their defensiveness by careful preparation and the creation of a mutually reflective space. Beyond that, the exploration of possible defences when analysing the data adds to understanding.

Skills of the interviewer

We list here some of the skills that we find important in socioanalytic interviewing. In providing a list, we encourage interviewers to check their own usual interviewing behaviours.

1. *Active listening* means that you should focus on what the interviewee says and regularly check that you have the interviewee's meaning correct.
2. *Prompting for extended detail* means that a first answer can nearly always be extended. "Tell me more about that", "Can you clarify that further?"
3. *Gaining specific examples* of what is talked about. Always try to ask, "Can you give me an example?" "Is there a story behind this?" Try to get narratives as well as more general ideas.
4. *Showing empathy* means trying to see the situation from the interviewee's point of view, not simply saying "I understand". Keep exploring until you actually "get it".
5. *Clarifying* means asking again if you do not understand the answer. Do not pretend to know (e.g., what is meant by an acronym or something in the news that the interviewee assumes you know about). You want their view anyway, and it is a problem to

assume anything. Ask until you think you have an understanding and then check again if needs be.

6. *Challenging* means extended clarification. If the interviewee has said one thing and later says another, you might ask what the two different perspectives mean. This does not mean that you have to point out that they are inconsistent, because the difference might mean that you are getting at the situation from a different perspective and you want to explore both. Do not avoid the exploration for fear of embarrassing your interviewee.

7. *Free association*—allow for the possibility of free associations to the material that has emerged. This might be through allowing the last ten minutes to consist of a mutual reflection on the interview process.

8. *Observation during the interview*. This is difficult because often the focus on content becomes all consuming. But try to be aware of the interpersonal context and how the interviewee is responding to you. Also observe you own reactions. Give yourself space for this. You will not have space if all you are doing is trying to remember your next question.

9. *Following the interview*, take process notes, even if you taped the interview/discussion. These should include separate listings of impressions and your own responses and reflections.

Analysis of interview data

Analysis using qualitative social science methods might involve the distillation of themes, categories, trends, and narratives in the interview data. This reduces masses of data to manageable "chunks". Such initial analysis might be done across many interviews, perhaps grouping the data into categories derived from the demographics obtained. In looking at organisational or social phenomena, this process involves discerning patterns across groupings (cross-sectional analysis), or over time (longitudinal analysis of reported incidents), or through narratives, stories, and myths held about the organisation. In particular, you might wish to examine critical incidents, both those described by the interviewees and those that occur in the process of the interview itself. Critical incidents in the interview process (from initial contact right through to completion of all interviews) might well mirror critical dynamics in your interviewee's organisational system. Fundamentally, this initial analysis involves looking for patterns in the data.

Beyond this, data analysis within socioanalysis is largely through *interpretation and association*. Some of the patterns discerned in the data will make more sense than others. However, a major tool is to apply conceptual sense making.

First, interpretation is theory driven. It helps to examine the data through the lens of theory and concepts: for example, transference, projective identification, etc. (Kleinian theory), or other theories (Lacanian, Jungian, etc.). And, of course, theory is developed through the group (of psychoanalysts and others exploring these issues) so that past theories are modified and new concepts are grown.

Second, interpretation is informed through experience and experience is understood (even occurs *as* experience) in the presence of, or alongside, others. Perhaps all experience is ultimately social. It is argued in this book that at an unconscious level, through the associative unconscious, all experience is linked.

Third, a method of analysis is also through access to the unconscious infinite (Bion, 1991), which is through free association. Free association gives potential access to unconscious experience and meaning. The further conceptualisation, hence, the further analysis of data, is then tested in reality, perhaps by a variety of means.

A model for all data analysis using socioanalytic methods is:

1. Discovering themes, narratives, and critical incidents (this is common to all social science research).
2. Discovering/identifying the dynamics (transferences, counter-transferences, projections, etc.) in the group/organisation/the data/the research or consultancy temporary system.
3. Discovering/formulating a hypothesis. This is the analytic tool of the working hypothesis (see Chapter One of this book), which may also be discovered through the analytic tool of the working note in organisational research (Miller, 1995).

Although all this may be done alone in one's own head, so to speak (if ever we are alone in our heads), it is better done in reality with others. This is achieved through discovering different perspectives on the data, different experiences and associations to the data, and having different theoretical light thrown on the data. This requires a steering group, reflection group, supervision team, or research team.

Conclusion

Socioanalytic interviewing requires the interviewer to carefully and rigorously design the interview experience. It requires discipline in undertaking the interview, paying due respect to the critical importance of time, task, and territory. Attention to these factors enable the possibilities of a shared experience in the interview setting whereby system data are created that might not have been previously conscious—data held in the experience of both the interviewer and interviewee.

This chapter has discussed a model for the socioanalytic interview and the rationale behind it. It offers the reader a way in to what is often a challenging but potentially rewarding opportunity to come to understand deep layers of organisational phenomenon.

References

Angyal, A. (1978). A logic of systems. In: F. Emery (Ed.), *Systems Thinking: Selected Thinking* (pp. 17–29). Harmondsworth: Penguin.

Bion, W. R. (1961). *Experiences in Groups.* London: Tavistock.

Bion, W. R. (1970). *Attention and Interpretation.* London: Tavistock.

Bion, W. R. (1991). *A Memoir of the Future* London: Karnac.

De Board, R. (1990). *The Psychoanalysis of Organizations: A Psychoanalytic Approach to Behavior in Groups and Organizations.* New York: Routledge.

Geertz, C. (2008). Thick description: toward an interpretive theory of culture (pdf). www.alfrehn.com/fahlner/tko/resources/Kultur/Thick-Description.pdf. Accessed May 2012.

Gould, L. J. (2001). Introduction. In: L. J. Gould, L. F. Stapley, & M. Stein (Eds.), *The System Dynamics of Organizations. Integrating the Group Relations Approach, Psychoanalytic, and Open Systems Perspectives* (pp. 1–15). New York: Karnac.

Hirschhorn, L. (1988). *The Workplace Within: Psychodynamics of Organizational Life.* London: MIT Press.

Hollway, W., & Jefferson, T. (2000). *Doing Qualitative Work Differently: Free Association, Narrative and the Interview Method.* London: Sage.

Jaques, E. (1955). Social systems as a defense against persecutory and depressive anxiety. In: M. Klein, P. Heimann, & R. Money-Kyrle (Eds.), London: Tavistock.

Katz, D., & Kahn, R. L. (1978). Common characteristics of open systems. In: F. Emery (Ed.), *Systems Thinking: Selected Thinking* (pp. 86–104). Harmondsworth: Penguin.

Kets de Vries, M. F. R. (1996). *Life and Death in the Executive Fast Lane: Essays on Irrational Organizations and their Leaders.* San Francisco, CA: Jossey-Bass.

Long, S. D. (1992). *A Structural Analysis of Small Groups.* London: Routledge.

Menzies Lyth I. E. P. (1988). *Containing Anxiety in Institutions. Vol. 1 Selected Essays.* London: Free Association Books.

Menzies Lyth, I. E. P. (1989). *The Dynamics of the Social. Vol. 2 Selected Essays.* London: Free Association Books.

Mersky, R. (2001). Falling from grace—when consultants go out of role: enactment in the service of organizational consultancy. *Socioanalysis, 3:* 37–53.

Miller, E. J. (1995). Dialogue with the client system: use of the "working note" in organizational consultancy. *Journal of Managerial Psychology, 10:* 6: 27–30.

Miller, E. J., & Rice, A. K. (1975). Selections from Systems of Organizations. In: A. D. Colman & W. H. Bexton (Eds.), *Group Relations Reader* (pp. 43–68). Washington, DC: A. K. Rice Institute.

Rubin, H., & Rubin, I. (1995). *Qualitative Interviewing: The Art of Hearing Data.* Thousand Oaks, CA: Sage.

Schein, E. H. (1984). Coming to a new awareness of organizational culture. *Sloan Management Review, 25:* 3–16.

Spradley, J. P. (1979). *The Ethnographic Interview.* New York: Holt, Rinehart and Winston.

Stacey, R. (2003). Learning as an activity of interdependent people. *The Learning Organisation, 10:* 325–331.

Wells, Jr, L. (1980). The group-as-a-whole: a systemic socio-analytic perspective on interpersonal and group relations. In: C. P. Alderfer & C. L. Cooper (Eds.), *Advances in Experiential Social Processes: Volume 2* (pp. 165–199). New York: John Wiley & Sons.

Winnicott, D. W. (1971). *Playing and Reality.* London: Tavistock.

CHAPTER SIX

Social dreaming

Lilia Baglioni & Franca Fubini

"I had been preoccupied with dreaming because it was felt that it could make a contribution, as a tool of cultural enquiry, to the quality of human living because it always seems to illumine the current problems of existence"

(Lawrence, 2009, p. x)

"Wordsworth says 'hearing often times the still, sad music of humanity'. I presume we are in contact with our fellow human beings"

(Bion, 2005)

The space in between

Thoughts, and particularly new thoughts, live in the space between minds, a space that does not belong to anybody and yet it is owned in common by all. The notion that ideas come from individual minds and, therefore, are a private possession is contradicted by the evidence of practice. A new thought or a new idea can be sensed by many people at the same time. Bion says,

> For example, take a group like this. We have a collective wisdom that
> is extraneous to the little that each one of us knows . . . I think there is
> something by which this combined wisdom makes itself felt to a great
> number of people at the same time. (Bion, 1980, p. 29)

The elaboration of a new thought depends on the readiness of the context; its surviving and thriving or being killed depends on the quality of the context and of the emotions that pervade it. How the idea of social dreaming (SD) itself was received is a good example.

It has been noticed that SD has developed and spread easily in Italy since 2001, when Lawrence was invited by Claudio Neri to host social dreaming matrices (SDM) at Rome University La Sapienza. Social dreaming, in fact, was taken to by Italians like "fish to water". Our hypothesis is that the Italian scientific community dealing with groups and psychoanalysis within its own cultural proclivities had become inoculated by some selected ideas of Bion that were also at the basis—and may even be a prerequisite—of the discovery of SD (Corrao, 1998; Neri, 2003). Moreover, in Italy, the practice existed of non-therapeutic psychoanalytic groups (experiential groups), in which the dreams of participants were construed as a major system of self-representation of the group's life and a window on its ever shifting unconscious emotional constellations. This might account for the instinctive welcome and integration of SD programmes in a variety of fields (universities, public and private agencies, professional trainings, etc.).

By contrast, at the Tavistock Institute in the UK, particular tools for enquiry into social phenomena had been developed, building on Bion's theory of group functioning. The prevailing and specific culture was preoccupied primarily with understanding what conditions would allow a group to pursue its task and what relationships would develop between the group and its leader. The theory of basic assumptions and work groups were considered central, and Bion's theory of thinking and the development of his thoughts after he left the UK were not fully integrated. This well developed body of knowledge, we suggest, might have saturated the field and, thus, presented an obstacle to the welcoming of this new idea.

The discovery of social dreaming has its roots in the study of groups and psychoanalysis, but, for the idea to find space in the mind of a thinker, a new way of construing the cosmos and the mind had first to come into existence in our Western culture. "Western", we say, because in other cultures, particularly in the East, the awareness of connectedness and interdependency has been a tenet since time immemorial (Capra, 1997). At the beginning of the past century, in fact, in the West the world appeared to be the product of law, order, and certainty. Yet, today, uncertainty and chaos are construed as essential features of the hidden order of the cosmos that is now seen as so complex as to be beyond our capacity to grasp and describe in an acceptably complete way (Briggs & Peat, 2000).

Moreover, such new theories and models cannot avoid the awareness that, as we study it, the cosmos changes, and we and our theories are bound to change with it. This means that in the fields of science, objects of study that in the nineteenth century appeared as discrete and independent entities appear now as parts of a non-linearly evolving whole. In the so-called hard sciences, as well as in the human sciences, the separation between mind and body, nature and culture, observed and observer, chaos and order—to mention but a few—has been questioned, giving way, in the culture at large, to movements towards integration and multi-disciplinary views.

An essential idea that has been advanced is that everything is connected to everything else and that only the frame of mind that relates to the I/ego with its observing stance creates distinctions and separations. From this vertex, the universe appears to be a complex web of interdependent and dynamic relationships (Capra, 1997).

What is social dreaming?

Social dreaming is a methodology developed by Gordon Lawrence in the 1980s. It allows a group of people to tap into the cultural knowledge and the thinking embedded in the dreaming of its members. Importantly, it focuses on the dreams and not the dreamer. It stimulates the capacity of the dreamers jointly to find social meaning.

Social dreaming is a tool of action research on social and collective processes. It is a tool of cultural enquiry and evolution, coherent with what Bion affirms about the function of psychoanalysis: that is, to be a probe that enlarges the field it explores. At the end of the 1970s at the Tavistock Institute, Lawrence, like others, was researching into groups and systems to examine the possibility of making larger society a more intelligible field of study. He was experimenting with different events with the aim of disclosing social and political realities: for instance, the Praxis Event for the group relations conferences (GRC) and the Listening Post, later developed by OPUS.

SD was the answer to the problem of devising an event that could allow not only a thorough experience of the unconscious processes at work in a group's life, but could also tap into their creative and generative core.

In Group Relations Conferences, which built on Bion's seminal work with groups, the unconscious was seen primarily as something that works against the task; the assumption was that the unconscious had to be made conscious so that a group could collaborate in pursuit of better contact with reality.

SD, instead, sees the unconscious as working in tandem with consciousness. Where, in GRC, the emphasis is on the unconscious defences against the task of the work group/reality, in SD, the emphasis is on the "unconscious as the source of creativity". SD capitalises on the power of conscious and unconscious processes to work in concert; it was, thus, a tentative solution to the problem of developing an instrument that could mobilise the group's potential for accessing its infinite, unknown, collective wisdom and use it to foster change.

In this respect, SD builds on Bion's intuition that a group's fundamental concern is with its knowledge and the group's ways of producing it and managing the new knowledge that might appear in its context.

> I am impressed as a practising psychoanalyst, by the fact that the psychoanalytic approach, through the individual, and the approach these papers describe, through the group, are dealing with different facets of the same phenomena. The two methods provide the practitioner with a rudimentary binocular vision. The observations tend to fall in two categories, whose affinity is shown by phenomena, which, when examined by one method, centre on the Oedipal situation, related to the pairing group, and, when examined by the other, centre on the Sphinx, related to problems of knowledge and scientific method. (Bion, 1961, p. 8)

SD takes the Sphinx perspective and focuses on the nature of the dreaming/thinking that human contexts produce. "Dreaming is the human way to access the unconscious with its unique logic. By making the patterns of dreaming part of our waking life, we enhance the bandwidth of consciousness" (Lawrence, 2005, p. 29).

SD opens a way of thinking of the infinite by accessing the subliminal mental life and the connections that people have in social systems. It is well known that most of our mental life is filled with unconscious information and that

> unconscious vision has proved to be capable of gathering more information than a conscious scrutiny lasting a hundred times longer . . . the undifferentiated structure of unconscious vision . . . displays scanning powers that are superior to conscious vision. (Ehrenzweig, 1967, p. 63).

Thinking/dreaming reality in context

Bion, focusing more than Freud on the process of dreaming itself, put forward the hypothesis that dreaming (Dream-work-α) occurs by day and by night and serves the reality principle as well as the pleasure principle and involves the collaborative activity of the primary and secondary processes (Bion, 1992).

In his theory, experience—including the experience of having a mind—must be dreamt before becoming real for the personality, in a process that is recursive and virtually infinite. This process is the weaving of the stuff of which a real self and a real world are made, using threads that are both material and immaterial.

As humans, we have a mind that is not capable of developing its functions in isolation, but, soon after birth, needs to pair with a more mature mind in order to develop a capacity to connect creatively to other minds for the rest of its life and to keep growing and contributing to the development of cultures favourable to life.

Everything in our organised environment is born from thoughts and thinking of individuals and of the groups they form. The way in which we perceive and explore reality itself is born from thinking: thinking that divides and sees the parts; thinking that unites, capturing the relationships between parts; thinking that establishes connections and new thoughts that dissolvesthem, generating new identities and new knowledge.

Thinking, then, can be seen as a continuous process in which the inhabitants of the universe engage. Thinking is the outcome of partaking of the deep structure of reality and of participating in the task of giving it shape and meaning.

In his theory, Bion postulated "thoughts without a thinker", which exist "wild" in the space "out there" (Bion, 2005). In the same text, Bion spoke of dream as an example of this kind of wild creature and free association as an example of thought with a name attached to it, found in an unexpected context; he was concerned with the genesis of these sensuous creatures that had a counterpart in the non-sensuous realm of mind. He would track them back to the "infinite" using an imaginative conjecture.

In *A Memoir of the Future* (Bion, 1990, pp. 274–282), an intriguing character—"Du"—has a nocturnal dialogue with sleeping Robin, oscillating between nightmare and dreaming. Such a dialogue might be seen as a description of the fateful intercourse between a thinker and the germ of a new idea, a wild thought. Shall it be dreamt or aborted? If dreamt (tamed and transformed into a provisional resident of the mind), it might survive and change the dreamer. We might add, if the dream were voiced, it might escape the prison of Robin's mind and change the social context.

Dreaming as the royal road to the unconscious knowledge of the collective

If it takes a group of people to understand a group, maybe it takes a dream (or many dreams) to understand the social meaning of another dream. In fact, "Dreams would speak to dreams" (Lawrence, 2003, p. 3) and

> When three or more people come together, the chances are that their unconscious mind will resonate; the unconscious images will echo one another . . . thus the social unconscious comes into existence . . . By concentrating on the flow of experience of the dream . . . a new domain of cultural significance is laid bare, which is based on the 'multiverse' of meanings . . . (Lawrence, 2007, pp. 15–16)

In the late 1970s, when he was joint Director with Eric Miller of the Group Relations programmes at the Tavistock, Lawrence noticed that when dreams were voiced during a conference, they usually seemed to be related to the way the participants experienced living in the group at that particular moment. The knowledge contained in the dreams was not addressed though, because, as he writes, "at that time it was difficult to work with them, because the analysis of the individual dreamer was taboo" (Lawrence, 2005, p. 2).

He started musing about how to deal with dreams in order to activate their potential for revealing the life and thinking of the group without focusing on the life of the dreamer. From his knowledge of anthropology, he knew that dreams' narratives could traditionally be used to gain collective knowledge. When he came across *The Third Reich of Dreams* (Beradt, 1968), he found the missing link and the evidence he needed for social dreaming to begin its journey. Beradt, a German journalist, had collected the dreams that her medical practitioner friends had recorded from their patients both before and during Hitler's dictatorship. When examined after the Second World War, they appeared to be clearly prefiguring and mirroring the political reality of the totalitarian society in which they were produced. She writes, "There is no facade to conceal associations, and no outside person need provide the link between the dream image and reality— this the dreamer himself does" (Beradt, 1968, p. 15).

In 1982, Lawrence and his colleague, Patricia Daniel, designed a "Project in social dreaming and creativity" to explore the proposition that "it is possible to dream socially". The hypothesis was that when a person dreamt in the role of citizen, the dream would be received as a social dream: indeed, it would provide the link between the individual and her/his ecological niche.

The idea was to explore a different context for dreaming—different from a psychoanalytical setting or a therapeutic group—nourished by a number of people who gathered for the purpose of sharing their dreams and free associating to them. They hypothesised that in such context the meaning of the dreams and of dreaming would expand, and thoughts would circulate more freely so that one and all could hear echoes of thoughts that inhabit the space of the mind where each of us is connected to the social, cultural, and natural environment.

Since the first programme at the Tavistock Institute thirty years ago, the theory and the practice of social dreaming has developed through the experience of many programmes held in various settings and in many countries of the world. Social dreaming, in fact, is a practice and a theory "in becoming"; a process in movement, alive and not yet too rigidly established.

Social dreaming matrix

A specific setting was devised to hold the process of social dreaming: the matrix, which is both a process and a form.

> As a process, the matrix is the system or web of emotions and thinking that is present in every social relationship, but is, for the most part, unattended and not acknowledged. It can be thought of as mirroring, while awake, the infinite, unconscious processes in waking life that give rise to dreaming when asleep. (Lawrence, 2011, unpublished manuscript)

A social dreaming matrix seems also to mirror the functioning of the mind. Matrix was the word chosen by Daniel in order to indicate a different container for social dreaming and differentiate it from the relational dimension of the group and its specific dynamics. Lawrence talks of having had to build in his mind a "Faraday cage, which would protect it from the interference of group dynamics and classical psychoanalysis" (Lawrence, 2005, p. 40), that is, from what he already knew about them.

A matrix, from the Latin word for womb, is a place where something can grow, a mental receptacle for creativity and discovery; it is the net where knowledge and thinking "won from the void and formless infinite'" (Lawrence, 1998) can be received and brought to consciousness. It corresponds to the space between minds, the space described by Winnicott as the transitional area of play between mother and baby that evolves in the space of culture (Winnicott, 1971). In form, an SDM is composed of ten to sixty or more people, sitting in a room where the chairs are arranged—if possible—in repeating clusters, like a beehive or a snowflake, so that dreamers do not necessarily need to look at each other. It lasts one hour or one hour and a half, and is convened by one or more hosts who help the dreamers to keep to the task, model it, and protect the boundaries. Most important is what the hosts do not do: they neither interpret a dream in terms of the individual dreamer's personality nor saturate the potential meanings that are developing in the matrix. Hosts dwell in "not knowing" until a pattern emerges; they cultivate negative capability, a concept Bion borrowed from Keats, meaning the capacity of being in uncertainties, mysteries, doubts, without any irritable reaching after facts, reason, and understanding (Bion, 1970). The intention is to facilitate the same frame of mind as the other participants.

Before initiating any matrix, the hosts explain very succinctly and simply, in language appropriate to the context, the basic elements of social dreaming: social dreaming focuses on the dream, not the dreamer, and looks for the social or system's meaning embedded in the dreams. Free associations can be contributed by any dreamer to any dream; there should not be any specific expectation about the outcome of the work; the dreams themselves should be set free to work for the members, undisturbed by premature search for meaning. This privileges the non-linear and synchronous mode of thinking and the unconscious/infinite dimension of the mind.

At every session the host states the primary task, as if it were an invocation of, or act of faith in, the existence of an unknown reality: "The primary task of the matrix is to transform the thinking of the dream by associating to the dreams offered in the matrix in order to find links and connections, and to discover new thoughts. Where is the first dream?"

The following dream, contributed by a participant in a matrix, is, in our opinion, one of the best ways of capturing the resonating essence of "matrix" using language as only dreams and poetry can do, since they contain an optimal balance between symmetrical and asymmetrical logic (Matte Blanco, 1988).

> . . . there is a cobweb, and at each intersection there is a spider in meditation; the web has the same sensitivity of the spider mouth and it resonates with the vibrations of all the other spiders on the web . . .

In fact, in the matrix there are many points of resonance, each dream and association resonating with some others in the room, each setting off a variety of responses. Some stand out more than others and, by clustering, may determine the flow of the discourse. In reality, all the strands are simultaneously present and move at their own pace, contributing to create the whole multi-dimensional picture.

Each SDM, in its own way, re-discovers how dreaming and reality relate to each other; how the boundaries between the two can be crossed; how one person can dream a fractal of the dream of another; how minds can probe and anticipate future events by connecting their dreams.

During the rapid eye movement (REM) phase of sleep, when we dream, the closely knit neural nets that characterise our awake and logical mind relax and let go of tension; in a sense, the neural nets become loose, a state that allows for new configurations and thinking to emerge. A social dreaming matrix, mirroring while awake the space of dreaming, is a space where the rigidity of boundaries can relax and allow free circulation among the minds of the dreamers. The process encourages and sustains the members to keep the door open to the unexpected and the new. The experience of an open space, of the infinite, of mobility and connectedness, is nourished as social meanings are discovered and explored. Dreamers can let go of the tight boundaries of their own ego and experience both the freedom of offering dreams and the unmonitored freedom of associating to them. Intuitively, members of the matrix realise that the task is not focused on the individual and that personal interpretations are not requested. They retrieve a long-lost natural way of dealing with dreams in a collective (see Hailes, 2010).

As the emphasis is not on the ego and its propensity for categories, interpretations, and separations, the matrix offers also a true experience of democracy in action. There is a democracy in social dreaming. No dream is more important than another; they all coexist in the space of the many, where they create a multitude of meanings. In addition, the matrix discourse is multi-faceted: one can hear it reflect on issues regarding the many shared contexts to which the participants belong: institution, community, nation, humanity, and the matrix itself. Each matrix, in fact, at some level, speaks of the matrix and of its own process.

One of the hypotheses that has been formulated on SD is that the first dream voiced in the matrix would contain in an implicate form (Bohm, 1980) all the dreams to follow and, therefore, could be considered a fractal of the whole dreaming of the matrix. At the same time, the basic hypothesis of SD is that one dream cannot release any meaning all by itself, unless the meaning evolves through the work of many interconnected dreams. "Dreams are related systemically, just as thinking is. Each dream is a fractal of the other . . . We attempt to find the pattern that connects the dreams" (Lawrence, 2005, p. 15).

In a similar way, we hypothesise that each matrix repeats the same process, but only when we are able to look at a number of them a pattern emerges, that can become manifest and be consciously sensed and described by the participants.

A few years ago, a student at La Sapienza University in Rome graduated in psychology with a dissertation on SD and titled it "The matrix dreams the matrix". She collected her material by participating in the ongoing SDM that we have hosted once a month in Rome for the past twelve years. Indeed, if ears are tuned in to what goes on in the matrix, after a while (as it does take time) one can hear, through dreams and associations, the matrix reflecting on its own process; at this particular level, meaningful conversations can take place, interesting thoughts about existential questions can appear, sustained by the developing capacity for thinking and by the emotional connectedness of the dreamers. When the matrix reflects about itself, it is possible to catch glimpses of the evolutionary process of humanity at the level of its thinking processes. The matrix reveals itself to be a living process that creates its own language and, at the same time, enters a pre-existing one (Fitzpatrick, 2003).

Dream reflection dialogue and dream reflection group

At the end of an SD matrix, there is a short time set aside for a "dream reflection dialogue", where participants can begin to put into words what the experience of being in the dreaming process of the matrix was like. This is very similar to when, in the morning, one wonders about the night dreams and their meaning. It is the moment when the I/ego, temporarily set aside during the matrix, can recover its conscious capacity of thinking in a linear mode, just as it does when waking up from its nocturnal dreaming. This is the time when the basic emotional pattern of the matrix can be made explicit.

Following this, a "dream reflection group" (DRG) takes place, which has the task of identifying the themes of the dreams offered in the matrix, finding the pattern that connects them, and advancing working hypotheses on what it might reveal of the shared context. It makes use of systemic thinking and, by revealing the connecting pattern, it works towards making a synthesis, a term borrowed from chemistry, that is, a way in which different elements can aggregate so as to form a substance, new and different from its original separate components.

The dream reflection group makes use of pieces of knowledge gathered from conscious and unconscious thinking and from different domains of knowledge, which, during the matrix, became linked. These new particles of knowledge can be used to formulate new working hypotheses. It is extremely important to combine these events with the SDM; because it is in this phase that the two complementary ways of the mind's functioning are put together, allowing the discerning mind to transform into new thoughts and new knowledge that which was harvested from the undifferentiated matrix of the unconscious.

Other events can be part of an SD programme: one is the "dialogue", where one of the hosts or a participant presents his/her reflections on a theme; the task for everybody is to be available for thoughts.

The other is the "creative role synthesis" (CRS) that allows individual participants to work through their chosen puzzles with the help of their fellow dreamers in the role of consultants. Its primary task is to identify a paradoxical challenge, or existential puzzle, or conundrum or issue, or problem or doubt about living, and to make a synthesis of the systemic elements involved in order to discover a creative role.

In a CRS, a small group can look at the individual member from the vertex of the Sphinx, building on the transformation of thinking achieved in the matrix. The socialistic experience of the matrix is, thus, applied to the individual without having recourse to logic and linear thinking.

Creation and destruction

When working in the group relations programmes at the Tavistock Institute, Lawrence had a particular interest in the large study group (LSG) and its capacity to mirror larger social phenomena (a glimpse of society). He writes of having been influenced by some of Pierre Turquet's ideas about the LSG. One was the concept of matrix as a place from which something grows, a concept distinct from "group". "The matrix holds the potential creativity of a large group and indeed the matrix qualities have yet to be explored experientially" (Turquet, 1975, p. 96).

Matrix, in this respect, appears to be a more inclusive concept, containing also the group configuration.

Another was the concept of "disarroy" (a neologism from the French *desarroi*), meaning "a state of complete bewilderment or confusion", a word

> . . . used in order to describe the actual experience of change, with an inherent notion of disintegration and collapse, but also to indicate the presence of a wish to return to the status quo ante, with further wishes not to know, never to return. (Turquet, 1975, p. 103)

Turquet was trying to capture the inner turmoil and the terror involved in change and learning, due to the difficulty of tolerating the empty space before something new appeared. Bion described a similar emotional configuration as typical of what he called catastrophic change (Bion, 1965). Our hypothesis is that Lawrence was looking for a quantum leap that would take the work of the LSG further, and for a way of being in the state of disarroy without necessarily triggering the psychotic side of the LSG.

Lawrence postulates that the experience of disarroy in the LSG is essential for learning, and that out of that experience one can tilt oneself in various directions for "knowing" and "not knowing".

> . . . I was dreaming of doors, a corridor of doors, the last one opens to the unknown . . .

And, in the words of the dream of a member of an institutional group facing a major reorganisation:

> . . . I am in a classroom. I open the door to go out at the end of a lesson and I see a parallel universe where a volcano is erupting fire. I turn and I see that my colleagues are very alarmed. They are shouting at me: "Shut the door! Make sure that you shut it for good!"

One of the ways the terror generated by contact with the unknown can be at least provisionally controlled by replication of the known is to form a barrier:

The problem about all institutions—the Tavistock Institute and every one that we have—is that they are dead, but the people inside them are not, and the people grow and something's going to happen. What usually happens is that the institutions (societies, nations, states and so forth) make laws. The original laws constitute a shell, and then new laws expand that shell. If it were a material prison, you could hope that the prison walls would be elastic in some sort of way. If organizations don't do that, they develop a hard shell and then expansion cannot occur because the organization has locked itself in. (Banet, 1976, pp. 277–278)

Growth, which is the outcome of creativity, is feared because it involves the destruction of the known order on which our feelings of safety and the idea of living in a predictable and controllable universe are based. It can be felt as an impending catastrophe.

In the SDM, dreams of watching erupting volcanoes and inundations, chain reactions usually accompany the sensed presence of a new thought. They are terrifying, but high energy laden dreams in which the dreamer as observer is also in the position of experiencing the loneliness and infinite sadness, mixed with elation, of the survivor.

> . . . I dream the 1995 earthquake in Umbria. I am with my family. I can see the town as it is destroyed, slowly and in complete silence. It is a soft demolition, it is not scaring: we don't die. My sister rings me on my mobile; it is the only sound; she wants to know whether we have survived and I reassure her.

The word catastrophe has a halo of meaning that captures at the same time the idea of destruction and the idea of a new beginning. The growth that is linked to creativity involves transformation. Bion spoke of transformations in O as different from transformations in K, of *becoming* truth as opposed to *knowing about* truth (Bion, 1965; Eigen, 1981). Transformations in K involve evolution of the already known and rely on a linear functioning of the mind, while transformations in O address a different order of reality: the unconscious, the unknown, the not yet differentiated.

O, ultimate truth or reality, cannot be known since it is not sensuous, but can be stimulated to evolve towards an apprehensible emotional realisation by "at-one-ment", that is, becoming it, incarnating it, so to speak. The emotional experience of contact with O requires total receptivity and is akin to awe.

One of the ways the terror generated by contact with the unknown, O, can be at least provisionally controlled is by replication of the known to form a barrier. In *Experiences in Groups* (1961), an early work of Bion, primary strong emotions, irrational thoughts, and phantasies are seen only as negative and inopportune perturbations of the work group. In *Attention and Interpretation* (1970) and following works, Bion devised the hypothesis that the experience of contact with a new thought necessarily involved the eruption of irrationality and the creation of a strong emotional turbulence.

The initial sharp distinction and opposition between the characteristics of the basic assumption and the work groups were modified, as was the concept of leader of the work group, giving birth to the concept of the "mystic" and later of "the artist" (Corrao & Neri, 1981; Neri, 2003). Moreover, the concept of observation was integrated with that of participation.

With the concepts of turbulence, transformation in O, and thoughts without a thinker, Bion pointed to the possibility of using "psychotic processes" in a creative way. Real growth of knowledge, in fact, both in the group and in its individual members, cannot happen without connecting the primitive with the evolved, thoughts with emotions. Growth, evolution of the system and of its individual members in a symbiotic relationship, is the basic aim of the SD enterprise. Dreams are something which, their meaning being unknown, can nevertheless be perceived as a possible object of knowledge and are one of the first evolved forms of O. In the matrix, it might be hypothesised that they gradually create in the collective the analogous of the "contact barrier" (Bion, 1962) in the individual: a permeable caesura keeping conscious and unconscious distinct, while allowing two-way traffic and correlation.

This is the way an eloquent dream summarised for a medical team, at the end of a cycle of SDMs, the dramatic process of going from an automatic and ineffective way of functioning in role to discovering unexpected wells of creativity and learning to protect and use them.

> . . . I am in an arid field, but I find some seeds in my pocket and sow
> them. I find some water; sprinkle the soil with it and the grass begins
> to grow fast, abundant and tall: it is like a tumultuous sea. A strong
> wind starts to blow as if the grass movement had been communicated
> to the sky. A storm is created and uninterrupted rain destroys all the
> crops. I see on one side a patch of short grass, like Irish grass, and go

to sit there and wait. After a while the storm subsides and the grass starts to grow again, but it is shorter. (Baglioni, 2010, p. 164)

Since the very first project in 1982, SD has been firmly connected to creativity, to the revelation of the unknown, and to discovering what facilitates the emergence of a creative process and what, on the contrary, hinders it in systems, in the collective as well as in the individual.

From a consultancy in a hospital, we offer an example of how members deal with the problem of inclining themselves towards change and meeting the rigid inner establishment as well as the very concrete outer one (Fubini, 2010).

After one year of consultancy, mainly using SD, the team of one of the hospital departments had to face what to do when the "new" is released but an inner as well as an outer "establishment" is not supporting it. It was worked out in the matrix through dreams and associations. The theme of death was present, but the emotional quality of the dreams was not congruent with the death of dear ones, as though those deaths were signifying something different, possibly the rigidity of the institution to which they belonged. The unformulated question was, "We are able to change, but what about our container?"

A sequence of dreams started to appear.

... My grandfather was dead and my two-year-old daughter was dead, too. They were rigid. I was trying to put clothes on them by pulling arms and legs, but it was impossible.

... My father-in-law had died at 1 a.m. I get angry because now it is 10 a.m. and it is hard to dress him; by now he must be rigid.

The dreams were pointing to something dead that could not be transformed.

At the same time, in the matrix, glimpses of change and freedom appeared; the transformation of thinking had taken place even if it was not yet clear in which direction it would go

My cat is dead: I hope I will be given one of the kittens of another cat, which have just been born.

I was going to the hospital, but it is no longer as it was before. They are restructuring everything.

My car has no doors, or boot, but the inner structure is sound and it works anyway.

I meet a man, we like each other. He says, 'I am married!' 'Me too!' I reply, and we can relax and be together. I see myself relaxed and beautiful. We don't need to think about a permanent relationship, just enjoying the moment.

Applications: SD does take time and has to be facilitated by expert hands

When access to the creative thinking of an organisation needs to be mobilised and sustained, when an existing culture needs to change and its possible "futures" need to be imagined and compared, when an organisation has reached the limits of its own comprehension, when there is a need, as in conflict resolution, to first give space to an unconscious affective field of resonance before addressing the conflicting issues, then SD is invaluable. We also hypothesise that comparing and correlating matrices held around the world at a given time might illuminate the pattern that connects apparently discrete and non-communicating systems in the larger social field. In this respect, each SDM could be seen as a fractal of an unconscious unbroken field of global dreaming at a given time, just as a Listening Post group can be taken as a fractal of the fantasies, fears, and expectations of the larger society.

The outcome of SD can be observed and evaluated when it is used for a time that is long enough to see the developments and the transformation of the thinking of the group. A short consultation can be effective, as it makes use of the matrix as a "diagnostic" tool: it usually reveals with accuracy the present situation and what the main problems might be. However, it is only when a consultation is sustained for a length of time that there is the actual possibility for the role holders to see and put to use the transformation of the thinking of the organisation and the development of its emotional connectedness. In an SD consultancy, the aim is to make the role-holders themselves capable of assessing the state of being and the state of becoming of their system and using this knowledge to promote change. This is what Lawrence refers to when he writes about the politics of revelation as opposed to the politics of salvation in consultancy (Lawrence, 2000). Lawrence's hope was that after the consultation has ended, the organisation itself would continue the SDM and make the dialogue with dreams part of its ongoing discourse. Ruth Silver in London, at Lewisham College, and our consultancy work in Italy, for example, do introduce regular use of SDM.

On some levels, SD has the kind of simplicity of Zen: a few lines in the sand of a Zen garden, a stroke of ink on the ricepaper. SD works with the frame of mind that can let go of the superfluous and go straight to the essence of things and phenomena. We have that potentiality, but very seldom it can be sustained without dedicated practice.

Lawrence maintains that SD was a discovery, not an invention; SDM, DRG, and CRS are methodologies he invented to best sustain the process and put to use the fruits of social dreaming.

Probably due to the very nature of its basic tenets, SD practices have never been institutionalised, although formal trainings have been held in Italy, the UK, and the US (Eden, 2010). Observing how SD developed in this respect, we notice that the collection, organisation, and transmission of its body of knowledge and basic principles, as well as research and innovation, has happened in rather small and sometimes isolated work groups. SD seems to be the kind of plant that grows where the wind blows the seeds, but resists, to some extent, being cultivated. As a movement, it appears to take a form akin to the spontaneous fleeting and sometimes unpredictable assembling and disassembling of social interest groups on the Internet.

At the moment, most SD hosts are also well trained in working with groups and in psychoanalysis, but all agree that it is necessary to develop one's capacity to tune into what is specifically required for hosting an SD matrix before doing it. It is, therefore, recommended that one should train oneself by participating in structured SD programmes in order to develop the capacity to help a collective to use their dreams to navigate safely between the unconscious and the conscious, to be curious about the new, and tolerant of uncertainty and doubt.

Where is social dreaming going as far as its potential for use in diverse societal contexts is concerned?

Increasingly, SD is being validated as a tool of cultural enquiry and presently appears to be a most appropriate answer to the needs that are perceived by organisations that have discovered the limitations of traditional methodologies to tackle their problems. In fact, there is increasing awareness of the role that unconscious processes play in the everyday life and decisions of organizations and role holders (Eisold, 2010). As Lawrence says, "There is no quick fix to find the truth, when we need to hold onto politics of revelation" (Lawrence, personal communication).

Moreover, SD offers an added value that consists in the capacity to address and mobilise the resources of the person as a whole and not just of the role-holder, so contributing to humanising the workplace.

Currently, SD is applied in many countries in the world, such as the UK, Italy, Germany, Australia, Israel, the USA, Latin America, and in a variety of contexts. In the field of education, from nursery schools to universities, SDMs are hosted both for students, as part of the experiential training of psychology, psychotherapy, and educational studies faculties, and for staff members in public health, the military, social services, political parties, and the church. SDMs, complemented by DRGs, are used as tools of action research and consultancy in private and public organisations and are increasingly being included in the design of group relations conferences. Many professional societies in the field of psychotherapy and socio-psychoanalysis have begun a practice of hosting SDMs at their conferences and professional meetings.

In the context of the performing and visual arts and in music SD has found fertile soil, often creatively combined with other group events that make use of their autochthonous languages. At this time, two new contexts of applications for SD are being explored: the spontaneous social protest movements worldwide (Occupy) and the virtual space of the Internet. Bipin Patel in London is starting a series of "Symbiont conversations using social dreaming off and online (Patel, personal communication). In the summer of 2011, some Israeli colleagues thought that the Occupy endeavour and social dreaming matrices could be a compatible match and organised a first programme in Tel Aviv. Soon after, in November 2011, a series of social dreaming matrices events (SDE) were held in London at Finsbury Square and St Paul's. (Full reports can be found at http://social-dreamingeventstentcityuniversity.wordpress.com/).

It is too soon to formulate conclusions about the outcomes of these experiences, but it is interesting to note a possible connection between

SD and these new social movements. As one of the colleagues who participated in the pilot experiences says,

> SD and social movements share some characteristics, a fractal DNA perhaps, which rises from the relocation of power to the many from the few; as a matrix differs from a group, so a social movement (such as Tent City) differs from a hierarchical and commissioned protest. (Silver, personal communication)

More experience and more sharing of results might illuminate, from a novel vertex, some of the psychosocial features that characterise the present times and, maybe, contribute to the development of the theory and the technique of SD.

References

Baglioni, L. (2010). Dreaming to emergence in a general hospital. In: W. G. Lawrence (Ed.), *The Creativity of Social Dreaming* (pp. 147–168). London: Karnac.

Banet, A. G. (1976). Bion interview. *International Journal for Group Facilitators: Group and Organization Studies, 1*(3): 268–285.

Beradt, C. (1968). *The Third Reich of Dreams,* Chicago, IL: University of Chicago Press.

Bion, W. R. (1961). *Experiences in Groups.* London: Tavistock.

Bion, W. R. (1962). *Learning from Experience.* London: Heinemann [reprinted London: Karnac, 1984].

Bion, W. R. (1965). *Transformations.* London: Heinemann [reprinted London: Karnac. 1984].

Bion, W. R. (1970). *Attention and Interpretation.* London: Tavistock [reprinted London: Karnac, 1984].

Bion, W. R. (1980). *Bion in New York and Sao Paulo.* London: Karnac.

Bion, W. R. (1990). *A Memoir of the Future.* London: Karnac.

Bion, W. R. (1992). *Cogitations.* London: Karnac.

Bion, W. R. (2005). *The Italian Seminars.* London: Karnac.

Bohm, D. (1980). *Wholeness and the Implicate Order.* London: Routledge & Kegan Paul.

Briggs, J., & Peat, D. (2000). *Seven Lessons of Chaos.* New York: HarperCollins.

Capra, F. (1997). *The Web of Life.* London: HarperCollins.

Corrao, F. (1998). *Orme.* Roma: Raffaello Cortina.

Corrao, F., & Neri, C. (1981). Introduction. *Rivista di Psicoanalisi, 27*(3–4) (Monographic Issue dedicated to W. R. Bion): i–vii.

Eden, A. (2010). Learning to host a social dreaming matrix. In: W. G. Lawrence (Ed.), *The Creativity of Social Dreaming* (pp. 177–186). London: Karnac.

Ehrenzweig, A. (1967). *The Hidden Order of Art: A Study in the Psychology of Artistic Imagination.* London: Weidenfeld and Nicholson.

Eigen, M. (1981). The area of faith in Winnicott, Lacan and Bion. *International Journal of Psychoanalysis, 62*: 413–433.

Eisold, K. (2010). *What You Don't Know You Know.* New York: Other Press.

Fitzpatrick, S. (2003). Theatre of dreams: social dreaming as ritual/yoga/literature machine. In: W. G. Lawrence (Ed.), *Experiences in Social Dreaming* (pp. 228–245). London: Karnac.

Fubini, F. (2010). Totalitarian toddlers. In: W. G. Lawrence (Ed.), *The Creativity of Social Dreaming* (pp. 131–146). London: Karnac.

Hailes, J. (2010). Spontaneity in social dreaming. Unpublished Doctoral Thesis, Swinburne University, Melbourne.

Lawrence, W. G. (2000). The politics of salvation and revelation. In: W. G. Lawrence (Ed.), *Tongued with Fire* (pp. 165–179). London: Karnac.

Lawrence, W. G. (2003). The social dreaming phenomenon. In: W. G. Lawrence (Ed.), *Experiences in Social Dreaming* (pp. 1–14). London: Karnac.

Lawrence, W. G. (2005). *Introduction to Social Dreaming.* London: Karnac.

Lawrence W. G. (Ed.) (2007). *Infinite Possibilities of Social Dreaming.* London: Karnac.

Lawrence, W. G. (2009). Foreword. In: J. Clare & A. Zarbafi (Eds.), *Introduction to Social Dreaming in the 21st Century: The World We Are Losing* (pp. ix–xvi). London: Karnac.

Lawrence, W. G. (2011). Lecture at the Tavistock Institute. Unpublished manuscript.

Matte Blanco, I. (1988). *Thinking, Feeling and Being .Clinical Reflections on the Fundamental Antinomy of Human Beings.* London: Routledge.

Neri, C. (2003). Anthropological psychoanalysis: Bion's journey in Italy. In: R. M. Lipgar & M. Pines: *Building on Bion: Roots.* London: Jessica Kingsley.

Turquet, P. (1975). Threats to identity in the large group. Cited in: W. G. Lawrence (2000), *Tongued with Fire: Groups in Experience.* London: Karnac.

Winnicott, D. W. (1971). *Playing and Reality.* London: Routledge.

CHAPTER SEVEN

Thinking organisations through photographs: the social photo-matrix as a method for understanding organisations in depth

Burkard Sievers

Introduction

The social photo-matrix (SPM) is an experiential learning method for understanding organisations in depth. Its aim is to experience, through collective viewing of digital photos taken by the participants of the social photo-matrix (and subsequent associations, amplifications, systemic thinking, and reflection), the hidden meaning of what in an organisation usually remains unseen and, thus, unnoticed and unthought.

The method of the SPM has grown out of my experience and work with social dreaming, developed by Gordon Lawrence (Lawrence, 1998, 1999, 2003, 2005; Mersky, 2012; Sievers, 2001, 2007a), and organisational role analysis (e.g., Newton, Long, & Sievers, 2006; Sievers & Beumer, 2006).

This method is based on the assumption that *photographs* are the medium for new thoughts and thinking while the photographer remains in the background and is usually unknown. This chapter describes the method, design, process, and some of the learnings from, and insights into, what it means to use photos as a means of understanding what might be below the surface of an organisation. I use two case examples. The first is a seminar with postgraduate students in a Department of Business and Economics at a German university, and the second in a penal institution for remand prisoners in Germany.

The experience from these two examples as well as from other SPMs gives encouraging evidence for the underlying assumption that this method allows organisational role holders to conceive their organisations differently in the light of new thinking and thoughts.

The social photo-matrix

In the SPM, people gather over a certain time period and freely associate to photographs that they have taken of their organisation. They make links between the photographs, which, in turn, generates new thinking about their organisation (Sievers, 2007b, 2008a, 2009, 2013; Warren, 2012).

Inviting participants to a social photo-*matrix*, not to a "group", is based on the experience with social dreaming. Unlike a group, which often is preoccupied with the maintenance of its identity, rivalry about power and reputation, and, particularly with a work group in an organisation, pursuing its task,

> the matrix, on the other hand, is a collection of minds opening and available for dwelling in possibility. It demands a different kind of leadership—one inspired by the recognition of the infinite, of not-knowing, of being in doubt and uncertainty, as opposed to knowing and repeating banal facts. (Lawrence, 2005, p. 40)

A "matrix is also to experience a democratic environment", not least because "free association means saying what comes to mind; it is not subject to rational control" (Lawrence, 2005, p. 38).

Although not "discovered" by Freud, free associations were the core of the psychoanalytic process with his patients. Whereas Freud focused on the relationship between analyst and analysand, the opportunity for his patients to free associate might, *cum grano salis*, equally be valid in the present, non-psychotherapeutic context. Freud encouraged the patient not to hold back any idea from communication, even if (1) he feels that it is too disagreeable or if (2) he judged that it is nonsensical or (3) too unimportant or (4) irrelevant for what is being looked for. (Freud, 1923a, p. 238, quoted in Bollas, 2009, p. 8)

In comparison to Freud who, in his psychoanalytic practice, referred almost exclusively to the individual unconscious, both that of the patient and the analyst, the SPM, in common with all other socio-analytic methods described in this book, explicitly deals with the unconscious at a systemic level. As Susan Long further elaborates in the Introduction and Chapter One of this book, the unconscious in organisations that the SPM attempts to reveal is part of the associative unconscious. Unlike the unconscious on the level of the individual, the associative unconscious allows SPM participants to experience the photos as something "social", as something the participants have in common; for participants in a SPM, this experience is often quite an unusual, if not totally new, one. It is the experience of a "we-identity" as Elias (1987), the sociologist, would call it, in comparison to an "I-identity". The photos help to "bridge the gap between the apparently individual, private, subjective and the apparently collective, social, political" (Vince & Broussine, 1996, p. 8, with reference to Samuels, 1993).

Whereas a group often tends to be dominated by tyrannical dynamics or individuals, in a matrix everyone can feel free to associate without the need for agreement or the obligation to reach a predominant opinion. There is space for as many associations as there are people in the room and, in comparison to a work group, there is no need to reach a consensus or to arrive at a shared meaning. To avoid the experience of being in a group and to facilitate the free flow of associations in the matrix, we usually set up the chairs around the screen in such a way that the participants are seated in staggered rows with sufficient space between the chairs, an arrangement which does not invite direct eye contact.

It usually takes a while at the beginning of the first matrix session, and the very first one in particular, for participants to allow one other to get into an associative mood. However, once they begin "to appreciate associative thought" (Bollas, 2009, p. 33) and dwell on it, the associations often gain a playful creativity (Winnicott, 1991, pp. 38–64). As Bollas (2009, p. 21) puts it, "free associating manifests the unconscious. It functions as an ever-sophisticated pathway for the articulation of unconscious ideas, regardless of their derivation". And, as he adds, "the logic of association is a form of unconscious thinking" (Bollas, 2009, p. 32).

Associations to the photographs provide many more insights than rational discussion and reveal part of the "unthought known" (Bollas, 1987), the "not yet thought" and the "not-known", both in the organisation and on the side of the role-holder. The photos allow access to the "organisation-in-the-mind" (Hutton, Bazalgette, & Reed, 1997), the "institution-in-the-mind" (Armstrong, 2005) or the "institution-in-experience" (Long, 1999, p. 58)—notions that refer to the inner landscape of organisations, that is, to the person's inner experience and perception of the organisation. These concepts contain, so to speak, an inner psychic model of organisational reality. This inner object forms and shapes the psychic space and, thus, influences actual behaviour. Organisation, in this sense, can be perceived as not just something "external", but also as an accumulation of experience and images that structures both the psychic space of a person and the social one of the organisation. In taking up a role in organisations, we introject parts of external reality and transform them into inner objects and part-objects. These objects build an inner matrix, which is only partly conscious and, not least because of its often frightening character, partly remains unconscious. The photographs can be a medium through which these inner objects and part-objects can be "externalized" and become objects for associations and sources for further thoughts and thinking. In this sense, the photographs are transitional objects (Winnicott, 1953).

The use of photos and photography in experiential learning for management education or organisational analysis is, as such, obviously not new (e.g., Parker 2009; Petersen & Østergaard, 2003; Ray & Smith, 2012; Rose, 2007; Schroeder, 2006; Vince & Warren, 2012; Warren, 2005, 2006, 2009). Whereas most approaches resemble that of an ethnographer or anthropologist in so far as they are based on the perception of an outside observer, the SPM is an action research method that uses the very eyes (hearts and minds) of organisational role-holders. They have the direct experience with the organisation and are the genuine source for giving meaning to the photos. While the photos of an external observer, researcher, or consultant can be a means of telling the client what the photographer sees at the very moment they are taken and/or a way of encouraging the client to find his own meaning, the photos in the SPM, so to say, speak for themselves and to those who have "collectively" made them.

Photographs in the SPM are not mere replicas of "reality", but means for opening up the transitional space between the real and the unreal, the finite and the infinite, the known and thoughts that have not been thought so far. Contrary to the common assumption that photographs are owned by the photographer, in the SPM the photograph, not the photographer, is the medium of discourse.

As the photographs are supposed to contribute to an understanding of organisations in depth, participants are encouraged to refrain from taking pictures which would be most likely to be published in a marketing brochure for their institution or found on the Internet. Participants are invited instead to make use of "a different way of seeing", guided by their own subjective perspective, which would make visible what usually remains invisible and the invisible imaginable in what is visible. During the SPM, the photos are displayed on a large screen and the participants are invited to freely associate to them. In the subsequent reflection sessions, participants have an opportunity to use the thoughts from the free associations for further thinking and to relate them to the hidden dynamics of their organisations.

Two case examples: an SPM in a business school and in a penal institution for remand prisoners

"You shall (not) make an image for yourself!": towards a socioanalysis of a university

The idea of using photographs as the means to grasp at what is beneath the surface of organisations grew out of a seminar series on organisational psychodynamics, which I offered in our Department of Business and Economics at the German university. After I had offered group relations conferences, organisational role analysis, and social dreaming seminars for some decades, it was above all the experience of working with students' drawings and dreams which fostered my idea to work with photographs as a medium for further understanding organisations in depth and our university department in particular.

Together with my colleague, Arndt Ahlers-Niemann, we invited students for a first "experiment" with the SPM. The seminar had the title (partly borrowed from Exodus 20: 4) '"You shall (not) make an image for yourself!"—Towards a socioanalysis of a university'. The students were asked to take photographs of the university (with digital cameras) and to add them to an electronic archive, from which photos were chosen for the SPM and shown via a projector.

The seminar was based on the working hypothesis that the photos of the university taken by the participants would allow access to the "unconscious of the university" to the extent that associating to, and amplifying, the photos would foster the thinking of thoughts that had not been thought before. The stated *aim* of the SPM as an experiential learning method was to experience, through visualisation (and subsequent associations, amplifications, and reflection) the hidden meaning of what in an organisation usually remains unseen and unnoticed. A one-hour session of the matrix was followed by a reflection session in which the participants had opportunities to relate and extend the thoughts and the thinking from the matrix to their experience of the university. This seminar went on for twelve weekly four-hour sessions during the term.

As it worked out, some six photos were appropriate for one matrix session. We had a student take notes during the matrices and during the reflection sessions; these notes, together with the photos from the respective matrices, were sent to all participants before the session the following week. These "minutes" made it easier to make links between the photos and the thoughts beyond the experience of a single session. My colleague and I took the role of host during the matrices and the reflection sessions, in the sense that we provided the required technology and the rooms, chose the photos from the archive, reminded students of the task of the respective sessions (if necessary), and helped to make links between the photos and the thinking from previous sessions. In addition, we also took the participant role and contributed our associations and amplifications to the photos.

In retrospect, it seems that the photos from the first SPM session—and the very first picture in particular—set the tone for most of the following sessions. While this was often the case in later SPMs, it might partly have been induced in this particular case by the fact that during this first "experiment", my colleague had chosen photos from the anonymous ones in the archive; we subsequently decided to select the photos randomly in order to avoid the impression of "manipulation".

Owing to the limited space of this chapter, I will refrain from giving a detailed account of the photos, associations, and amplifications (cf. Sievers, 2008a, p. 238ff.); instead, I will give some impressions from the first session.

All photos in this session showed parts of buildings and empty, sterile, mainly frightening spaces. The very first picture portrayed a view through a glass door with a sign asking that the door be kept closed in order that smoke from a potential fire would not seep into further parts of the building. Beyond was an empty hallway in front of an elevator. Like most of the subsequent photos, it raised associations of prison, clinical laboratory, and psychiatric hospital, and fantasies of persecution and annihilation (Figure 7.1):

"This is a zone of high danger."

"The atmosphere is precarious."

Figure 7.1.   The door to the elevator.

"Maybe the students are already evacuated."

"My immediate impression was hospital, clinic and sterility—like staying in front of a door that protects against an epidemic."

"The picture reminds me of the movie *One Flew over the Cuckoo's Nest*"

. . .

"or *The Cube*, in which people were trying to escape."

"Smoke and fire alarms are the only security and safety devices the university provides."

The second picture showed part of an iron fence in the car park, which was erected in front of an area that was under construction; other photos from this first matrix showed a rusty pipe that was part of the ventilation system, the view up an empty staircase, and another view into a hall where rubble was temporarily deposited.

The subsequent session provided space for reflection on the associations during the preceding first SPM. It raised the following thoughts:

"Taking photos is an unconscious process. There is a difference between what one wanted to catch and what actually has been caught."

"Do you remember who took the photo? I can't."

"It is interesting to notice that others have seen things differently to those photos I wanted to present."

"The photos are almost always reflecting how ugly the building actually is."

"There are no spaces to linger."

"It is like a factory."

"It well may be that the depression that is there is privatised. One does not have a choice. Why grumble? And thus it disappears."

"Even though I did not make the photos, I easily could have made many of them."

"Towards the end of the session we no longer talked about the photos. But a lot about the university."

"Yes, and would we have been able to do so without the photos?"

The frame of this chapter is not sufficient to go through all the sessions to the same extent. What follows is, therefore, a summary of some of the main issues and thoughts we addressed.

As the work with photos progressed from session to session, the photos gained another meaning: they were increasingly seen as the means for new ways of thinking about the university.

> "We are just thinking the university through the pictures. The photos actually are not what we are interested in, what really counts is disclosing our inner pictures."

> "There is no room in traditional science (and the humanities) for this kind of work and for free associations in particular."

> "The photo matrix allows speaking about what cannot be expressed officially."

There was also an acknowledgement that the thinking initiated by the SPM creates awareness for those processes and connections that are better kept unknown or not obvious. This work is seen as giving access to the university's (and the department's) shadow (Bowles 1991; Denhardt, 1981).

Much favours the assumption that we, both individually and collectively, have become so accustomed to subjugating ourselves to an "organizational familiarity with death, violence and injustice" (Marcuse, 1965, p. 94) that it is difficult, if not impossible, to admit how much we are suffering from the "building" and, above all, from the way that teaching, learning, and research are organised and undertaken.

This first attempt at working with the SPM convinced me, my colleague, and, apparently, most of the student participants that it is possible to gain access to the unthought known and, thus, to the unconscious in organisations through photos taken by their role-holders. Meanwhile, this insight has been reconfirmed in other SPMs with students of the Business School, the management of a major German enterprise, and as part of the Professional Development Programme during some Annual Meetings of ISPSO, *The International Society for the Psychoanalytic Study of Organizations.*

Another way of seeing: an SPM in a penal institution for remand prisoners

The following case is an SPM in a penal institution for juvenile remand prisoners. If this had been my very first experience of this methodology, I probably would have rejected it as a method suitable for learning about organisations in depth. For various reasons, which I will indicate below, it was very difficult to gain the acceptance and commitment of some of the participants to engage with this method and the stated aim of this SPM, that is, to experience, through visualisation (and subsequent associations, amplifications, and reflection), the hidden meaning of what in the prison usually remains unseen and unnoticed. Although, at times, we considered bringing this project to an early end, we eventually achieved a "good enough" ending. As I will briefly indicate, this SPM was actually not a waste of time and energy. I have chosen this case here as it raises some important insights into the impediments and possible failures in using this method.

Through a student who had taken part in an SPM at the university and also worked voluntarily in the prison, we—some eight students, my colleague Arndt Ahlers-Niemann, and I—were invited by the Catholic minister of the prison to undertake an SPM with a small group of male remand prisoners, that is, prisoners held in detention while awaiting trail. Most of them were juveniles, who committed their offences when they were between fourteen and seventeen years old; a few others were adolescents between the ages of eighteen and twenty.

While my colleague and I had previously consulted to prisons (Ahlers-Niemann, 2007; Bredlow, 2009) and had some experience of what it means and feels like to be in prison, and also "the prison" had already appeared in various association in the university case above, most of the students were quite frightened and shocked on our first visit, when we were guided through to take photos for the matrix. For most of them, the inside of a prison was a new, unfamiliar, unknown, uncanny, and frightening place.

With this SPM, we used a design quite similar to the one described in the previous case. We also had students take notes in the matrices and reflection sessions, which, together with the respective photos, were sent to all participants before the next session; surprisingly enough, the documents sent to the prisoners were not censored by prison security.

Being aware that the prisoners were unfamiliar with this methodology and that their primary interest might have been to meet and socialise with young people from outside, we held a social event before the first matrix. On this occasion, all participants had an opportunity to introduce themselves, to be familiarised with how we would be working together for the next few weeks, and to make drawings of how they see the prison. This experience was discussed in heterogeneous groups; however, it was obviously—in hindsight—not sufficient for gaining the prisoners' commitment to join the task of the SPM.

We worked on a weekly basis for six weeks. Between the matrix and reflection sessions we had a "smoking break", which also provided opportunities for conversations. At the end of the very last session, after an evaluation of the common experience, we had a party for which the students brought beverages, pizza, and cake.

Before the first session, we, the "visitors", were led through the prison in a group by the minister to take photos. The prisoners, probably for security reasons, were individually accompanied on their photo tour by the minister. We were not allowed to take photos of security devices, prisoners, or wardens.

Walking along seemingly endless corridors, led into empty prison cells (including the cooling-off one), shown workshops and the courtyard where the prisoners spent part of their "leisure" time, we, the visitors, were continually confronted with the depressing and, at the same time, fascinating aesthetics (and unaesthetics) of the power and authority of the state and judiciary. In a paradoxical sense, many of our photos showed a "perverse beauty", an aesthetic view of the uncanny, ugly, and frightening. The photos taken by the young remand prisoners were often more reflective of the ugliness of the place, its incarnated violence, and were, thus, an expression of their hopelessness, lament, revolt, and despair (Figure 7.2).

Whereas the remand prisoners were at first delighted to be released from the solitude of their cells and meet "normal" people (the female students in particular), this enthusiasm soon began to dwindle once they felt confronted with the task of associating to the photos shown on the screen. While most of the students had previously taken part in the SPM and/or other experiential and action research-orientated

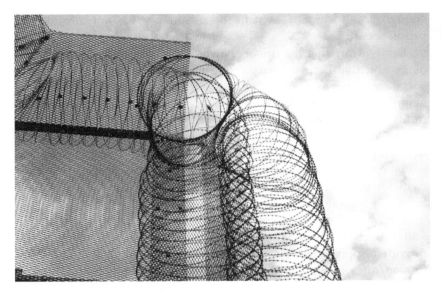

Figure 7.2.   Even the sky is grated.

methodologies at the university, this way of working was totally unknown to the prisoners. For them, learning from experience was largely limited to protecting oneself from attacks from co-prisoners and punishment from wardens. The more the students became aware of this gap, as well as of the enormous differences in verbal competence between themselves and the prisoners, the more they restricted their free associations and sanitised them according to their fantasised limitations of their prisoner participants.

For the prisoners, associating to the photos more often than not appeared to be absurd. Most of them insisted that what the photos showed was nothing but "reality" and using the photos for a wider range of thoughts and fantasies was mere nonsense—a conviction that served at least to protect them from experiencing their own emotions, fantasies, or thoughts. The more the prisoners became confused and frustrated by the associations of the students and our ongoing invitation to freely associate, the more stuck they became in their own "reality principle". The prisoners, so to say, wanted to convince us that a grid at the window of a cell is but a grid. The photos and—above all—the associations confronted the prisoners with a different reality, which largely they were unable to face. They also were not at all accustomed to persevering with a single photo for up to ten minutes; staring at a photo for that long was, with very few exceptions, a clear contrast to their normal experience of photos and images.

On the other hand, however, the invitation to freely associate to the photos—to express freely and uncensored as much as possible the thoughts, fantasies, emotions, images etc., that come to one's mind— is, in the context of a largely totalitarian institution, a paradox and almost impossible to accept. Even though a prisoner is free to think whatever he wants, more often than not it appears more appropriate to keep one's thoughts to oneself.

During the reflection sessions in heterogeneous groups of prisoners and students following the matrices, the former often were able to talk about some anxieties. Their main fear was about their future, that is, the outcome of a forthcoming trial, whose actual date seldom was set, the uncertainty as to whether they would be convicted or acquitted, and, if convicted, how long the sentence would be and what kind of life they would be able to lead afterwards. Animated by some of the photos, they also shared their daily anxieties, such as violence both from the wardens and other prisoners and the rejection of relatives and friends both during the time of their imprisonment and afterwards:

"Of course, one is anxious once one gets out. One has to change one's life."

"Maybe everything is lost then."

"Will someone be waiting for me? Will friends accept me as I am?"

"They don't know you as you are now; they just know you as you were when you went into the clink."

"I'm afraid that everything will happen all over again."

Not the least of their fears was that ultimately they would not be able to stay sane but would become mad—and therefore end up in the cooling-off cell.

It appeared that the prisoners often felt helpless in the matrices and did not think that they could cope:

"If one does not have any thoughts one prefers to stay silent."

"No feelings with some of the photos."

"Anxieties about saying something wrong."

"We, the inmates, are seeing these pictures day in, day out."

"One is thinking less in reaction to familiar images, new photos would have been better."

"One had to force oneself just to express one's current thought."

"The two parties do not start on the same level."

"The knowledge of the prisoners inhibits free thoughts."

As indicated above, owing to our ongoing failure to get both the prisoners and the students to commit themselves to the given task and method, my colleague and I wanted to end the SPM prematurely after the fourth session. We were, however, very grateful to the minister for encouraging us to stay on, but to slightly change the design and the setting of this event.

Instead of continuing to work in heterogeneous reflection groups, in which both prisoners and students took part, we had the participants work in homogenous groups. Their task was to reflect on the previous events and their possible learnings, and to make suggestions for how the forthcoming last matrix and reflection session could be designed differently. The minister joined the prisoners, and my colleague and I worked with the students.

The group of prisoners came up with two main suggestions. The first one was about the beginning of the weekly sessions. Before, we—the students, my colleague, and I—had first been led by the minister from the reception area to the chapel, where the SPM took place. There we waited for the prisoners, who were fetched from their cells by the minister. Following the prisoners' suggestion, during the remaining sessions we met the prisoners at their cells and went to the chapel to arrange the chairs for the matrix together and then had a smoking break in front of the chapel. They also suggested that every photo should first be explained by one of the prisoners before we could all associate to it. They did not realise that once the meaning of the photos had been nailed down by their descriptions and/or interpretations, any other possible meanings would be eliminated.

Those of us familiar with the SPM were afraid, if not convinced, that explaining the photos in advance would jeopardise the possibility of freely associating to them. However, for the sake of peace, we agreed, hoping at the same time that the prisoners would soon experience how inappropriate their suggestion was in light of the given task.

In comparison to the SPM at the university, where students were, to a major extent, able to join the matrix and freely associate to the photos, in this project we soon realised that the prisoners and students alike were broadly unable to refrain from their "groupishness" (Bion, 1961, p. 168). Although the matrix is supposed to provide equality, more often than not it turned into an inter-group event and tended to be dominated by tyrannical dynamics among the subgroups and/or between individuals. In a sense, despite our "good intentions", we were mirroring and re-enacting the fundamental split of "them and us" which is constitutive of the relatedness (and non-relatedness) of wardens and prisoners in a prison—and also for society and prison inmates.

This prison SPM also made obvious to what a limited extent feelings and emotions could be experienced, admitted, endured, contained, and reflected by the prisoners, in particular, and by "us" as well. We became aware again and again to what extent this "institutionalised insensitivity" had a restrictive, if not destructive, impact on the participants' capacity to think.

On the other hand, it seems very likely, from what some prisoners said at the very last session in the prison, that the SPM had set some of them thinking:

"I felt inclined to think more intensively."

"The thoughts that one had kept to oneself got confirmed. Therefore my own thoughts can't be totally wrong."

"There were similar thoughts from both sides [prisoners and students]—even though one group is not living in the clink."

While "our" experience with the prisoners was limited to the six sessions of the SPM, the minister experienced them in his daily work both before and after the event and was better able to recognise the impact of the SPM on them. In his "Attempt at a résumé" (Uellendahl, 2009, pp. 125ff.), the minister wrote that he experienced the SPM, despite all its difficulties and the ongoing threat of a premature ending, as very different from what transpires when groups of visitors come to get an impression of the prison or to "entertain" the prisoners by liberating them temporarily from their daily experience.

> Particularly on the side of the prisoners, I experienced a depth of and change in thinking which I previously would not have believed possible. Even long after the end of the SPM, it remained a topic of conversation and was moving to the juveniles. (Uellendahl, 2009, p. 129)

The minister noted that the SPM made experiences possible which would not otherwise have taken place.

> The prisoners did not get stuck in their permanently repeating circles around the "reality of the clink" but, animated by the associations, allowed themselves new ways of seeing and thinking about the penal institution. (Uellendahl, 2009, p. 130)

This was, as far as the prisoners are concerned, an SPM with people "who had never before associated in a guided way nor freely" (Uellendahl, 2009, p. 130).

After the end of the SPM in the prison we, the students, the minister, my colleague, and I, met at the university for two sessions to reflect upon the experience of the SPM and to evaluate it. Relating the experience in the prison to the previous one in the university, one student, probably on behalf of several others, stated,

> "I no longer see the university as being that bad. Due to the experience of the clink, I know what clink really means. However, I still see some similarities between the university and the clink; after having experienced the clink the university is only half a clink."

Two of the students had dreamt about the prison: in the first dream, the dreamer met someone who had been imprisoned for eighteen years even though he was innocent; the second dreamer had been in a prison where he and others had freed some prisoners. Other students referred to their experience:

> "For the inmates it is very difficult to say much in the clink; for me it was also difficult to freely associate, because I did not know how the prisoners would react."

> "Looking at the prison and experiencing it together with the prisoners is totally different from looking at it from outside."

"I was reminded of the time of my military service: being herded into a cage, barbed wire, the endless corridors, the stench, being subject to permanent constraints, always being at someone's mercy; all of this I had pushed away so far and suddenly it was there again."

"When one of the prisoners told us during the break that it would be the most normal thing in the world to hold a weapon to someone's head in the course of a raid, I felt helpless and it became clear to me that my rational logic was not applicable here."

While those students who previously had participated in the SPM at the university saw the SPM, despite its enormous challenges and difficulties, as an important experience both for themselves and the prisoners, the two students for whom it was the very first SPM did not regard it as an appropriate method in the given context. Be that as it may, we probably did endorse what one student said:

"It is quite difficult in any totalitarian organisation to work with the SPM—to gain access to what is unconscious underneath the surface of such a system."

The underlying assumption of the SPM as a method for experiential learning is that photographs taken by organisational role-holders promote an understanding of the unconscious in their organisations by revealing and putting into thoughts and thinking the hidden meaning and deeper experience of what usually remains unseeable and unthought. The prison SPM was, for various reasons, not easy to maintain and could only be brought to a "good enough" end with some modifications of the method and the design. Although this SPM was certainly not a "masterpiece", in paraphrasing Christopher Bollas's (1987) notion of the "unthought known", it brought the prison's "unseen visible" into awareness and allowed for it to be "seen" and to raise thoughts that, at least on occasion, were used for further thinking.

Instead of a conclusion

These two case examples make it obvious that the degree of the participants' commitment and their ability to temporarily abandon their individuality in order to dive into the associative unconscious by means of free associations are certainly preconditions for an SPM to succeed. They revealed so far unknown and unnoticed unconscious aspects and dynamics in organisations. It also shows the importance of the hosts' capacity to provide the space and containment necessary for such a venture. While a university setting, with students who are familiar with searching for the unconscious in social systems by using experiential learning methods, may be an almost ideal situation for an SPM, the penal institution gave ample evidence of the impediments for such work. Although the remand prisoners had no experience of freely associating "in public" and, apparently, were far less articulate than the students, it would be much too easy to blame them, the prisoners, for all the difficulties during this SPM and the ongoing threat of a premature ending. In fact, we, the students, my colleague, and I, more often than not felt dissociated from our capacity to think, withheld our spontaneous associations for fear of the prisoners' disapproval, and were only to a very limited extent able to acknowledge and address the continuous splitting of "them and us", giving rise to the assumption that the behaviour and thinking of all of us in our role as participants in the SPM were, to a major extent, crippled by the penal system and its prevailingly totalitarian mindset. A totalitarian-state-of-mind (Lawrence, 1995) reduces a broader reality to what is bearable and diminishes the capacity for thinking. It also fosters a high degree of violence, both towards others and the self, and threatens to turn those inside a totalitarian organisation into mere zombies, the living dead, without a soul, with no sympathy for others, and no valency for the unconscious. That the SPM in the prison, despite its apparent difficulties, was possible and, at the end, meaningful for most participants might, in retrospect, be explained by the presumption that the two sponsoring institutions, the university and the church, were unconsciously perceived by the participants as far less totalitarian than the prison.

In organising an SPM, sponsors and hosts of such an event have to be aware that it might be, at best, quite difficult and, at worst, dysfunctional and harmful in an organisational context in which totalitarian, perverse (Long, 2008), or psychotic mindsets and dynamics (Sievers, 1999, 2006, 2008b) prevail.

In the two SPMs presented here, we were working on a weekly basis for six to twelve four-hour sessions. This time frame and the continuous documentation had the great advantage that photos, associations, and thoughts from previous sessions were often remembered and referred to in the following sessions; ideally, the weekly sequence of sessions, as well as the intermediate breaks, can create a flow of thoughts and thinking and, as happened in the SPM at the university, inspire participants to make new photographs, which can be added to the archive and shown in one of the following sessions.

On other occasions, my colleagues and I have hosted SPMs for two- to three-day workshops, either with homogeneous groups of participants from one particular organisation or with heterogeneous groups of participants who wanted to experience and learn about the methodology. In the latter case, we chose themes for the workshops such as "Men and women at work", "The city" or "Transitional spaces". When a workshop is part of a larger conference, we use a theme that is related to the one of the conference. Working with role-holders in an organisation, we develop the theme together with the sponsors of the SPM; previous themes have, for example, been "What does it mean to work here?", "Where will our organisation be in five (or ten) years time?", or "Safety and insecurity at work".

In the first case example, the SPM at the university, I have already briefly circumscribed the role of host in providing the required technology and the rooms, choosing the photographs from the archive, reminding participants of the task (if necessary), and helping to make links between the photos and the thinking from previous sessions. From this, it might at first appear that the role of the host is only a minor, mainly facilitating, one. Although this may be the case "ideally", I want to emphasise that this role can only successfully carried out if the role-holder has ample experience in, and competence for, working with the unconscious in social systems. Hosting a SPM also requires sufficient competence and experience in working with social systems from a psychodynamic perspective (e.g., through participation in group relations conferences) in order realise when participants in the matrix tend to be preoccupied by their "groupishness" (Bion, 1961, p. 168) and/or their narcissistic tendencies, and to encourage them to keep them at bay and stay on the task (see Mersky, Chapter Eight, in this book).

Hosting an SPM is quite different from facilitating or moderating a (discussion) group or the role of process consultant. As already emphasised above in the more general description of this methodology, the matrix is *the* crucial element of the SPM. The second case, the SPM in the prison, illustrates how the preoccupation with a group identity of either prisoners or students might impede the ability of the participants to think and speak for themselves. Also the apparent split and broadly concealed quarrel between and among the groups more often than not prevented participants from going with the flow of associations without rational and/or social control. Not least the "reality principle", with which the prisoners often referred to the photos (a grid in the cell window is a grid, is a grid), made it difficult, if not impossible, for all participants to go beyond "the real" and the finite, beyond what is already known and the repetition of banal facts.

In contrast to a group and its conscious and unconscious dynamics, the matrix is, as Lawrence (1999, p. 18), referring to social dreaming, puts it, "a place out of which something grows as in a uterus". The matrix is based on the assumption that participants temporarily suspend their individuality and their ordinary (and/or scientific) rational logic; they are prepared to dive into the endless chain of associations and amplifications, "a line of thought . . . linked by some hidden logic that connects seemingly disconnected ideas" (Bollas, 2009, p. 6). Hosting an SPM, therefore, demands, as already mentioned, "a different kind of leadership—one inspired by the recognition of the infinite, of not-knowing, of being in doubt and uncertainty" (Lawrence, 2005, p. 40). The host has to provide sufficient containment for the participants to make it possible for the aim of the SPM to be accomplished, that is, to experience—through collective viewing of digital photos taken by the participants (and subsequent associations, amplifications, systemic thinking and reflection)—the hidden meaning of what in an organisation usually remains unseen and, thus, unnoticed and unthought.

The social photo-matrix is an action research orientated experiential methodology in the making. Future experiences with it, my own and those of other colleagues, will, I hope, contribute to both deepening this method and extending it to further demonstrate how insights and learnings from an SPM can have an impact not just on individual role-holders, but on organisations as a whole.

References

Ahlers-Niemann, A. (2007). *Auf der Spur der Sphinx. Sozioanalyse als erweiterter Rahmen zur Erforschung von Organisationskulturen*. Norderstedt: Books on Demand.

Armstrong, D. (2005). The 'organization-in-the-mind': reflections on the relation of psychoanalysis to work with institutions. In: D. Armstrong, *Organization in the Mind: Psychoanalysis, Group Relations and Organizational Consultancy*, R. French (Ed.) (pp. 29–43). London: Karnac.

Bion, W. R. (1961). *Experiences in Groups and Other Papers*. London: Tavistock.

Bollas, C. (1987). *The Shadow of the Object: Psychoanalysis of the Unthought Known*. New York: Columbia University Press.

Bollas, C. (2009). *The Evocative Object World*. London: Routledge.

Bowles, M. (1991). The organization shadow. *Organization Studies, 12*: 387–404.

Bredlow, K.-H. (2009). 'Bilder und Worte'. Ein Vor-Wort. In: B. Sievers (Ed.) *Hier drinnen sind irgendwie alle Türen zu. Eine Soziale Photo-Matrix in einer Justizvollzugsanstalt* (pp. 7–13). Münster: agenda.

Denhardt, R. D. (1981). *In the Shadow of Organization*. Lawrence, KA: Regents Press of Kansas.

Elias, N. (1987). Wandlungen der Wir-Ich-Balance. In: *Die Gesellschaft der Individuen* (pp. 207–315). Frankfurt: Suhrkamp.

Freud, S. (1923a). Two encyclopaedia articles. *S.E., 17*: 233–260. London: Hogarth.

Hutton, J., Bazalgette, J., & Reed, B. (1997). Organisation-in-the-mind: a tool for leadership and management of institutions. In: J. E. Neumann, K. Kellner, & A. Dawson-Shepherd (Eds.), *Developing Organizational Consultancy* (pp. 113–126). London: Routledge.

Lawrence, W. G. (1995). The seductiveness of totalitarian states-of-mind. *Journal of Health Care Chaplaincy, 7*: 11–22.

Lawrence, W. G. (Ed.) (1998). *Social Dreaming @ Work*. London: Karnac.

Lawrence, W. G. (1999). The contribution of social dreaming to socio-analysis. *Socio-Analysis, 1*(1): 18–33.

Lawrence, W. G. (2003). Social dreaming as sustained thinking. *Human Relations, 56*: 609–624.

Lawrence, W. G. (2005). *Introduction to Social Dreaming: Transforming Thinking*. London: Karnac.

Long, S. (1999). Who am I at work? An exploration of work identifications and identity. *Socio-Analysis, 1*(1): 48–64.

Long, S. (2008). *The Perverse Organisation and its Deadly Sins*. London: Karnac.

Marcuse, H. (1965). Das Veralten der Psychoanalyse. In: *Kultur und Gesellschaft (Vol. 2)* (pp. 85–106). Frankfurt: Suhrkamp.

Mersky, R. (2012). Contemporary methodologies to surface and act on unconscious dynamics in organizations: an exploration of design, facilitation capacities, consultant paradigm and ultimate value. *Organizational & Social Dynamics, 12*(1): 19–43.

Newton, J., Long, S., & Sievers, B. (Eds.) (2006). *Coaching in Depth. The Organizational Role Analysis Approach.* London: Karnac.

Parker, L. D. (2009). Photo-elicitation: an ethno-historical accounting & management research prospect. *Accounting, Auditing & Accountability Journal, 22*: 1111–1129.

Petersen, N. J., & Østergaard, S. (2003). Organisational photography as a research method: what, how and why. *Academy of Management Conference Proceedings* [Submission identification number: 12702 Division: Research Methods].

Ray, J. L., & Smith, A. D. (2012). Using photographs to research organizations: evidence, considerations, and application in a field study. *Organizational Research Methods, 15*: 288–315.

Rose, G. (2007). *Visual Methodologies.* London: Sage.

Samuels, A. (1993). *The Political Psyche.* London: Routledge.

Schroeder, J. (2006). Critical visual analysis. In: R. Belk (Ed.), *Handbook of Qualitative Research Methods in Marketing* (pp. 303–321). Cheltenham: Edward Elgar.

Sievers, B. (1999). Psychotic organization as a metaphoric frame for the socio-analysis of organizational and interorganizational dynamics. *Administration & Society, 31*: 588–615.

Sievers, B. (2001). "Im Traum erscheint alles als normal und logisch": Die Matrix Sozialer Träume. In: B. Oberhoff & U. Beumer (Eds.), *Theorie und Praxis psychoanalytischer Supervision* (pp. 124–142). Münster: Votum.

Sievers, B. (2006). Psychotic organization: a socio-analytic perspective. *ephemera, 6*: 104–120. www.ephemeraweb.org/journal/6-2/6-2sievers.pdf. Accessed 25 February 2012.

Sievers, B. (2007a). "There's nothing more worth fighting for." Social dreaming with Social Democrats in Austria. In: W.G. Lawrence (Ed.), *Infinite Possibilities of Social Dreaming* (pp. 18–28). London: Karnac.

Sievers, B. (2007b). Pictures from below the surface of the university: The social photo-matrix as a method for understanding organizations in depth. In: M. Reynolds, & R. Vince (Eds.), *Handbook of Experiential Learning and Management Education* (pp. 241–257). Oxford: Oxford University Press.

Sievers, B. (2008a). Perhaps it is the role of pictures to get in contact with the uncanny. The social photo-matrix as a method to promote the understanding of the unconscious in organizations. *Organisational and Social Dynamics, 8*: 234–254.

Sievers, B. (2008b). The psychotic university. *ephemera*, *8*: 238–257 www. ephemeraweb.org/journal/8–3/8–3sievers.pdf. Accessed 25 February 2012.

Sievers, B. (Ed.) (2009). *Hier drinnen sind irgendwie alle Türen zu. Eine Soziale Photo-Matrix in einer Justizvollzugsanstalt.* Münster: agenda.

Sievers, B. (2013, in press). A grid is a grid is a grid is a grid . . .: a social photo-matrix in a penal institution for remand prisoners. In: G. Lightfoot, P. Pelzer, & J.-L. Moriceau (Eds.), *Demo(s): Against Organization.* New York: Peter Lang (in press).

Sievers, B., & Beumer, U. (2006). Organisational role analysis and consultation. The organisation as inner object. In: J. Newton, S. Long, & B. Sievers (Eds.), *Coaching in Depth: The Organizational Role Analysis Approach* (pp. 65–81). London: Karnac.

Uellendahl, K. (2009). "Was hat es gebracht?" Versuch eines Resümees. In: B. Sievers (Ed.), *Hier drinnen sind irgendwie alle Türen zu. Eine Soziale Photo-Matrix in einer Justizvollzugsanstalt* (pp. 125–135). Münster: agenda.

Vince, R., & Broussine, M. (1996). Paradox, defense and attachment: accessing and working with emotions and relations underlying organizational change. *Organization Studies, 17*: 1–21.

Vince, R., & Warren, S. (2012). Participatory visual methods. In: C. Cassell & G. Symon (Eds.), *The Practice of Qualitative Organizational Research: Core Methods and Current Challenges* (pp. 275–295). London: Sage.

Warren, S. (2005). Photography and voice in critical, qualitative management research. *Accounting, Auditing and Accountability Journal, 18*: 861–882.

Warren, S. (2006). Hot nesting? A visual exploration of personalised workspaces in a 'hot-desk' office environment. In: P. Case, S. Lilley, & T. Owens (Eds.), *The Speed of Organization* (pp. 119–146). Copenhagen: Copenhagen Business School Press.

Warren, S. (2009). Visual methods in organizational research. In: A. Bryman & D. Buchanan (Eds.), *Handbook of Organizational Research Methods* (pp. 566–582). London: Sage.

Warren, S. (2012). Psychoanalysis, collective viewing and the 'Social Photo Matrix' in organizational research. *Qualitative Research in Organizations and Management: An International Journal, 7*(1): 86–104.

Winnicott, D. W. (1953). Transitional objects and transitional phenomena—a study of the first not-me possession. *International Journal of Psychoanalysis, 3*: 89–97, reprinted in: *Playing and Reality* (pp. 1–25). London: Routledge, 1991.

Winnicott, D. W. (1991). *Playing and Reality*. London: Routledge.

CHAPTER EIGHT

Social dream-drawing: "Drawing brings the inside out"

Rose Redding Mersky

"All representations are transformations"

(Bion, 1965, p. 140)

Introduction: from the depths to the drawing pad

The use of individual dreams and dream material to illuminate social processes was pioneered by the work of Gordon Lawrence and his social dreaming methodology (1999b). Participants in the matrix are invited to share recent dreams, and members of the matrix make associations to them. The hosts of the matrix "take" these dreams, offer hypotheses that link the dreams thematically, and suggest possible underlying meanings relating to the social or organisational world of the matrix. It is this use of dreams to explore the underlying issues of social systems that has led to my interest in developing a related methodology, social dream-drawing.

For a period of years, I have been working with groups of colleagues and professionals in related fields to develop this methodology as a means of illuminating and potentially helping to resolve emerging, but perhaps not as yet fully conscious, professional issues.

I have worked with groups in the Netherlands, Chile, Germany and the UK. Some workshops were one-day, others extended over multiple sessions and a span of months. In 2009, I entered the doctoral programme of the Institute for Psycho-Social Studies at the University of the West of England in Bristol, specifically to undertake further research on this new methodology. This chapter contains extensive interview material with six of these participants, whose comments appear in quotations throughout, as well as quotes from the original transcript of the Chile workshop group. I am very grateful to all of these participants.

Beginning with the dream . . .

As one's original dream makes its journey from a totally unique internal experience to its "presentation" to the world through drawing, it becomes transformed. The delicate and mysterious "decision" of the dreamer to attempt to recall his or her "latent not material unmaterial dream"—usually while still in bed and just awoken—begins this process. The dream material becomes lodged imperfectly into some sort of disconnected narrative "in the mind".

From this first "achievement" comes the opportunity for further transformation, either through language (by telling another or by writing it down) or through drawing. This is not an easy process. Said one interviewee, ". . . it's hard to come through to get in touch, or come in touch with the dreams. To come in touch with your own unconscious material, it's not such easy going!"

Sometimes, the dream is drawn and further elaborated by the written word. When the fleeting, often chaotic "pictures" in the unconscious are represented on paper, they enter an arena of transformation. It is there that the dreamer has brought to physical reality what has already uniquely emerged from the unconscious. For every immediately forgettable bit, rejected fright, illogical and, therefore, impossible "lost" dream fragment, come those that we somehow feel able to refine, reframe, and represent to others.

One London participant described her process of drawing a dream this way:

"I wouldn't be able to do it straight away . . . because I needed to collect it together . . . it didn't go away . . . it sat there in my mind . . .

if I'd put it down straight away . . . I couldn't have done it . . . actually any creative activity . . . if you had an idea in your head . . . all the time you are working on the idea but you don't put it in the external until somehow it's formulated in a way in your mind . . . and it can just sit there."

For this participant, "If you have a clear image somehow embedded in your mind, which might take a couple of days to do, then that's your starting point."

Any step in bringing forward the dream from the original is an act of transformation. Bion (1965), in his theory of transformations, uses the example of the artist who paints a field of poppies. When he/she does so, elements of the original field (what he terms "invariants" (Bion, 1965, p. 4)) remain unaltered (i.e., the red colouring), in order for the painting to be recognisable as a representation of that particular landscape. Just so, the transformation of the original dream material contains invariants that link the original images to the drawing and make it recognisable. In this process, one can say, a kind of transformation in the psyche of the dream drawer also takes place.

However, there are challenges. How can one possibly "match" the experience of the dream with the materials of drawing, especially if one does not see oneself as a good enough artist? One must somehow translate a three-dimensional experience into a two-dimensional one. Can one's coloured pencils really capture the colours? Must a "story" (as a cartoon) be made out of unrelated images? Will the effort over-tax one's artistic abilities? How can one stay "true" to one's original dream experience? As one interviewee put it, "I can't paint the dream in the way that I dream it . . . It's more complex than I . . . can ever bring . . . to this two-dimensional sheet."

Hau (2002, cf. 2004), a psychologist and member of the research staff at the Sigmund Freud Institute, Frankfurt am Main, Germany, did an experiment designed to compare what were termed "free-imagination drawings" and "dream drawings". He and his colleagues asked sleepers to wake up and immediately draw what, if anything, they had just dreamt. He later asked them to make "free-imagination drawings" during a conscious state. Then he compared the two kinds of drawings.

He found that the dream drawings had a childlike quality and represented a regression into earlier childhood stages (the average age for dream drawings being 8.6 years and for free imagination drawings 10.2 years). The dream images, he says, are from earlier developmental stages, even though they may represent much more complex material.

Hau sees dream drawing as being mainly concerned with drawing a story and creating some kind of connecting cord. The line of thoughts from the remembrance and the sequence of images of the perceived and remembered dream experience are supposed to be brought together and shown. Breaks, summaries, changes of perspectives, sequences of action, the space and time of the dream, are condensed in the image, which does not give room or space for perspective representation. What happened in the dream is condensed, just as "dream-thoughts" have "undergone an extensive process of condensation in the course of the formation of the dream" (Freud, 1900a, p. 279).

Despite these limitations, however, Hau and his colleagues make the important observation that, by drawing a dream, one is closer to the original experienced image (Hau, 2002, p. 199). At the same time, the potential for distortion lies in overly elaborated or "sanitised" drawings, those that are meant to show good drawing or good imagination instead of the "messier stuff", as one interviewee put it. These might not be very well linked to the original experience.

Here is how one participant in the German group put it:

"I think for me it's in the core . . . to bring ideas to the point of being visible. To bring it into materialised manifest form and then you can work in another way about it or with it. But I think in this it's a step from one part to the other and there are some things in this transformation if you have to express it in the language, maybe also in the symbolic language. I guess something will be lost in this transformational process. I have the idea that I have a dream, then I start to draw the dream, and then next I go to Solingen and I start to talk about the dream. In this step-by-step process I can't take all the content or all the ideas or all the parts with me. Some will be lost and other ideas, other parts, will be found. So, when I start to paint the dream, there is a form of selection. I can't paint the dream in the way that I dream it. That was sometimes very hard for me, because I thought there would be every possibility to bring this inner picture to the paper. It's more complex than I ever can bring to this two-dimensional sheet. So that's what I meant. Something is lost . . . I'm not sure what is the significance of losing or finding some new parts. I don't know."

Additionally, there is the risk that, when being worked with in the group, the dream itself becomes distorted. As two interviewees put it (one from the German group and one from the London group):

"As soon as you put it in the external, it becomes layered with other meanings . . . your own idea gets submerged, or emerges absorbed into other people's . . . It's obviously got to do that to grow and have other meanings."

"And also when you then start to get into talks with the other group members, they will talk about your dream . . . And sometimes maybe it's strange to remain calm, to listen what are they saying [sic] about my dream. 'So interesting, I did not see that in my dream.' So it's a present to hear these other associations and other approaches and also the other symbolic offerings . . . I was not forced to adopt any opinion which was offered or any interpretation which was given by the others."

Despite these limitations, however, these drawings do represent an unconscious event for the dreamer and this methodology is based on capturing that.

Dead babies in the mud: group associations to a dream drawing of my client

The first time I recognised the power of the drawings of dreams for my work was in 2003, when I presented a consultation case with a client who would only work with me over the telephone (Mersky, 2006). The client is a very ambitious female in her mid-forties, who is quite fastidious about her appearance. A few days after the presentation, "J", a student in the class, had a vivid dream about my client. One part is as follows:

We ["J" and my client, Leslie] are now standing hip-deep in brown, muddy water and there are small, soft and wet-looking little islands with some sort of grass on it like in a moorland. Here everything, including our former business-like clothes, are in brown and pale green colours . . . Leslie is at my right side and now I can see her for the first time. She looks a bit like Winona Ryder, big eyes, short brown hair and a desperate look on her face. She is close to tears, pulls my sleeve at the right arm and is trying to tell me something. She seems afraid I could punish her or be angry with her, but she wants to tell it no matter what. Then I can make out what she is constantly saying: "I killed all the babies, hear me? I killed them." At first I do not understand what she is talking about, but then I can make out many little baskets swimming near the islands. Leslie grabs such a basket and shoves it over to me and in it is a dead baby, pale, dead and cold with mud and grass on it. In the dream I have the impression that she killed them a time before by pulling the whole basket under water. Surprisingly I do not feel any anger or that she should be punished. In fact I sort of expected this and take it as a plain fact. I just want to tell her that it is no surprise to me that she did this and that everything in her appearance tells this, as if it was written in her forehead and that I wonder why she is making such a big deal out of it. . . as the dream ends . . .

"J" emailed me the dream and offered to bring pictures of the dream to a subsequent class for our reflection. She brought four big drawings of this dream and talked us through them. One of her drawings is shown in Figure 8.1.

The associations to this picture dealt in large part with the mud and dirt of the dream and also on Leslie's deep shame for having killed babies and covered them with mud. We tried to connect these associations to two important facts about her: she is a paediatrician and, though married, has no children. The drawing of the dream was noted as being "cleansed" in a certain way, as if the material was just too difficult to look at.

In my work with Leslie over the past few years, I knew that she was very concerned about how she looked, what impression she made, and how she was seen—whether she had, for example, the right expression. She would often discuss preparations for forthcoming unstructured situations, where she would be quite visible, such as office parties or workshops. She was also terrified of those times when she was tired and would lose her temper or do something destructive in her interactions with others. She had been reprimanded more than once for being unable to work well with other people.

The idea of being covered with mud for having done some unforgivable act (that must always be hidden) was an important metaphor for my subsequent work with her. I was confirmed in my ongoing hypothesis that her self-representation was strongly influenced by an early trauma of some sort. To be clean and fresh, not dirty, with the right expression and, especially, to be kept pure by the distance

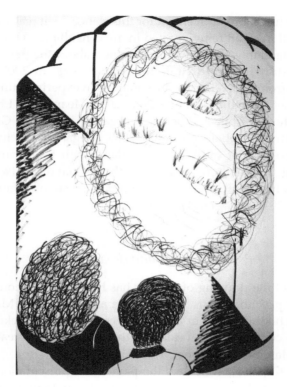

Figure 8.1.   Dead babies in the mud.

conferred by the phone line made more sense and also helped me to accept that, for her, this was the closest intimacy she could handle. I became less judgemental of her choice to work only by phone.

The associations to this dream picture provided a kind of "third eye" on the consultation. A great deal of space was opened for me to work with Leslie, not in the sense of sharing this experience with her, but in the sense of being able to develop and hold more hypotheses about her and her inner world. I grew open to the idea that "J" had actually had a dream on behalf of the consultation. I felt identified with the figure of "J" in the dream, who heard my client's deeply shameful confession and saw the evidence of my client's terrible deed. What was especially important was that "J" offered her forgiveness and acceptance. Although I had never articulated it, I realised that, as a consultant, I was taking a similar role with Leslie and that "J's" dream provided a further reinforcement for this stance. I felt reaffirmed in my professional role and reinvigorated in my consultation work.

Understandably, I became quite excited about the possibilities for exploring drawings of dreams for future work. In 2005, I invited colleagues from the Netherlands to join me in experimenting with this idea. We met three times from 2006 to 2007. Meanwhile, I held a one-day workshop in Chile and began to organise a group in Germany. In the northern hemisphere autumn of 2009, I began my doctoral studies at the University of the West of England with the express goal of developing this methodology. Since then, I have run two one-day workshops in Bristol, and a four-session workshop in London from September 2010 to December 2011.

Psychoanalysis and dream drawing

The value of the drawing of dreams has historical and contemporary support in psychoanalysis. Freud wrote about the Wolf Man's drawing of his childhood dream about wolves, and he also acknowledged that latent content was revealed in the drawings of dreams undertaken by Marcinowski (Fisher, 1957; Hau, 2004).

Bion (1977[1965]) considers the painter's representation of a field of poppies similar to an interpretation of a patient's unconscious material, wherein "the facts of an analytic experience (the realization) are transformed into an interpretation (the representation)" (Bion, 1977, p. 4), whether by patient or analyst. From his perspective, the key aspect of this transformation is that "an experience, felt and described in one way, is described in another" (Bion, 1977, p. 4).

Bion's notion that the painter's representation transforms the original landscape in the same way that an interpretation transforms analytic material suggests support for the idea that the dream drawer is also transforming unconscious material. Not only is unconscious material made available to the dreamer (and the group), it is being worked on, worked through, and elaborated in the course of bringing it into the social arena.

Based on his work with patients' drawings, Fisher (1957), a psychiatrist at Mount Sinai Hospital in New York, believes that the act of creating images of one's dream evokes dream images that would otherwise not come to awareness. He writes,

It is an interesting feature of these experiments that some of the latent content of the dream emerges and becomes evident through the process of drawing the dream. It is very likely that this content would not become evident if the dreams were reported only verbally and not drawn. . . . There is no doubt that because dreams are largely visual in structure the usual purely verbal analysis results in the overlooking of significant latent content. (Fisher, 1957, p. 36)

Linda Brakel, a psychoanalyst and faculty member at the Michigan Psychoanalytic Institute, proposes that dream drawing be officially integrated into analytic treatment. She compared patient verbal-only reports and associations to their dreams to their verbal associations to drawings of these same dreams. She documents the greater depth of material and detail revealed by the combination of "verbal association and pictorial renderings" (Brakel, 1993, p. 368). In her view, this combination provides greater access to the time in the patient's life when pictorial representations were more dominant and, thus, tap into earlier material that would otherwise not be accessed by purely verbal means. Furth (1998, p. 12) takes another step when he notes that "pictures from the unconscious represent primitive, raw material taken directly from the unconscious, undeveloped, yet filled with the unconscious content closely connected to the individual's complexes".

Unconscious revealed: using drawings in consultation and research

In the traditional organisational development field and in the field of socioanalytic research and consultation, the use of drawings has proved extremely useful (see Chapter Three of this volume). The risk one takes in using this methodology is client resistance, due to a fear of infantilisation and scepticism that anything practical can truly be gained by such a methodology. Because one is engaged in an activity associated with childhood, there is a natural fear of regression and of appearing too childish, or of revealing something that is better kept private. Very often, the success in convincing a client or research subject to undertake such an activity is based on the existing trust between consultant/researcher and client/subject, perhaps through previous work projects or previous participation in training programmes, workshops, or group relations conferences. And, because this activity often produces anxiety in the client system (inside and outside the group), the role of the facilitator in explaining the purpose of such an exercise and conducting the intervention in a well-bounded and contained way is extremely important (Mersky, 2012).

In terms of methodologies, a common assignment is to ask a group to draw a picture of an animal or a machine that represents one's organisation (Morgan, 1993) or, simply, to make a picture of their organisation. One way these drawings are then worked with is as follows (Sievers & Beumer, 2006). Finished pictures are mounted and displayed around the room, and each one is explored in depth. The first step is for the drawer to explain the drawing. After initial clarifying questions are answered, group members associate to the picture, while the drawer remains silent. After a period of fifteen or so minutes, the drawer responds and shares his/her reflections. From that experience, a general discussion or set of associations at the group level may take place, facilitated by the consultant or the researcher. Often this is an opening exercise with a group that will subsequently be working at a concrete level in a change management or a strategic planning process (Sievers & Beumer, 2006).

Practitioners and researchers using pictures are trying to elicit material that lies out of awareness and that generally underlies current problems and challenges. Whether approached from the perspective of Jungian analytic art therapy (Broussine, 2007; Furth, 1988), psychoanalysis (Brakel, 1993; Fisher, 1957), or socioanalysis (Gould, 1987; Nossal, 2003), bringing "unknown and unconscious material to the attention of the consciousness" (Furth, 1998, p. 9) is the goal.

In describing the methodology of mental maps, where participants are asked to draw a mental picture of their organisations, Gould notes that the idea is "namely, to make unconscious or covert experiences, conflicts and fantasies conscious, and thereby available for interpretation, explication and insight" (Gould, 1987, pp. 5–6) and to "elicit previously inchoate, unorganized and/or preconscious assumptions and fantasies, and to give them sufficient form for scrutiny and analysis" (Gould, 1987, p. 3). In order to make this possible, adults are encouraged to playfully regress by drawing, which is in the service of the overall task of bringing this material to awareness. It is the work of the consultant, in an ongoing way, to help the client group link this material to their organisational reality. This is often done by identifying themes that emerge from the material through making links between drawings and by offering what appear to be contradictory hypotheses from the data.

At the group level, such work offers the possibility of developing a shared understanding of one's organisation, as associations to individual pictures become linked with one another and themes begin to emerge in the discussion. Morgan (1993) finds this a critical advantage. As he puts it, "The challenges in times of change is [sic] to find shared meanings that are themselves in flux, so that people are encouraged to find an intelligent place in the world around them" (Morgan, 1993, p. 11).

A well-contained group environment, with a clear task and well-bounded facilitation, can become a place for creativity and new thinking, as well as a safe environment to experiment with other aspects of one's identity and personality in role. Nossal (2003) terms such an environment a "'thinking space' where there is openness to sharing and exploring in a different way" (Nossal, 2003, p. 3). In this space, which is "characterized by a great deal of individual and collective creativity, and a spirit of playful competitiveness among the participants" (Nossal, 2003, p. 6), there is the opportunity to explore serious ideas and problems.

Through this kind of playful and creative methodology, complex data (often too complex to completely process at once) emerge. Often, contradictory images and deep anxieties are reflected and participants are awash in the complexities of their organisation. One major advantage of working with both visual and verbal data is that "the brain is able to both store and give expression to far more complex data in a visual form, such as a picture, than it is able to do verbally" (Nossal, 2003, p. 4). More parts of the brain are stimulated and are also required to sift through what emerges.

There is also an important benefit to focusing on something separate from the individual (i.e., a drawing) as opposed to what is being said at the moment. Once the picture is drawn (as my colleague Martina Joachem points out), it cannot be revoked. One cannot change one's mind and "take it back". On the other hand, it leaves the drawer and the group with something that is outside and to which all can relate together. This is termed the "third factor", that is, the drawing as a mediating or an intermediary device . . . [that] . . . enables the data to be out there in the drawing rather than in the immediate exchange between individuals and in this way it allows difficult material to be explored in a way that is less threatening. (Nossal, 2003, p. 7)

That fact that working with drawings helps to "contain the play-ful as well as the serious" (Vince & Broussine, 1996, p. 17) is well illus-trated by the following example from colleague Stephanie Segal:

It was through my first exposure to her [Virginia Satir's] work that I saw how powerful using drawings can be in an organisational role. One of the workshops that I attended encouraged a group of public sector professionals to spend an hour each drawing their work roles. Lots of lovely huge sheets of paper and colourful pens were placed around the room. One of them, a Headteacher, who was feeling very jaded, drew a cruise liner with herself at the helm of the wheel on the top deck with lots of teachers peering out of all the cabin holes. There was not one child in sight. When the facilitator asked the Headteacher what she saw in the picture, she was unable to see the absence of the children (the primary task of the school) and only when others in the group pointed it out did she realise how managerial and bureaucratic her post had become, why she was disliking it so much and how removed she felt from the children. It was so dramatic and she was very choked. It really was an enormous moving point for her; she eventually resigned as a Headteacher and moved to a position as a locum where she had far more contact with the children, which was the part of the work she adored. (Segal, 2007)

Ultimately, the true value of such a methodology lies in its effec-tiveness in organisations. Morgan (1993, p. 9) documents the advan-tage and the learnings such a request can bring. Perhaps he does not state the case too dramatically when he writes, ". . . imagery can be used to create breakthroughs on organizational problems and find new initiatives in difficult situations".

Access to the unconscious feelings of groups and organisations serve as a prime motivation for the use of drawings in research. Broussine (2007) summarises the many advantages:

. . . the use of art as a research approach enables people to communi-cate multifaceted information and feelings about their experiences in organizations and other social settings. It legitimises the expression of

complex, subtle and possibly irrational facets of organizational experience. This may be important within certain settings where it is 'not
done' to give voice to feelings and irrational aspects of life. . . . It is the
dialogue, reflection and sense-making that is provoked in an individual or in a group by the production of expressive images that can be
as important as the images themselves. (p. 78)

So, for those organisations that wish to know more about, and
make use of, the underlying dynamics in their systems, pictures are a
well-researched and well-documented source of valuable information,
and provide a non-threatening and often playful/serious look at what
is going on. Documenting these events by taking photos of each
picture and perhaps providing a written record of the associations are
ways to allow clients/subjects to return to the material again and
again over time and to continue their integration of the possibilities
and insights.

Dream- and photo-matrix with associations and amplifications

My work with the drawings of dreams is based on the pioneering
work of Gordon Lawrence and his development of social dreaming.
His critical insight is that dreams have a social meaning and that this
social meaning can be uncovered in an environment where association
and amplification are possible (the matrix). This idea is a major underpinning of the work on dream drawings. As Bain points out, "There
is a waking life relationship with the Organisation, and a dream life
relationship to the Organisation" (2005, p. 1) and ". . . the dreams of
members of an organisation contribute to an understanding of that
organisation, and its unconscious" (Bain, 2005, p. 5).

Lawrence's work is based on the assumption that people ". . . live
in an ecosystem in which there are linkages that have been unimag-
ined hitherto, that they exist in a 'wholeness' that can be but dimly
perceived because of their own experiences of fragmentation" (Lawrence, 1999b, pp. 38–39). Through his work and his many publications,
he has demonstrated that these disconnected and fragmented parts
can be brought to some sort of larger consideration in the work of a
social dreaming matrix and can be made sense of, at least in providing material for possible organisational hypotheses.

The use of social dreaming as an organisational intervention to bring about not only consciousness and awareness, but also important change, is more and more being documented. The work of Sievers (2007) with the Austrian Social Democratic Party and that of Michael (2007) with a community mental health centre in the USA are two good illustrations.

Lawrence's pioneering work, developed in conjunction with colleagues from around the world, including Burkard Sievers, has formed the basis for Sievers' own elaboration, the social photo-matrix. Here, the matrix associates to, and amplifies, thoughts in relation to photographs taken by the participants themselves, often of an organisation they have in common, such as a university. They work to create links between photographs. This is an experience that grows in meaning over time. Sievers' innovation emphasises photos as a collective representation, rather than belonging to the individual. Thus, "the photograph—and not the photographer—is the medium of discourse" (Sievers, 2008, p. 235, and Chapter Seven of this book).

The methodology

For the social dream-drawing workshops, three or four participants are invited to bring a drawing of a dream related to a particular theme. The current theme I am using is, "What do I risk in my work?" We sit at a table and follow the same procedure for each dream drawing. The dreamer first describes the dream. Then he/she shows the drawing. Clarifying questions to the dream drawer are asked and answered. For approximately twenty minutes, all participants, including the dream drawer, offer associations and amplifications to the drawing. Very often, during this process, the dreamer recalls more original dream material. The drawer then offers his/her reflections on this associative work. We stand up and switch seats for a general discussion relating to the theme, the reflection section. We work on each dream drawing for approximately forty-five to sixty minutes.

Free association, considered by Freud (1916–1917, p. 287) as "this fundamental technical rule of analysis", involves anything that comes to one's mind in relation to the drawing or the dream material. Rather than the traditional psychoanalytic use of free association as a means to help the individual patient reveal repressed unconscious conflicts, this use of free association here is based on the concept of a group or a system's associative unconscious (see Chapter One of this book).

Amplifications are those cultural and political elements that come to mind, such as current events, music, literature, and film.

A transcript of each workshop is created. It includes photos of the dream drawings, the dreamer's presentation of the dream and the drawing, the group's associations and amplifications, and the reflections on the theme. Such a transcript can be produced in many ways. Sometimes, participants rotate the role of taking notes, which produces not necessarily a word-for-word transcript, but a series of summaries of what is said, such as the transcript from Chile (see example below). For my doctoral studies, I have more and more relied on tape recordings, which have been transcribed professionally. This has meant receiving the consent of all participants in advance.

An example from a one-day workshop

In a recent dream-drawing workshop in Chile, "C" brought a drawing with images from two different dreams, which he had three days apart (Figure 8.2).

Figure 8.2. Chilean dream.

The transcript describes C's presentation of his first dream:

C. depicts a fragment from a dream he had one day after receiving the theme. In the dream, the dreamer sees himself facing forward and then from above. He has plenty of hair on both sides of his head and in the front in the middle, but he has almost none, or just fuzz, on the top of his head. When looking at himself head-on, the dreamer could not realise he had lost his hair. This happened only when he looked from above or from behind. The dreamer developed a feeling of anxiety and distress, since he was not able to tell what was happening when looking at himself head-on.

C's second dream:

The second fragment is related to a dream the dreamer had three days after the previous one. In this dream he sees three women (students of his class), who, at the end of a class, approach him and remark on how interesting the lesson was. While this takes place, he realises he forgot to put on his belt and his trousers are falling down. This generates distress but also an erotic feeling.

C's immediate association to his first dream and his drawing had to do with "the excess of work and the anxiety it generates". He noted that "baldness is associated with an illness (alopecia) produced by stress, an illness that his father also has" and his anguish about this. His associations to the second dream "refer to a sense of eroticism and the seduction of others, especially women, in his role of professor".

The associations and amplifications of other group members, all of whom were affiliated with the university, noted the connections between the two dreams and their drawings: for example, "I see in the drawing the psychopathic behaviours people develop at work. On the one hand, one smiles and, on the other, one loses one's hair". The complicated relationship between a young professor and his/her students was also referred to, noting, for example, how "powerfully ... stress and eroticism is associated to the concept of a 'good professor'", and that a "Professor's role and adviser's role ... promote a seductive and omnipotent role where you can't be yourself".

The dreamer talked of his struggle to connect with his students. His trousers are falling down because he is not absolutely sure if what they are saying is true. In a sense, he does not have the capacity yet to know what to trust and what not to trust.

The group discussion in the reflection session reinforced the dreamer's insights and noted two important risks. One is the risk that work will make one unhealthy, and that one needs to keep a good balance between work and personal life. The other is the risk of being perceived as irrelevant or unable to succeed in a new role. One can feel totally naked in this circumstance.

In a follow-up interview a year and a half later, the dream drawer recognised even more deeply how significant a time this had been for him. What connected the two drawings was the difficult transitional experience he was going through from clinical to business school professor. Not only was it ". . . very difficult in terms of the students and how to connect with them" and the "process of finding a role as a teacher", there were also strongly erotic aspects to this work. He felt "trapped probably in this seductive role". The drawing of these two dreams and working on them with the group seemed to help him recognise these two difficult experiences that were taking place simultaneously.

> "So it's complicated because when I had troubles with my role as a teacher, probably sometimes I felt quite lost with the audience. When people just really are out of mind, interested in other stuff, when I teach, probably playing with their mobile, or reading on the computer other stuff, and one has to really fight it out, to really get them connected to myself and to the learning process."

From his perspective after the passage of time, he had now made this transition. The work on his dream drawings was for him helpful in recognising the frightening implications of the stress he was under at the time.

Theoretical grounding: practice and meaning

One key focus of my research, in addition to developing the practice of this methodology and attempting to identify its benefits, if any, is to articulate a theoretical basis for this way of working. I see the value of this methodology—along with the others in this book—as helping participants increase their capacity to think about the difficult realities they are facing, rather than suppressing them or allowing them to be acted out in other ways, and to take actions and make decisions based on these insights. By accessing a group's unconscious thinking using the stimulus of the dream drawing, participants can be helped to see reality, mourn losses, and work them through.

Accessing unconscious thinking or the associative unconscious of a group takes place through the free associations to the dream and the drawing. Two forms of unconscious thinking, as posited by Lawrence (1999a), are being made available:

1.   Dreaming as thinking,
2.   The unthought known.

"Dreaming as thinking" is made available by the dream material brought in by participants, both as they recite the dream and as they show their drawings.

"The unthought known", originally conceptualised by Bollas (1987), is defined by Lawrence as "that which is known at some level but has never been thought or put into words, and so is not available for further thinking" (Lawrence, 1999a, p. 8). The individually created third object (the dream drawing) functions as a catalyst for associations and amplifications, which reveal the unthought known from the unconscious: as one interviewee put it, "The drawing in itself is only the tool that you're using for the exploration."

The reflection section that follows this free association period, I believe, is where participants are able to think about the theme we are exploring, informed by the unconscious thoughts that previously emerged. Here, I apply Bion's notion (1988, p. 179) that thinking is the result of "two main mental developments. The first is the development of thoughts", which I see as arising in the associative processes. The second is the "apparatus to cope with them".

As I see it, the reflection section makes it possible for this apparatus of thinking to undertake its task of transforming the thoughts from the infinite into actual thinking relating to reality, that is, the chosen theme of "What do I risk in my work?" From Bion's perspective, "thinking is a development forced on the psyche by the pressure of thoughts and not the other way around" (Bion, 1988, p. 179), meaning that we cannot call thoughts into being by the act of thinking, but can only think once thoughts arise.

Bion viewed these arising thoughts "as if they were objects that had to be dealt with" (Bion, 1988, p. 184). This is because "(a) . . . they in some form contained or expressed a problem, and (b) because they were themselves felt to be undesirable excrescences of the psyche and required attention, elimination by some means or other, for that reason" (Bion, 1988, p. 184). In applying this to the dream-drawing workshop, one could say that the unconscious thoughts that arise are clues to important underlying problems of the dreamer (and perhaps of the group as a whole), and they represent what has been projected as unwanted into the dreamer's unconscious. The work of the Chile group illustrates this. The issues of personal health and the difficulty of connecting with students illuminated by the dreamer were clearly familiar ones to group members, although presumably never previously articulated among them. The "inside" of the dream was directly relevant to the outside work of the university.

In addition to theorising the content of this methodology, I have been focusing on how it is designed and facilitated. This is a methodology designed to access unconscious thoughts and to bring them to the fore, so that they can be thought and eventually acted upon. This process is a delicate and difficult one. Dreamers must feel safe enough in all ways to bring their material forward and participants must feel sufficiently contained in order to freely offer their associations and amplifications.

A major task of the facilitator is to provide sufficient containment so that the group can undertake its task. To "contain" and "containment" are concepts that describe the capacity of any entity to keep within itself parts that arouse anxiety (Nutkevitch, 1998). These events are not designed to provide a retreat; we want participation. As they all deal with the infinite, it is not possible to know what will arise. Hence, it is important that the event (which often includes unfamiliar experiences for the participants) is experienced as safe and sufficiently contained. That is the role of the host. We want participants to be able to regress sufficiently to associate, but also to stay on task (Mersky, 2012).

The theme itself is an aspect of the containment and can be identified in advance by the group or separately by the facilitator. One important value of a theme is the containment it provides, which helps the system and participants contain anxiety relating to the regressive associative experience. None the less, two participants have raised important reservations about using a theme. One found it too artificial, not relevant to her particular situation, and would have preferred that we had developed the theme as a group. For her, it was too sharp a transition between the deep associative work and focusing on a (to her) non-relevant theme. Another participant, who used this methodology with a group he was supervising, felt that a theme might have been unproductive and experienced by group members as an attempt to lead them "in a particular direction". Instead, he just asked, "How might this relate to our work?" This worked extremely well. So, while designed to provide a focus for the learning and discussion in the reflection section, a theme might not be necessary, especially when used as an organisational intervention.

I have been very much guided in my work by socio-technical thinking. The socio-technical perspective holds that there is interrelatedness between the social and technical components of organisations. The technical components that it most emphasises are role, primary task, organisational structure, and boundaries.

The drawing of clear time and task boundaries is essential in mounting these methodologies, in order that participants experience the leadership as clear, responsible, and competent. It seems there is a direct relationship between the confidence to regress creatively and the experience of leadership as taking its role in a clear and competent way.

There is always a task here, which is to help participants individually and collectively better understand what is being experienced as risky in their organisational life. What is required is a group experience, as it is through and by the associations of group members that a deeper meaning is discovered. Two interviewees eloquently expressed this point:

> "When you share it with others, you see it again yourself . . . and I think seeing it through other people's eyes really struck home and made it very, very powerful."

> "I think the richness was sitting there and looking at people's drawing in huge detail and trying to pick out what was in those drawings. You can't do it in isolation."

In fact, it is the depth of understanding that is mentioned over and over again in the interviews. One German participant likened the process to a Russian Babushka doll.

> "The doll in the doll in the doll. And so the idea [sic] that it's going deeper and deeper and deeper."

She continues,

> "It's looping like the snake, the picture. It's not this working straight on. It's not 'There's the aim and we have to go there in the shortest way and [using] the most optimal possibility'. And that's the part where I can say I feel it like seductive work. You can take the time and loop back and meet an idea or a feeling which you've just found half an hour before or an hour before, and then it comes back and it gets another form. In the group work it's a sort of transformational process. So when we start, OK, that's the dream we hear. That's the first step. But when we ended, the room was wider . . . And it's like a knapsack, it's getting fuller with more and more you can carry out and take home."

Somewhat freed from the immediate experience of the dream, the dream drawer is able to take a role as a member of the group and to offer associations and amplifications. In this way, the drawing lives in two worlds: the world of the dreamer and the world of the group undertaking its task. As such, it takes on an important mediating role between the unconscious of the individual and the underlying dynamics of the system. The drawer, as part of the group, can use his/her own capacities for association and thinking.

Concluding thoughts

To this point, I have been using this methodology with groups of professionals in the same or related professions. The explicit goal has been to provide a transitional space in which they can work on both collective and individual professional issues. One participant has taken this methodology a step further, and used it as a sort of organisational intervention with a group of child therapists that he supervises once a month at a community mental health service for children. One participant mentioned that she had had a very vivid dream, so he suggested that they do a session of social dream drawing. He invited them next time to bring a drawing of a recent dream. Despite some initial doubts, it turned out that "people got an awful lot from that session and were quite taken aback", particularly because they had never expected that so much learning could come from a drawing of a dream. "They were absolutely stunned about what they came up with" and how the work really made it possible to see a larger "systemic dilemma". The leader felt that it was very effective in revealing to the participants their "organisation in the mind", even though they were, in many ways, very loosely connected to the central organisation. "It suddenly opened up a completely different landscape." And they very much enjoyed the experience. "They absolutely lapped it up, to be honest. They got a tremendous amount from it."

I am very gratified to know the potential use of this methodology in systems. From a theoretical basis, I am convinced that this can be a very helpful organisational tool. I have written about how to undertake such an intervention elsewhere (Mersky, 2012).

In the course of my experience and research with this methodology, one aspect of it stands out very strongly: the power of the drawing. As one interviewee put it, in describing the process,

"You have the original dream. That goes through a process. And you draw that drawing. Then you make that drawing, which is a kind of abstract from your dream, a very special abstract, not just any abstract. Then you go into the group and you know that you are going to work with that picture in a very special way. And these are always these two layers, the very rational thinking, talking about it, understanding, analysing, in the situation itself . . . The picture always reminds you of the fact that you can't express everything in words. It's a reminder of that. It's not the fact itself."

From what I have learnt in interviewing participants subsequent to these workshops, it seems that dreams are better remembered by their drawings than by their descriptions. When first asked for an interview, former participants usually say that they cannot remember anything of the experience. However, once they see the drawing again and read the transcript, the experience comes alive. And, this time, they and we have the benefit of the passage of time and the ability to look back on the experience from the perspective of what has followed.

What characterises these experiences is that of having somehow mastered or contained some sort of deep transitional experience, usually professional, but not always. Interviewees comments include:

"The process enabled all of us to witness, I guess, a . . . kind of personal and life transition, for me that was the common theme."

"It's the possibility to bring life and work very close to each other."

"The process started then. It sorted itself out."

One participant noted that, as a result of participating in this methodology, he has started to dream more and is "far more aware of my dreams and the richness of them".

Somehow, this experience is felt as safe, even for those who were at the time going through a very difficult personal period. One interviewee, who went through a tragic life experience during the eleven-month span of the workshop, referred to a "fine line". "I couldn't define this fine line. But there is a fine line" between staying on a clear task and regressing deeply into private material, which she did not want to do.

Having the freedom and the authority to choose which drawing of which dream to bring to the group affords a kind of safety for participants. The drawing is always created before the session. The act of drawing and the physical object places the material more "outside" the personal reality of the dreamer, thus creating a kind of buffer, or "third factor". In addition, the structure and process itself, with its focus on a theme relating to work, seems also to provide safety. As one interviewee expressed it,

"It's like you know you have something that's gone through that process and that enables the group which is very clear about, OK, this is not therapeutic and this is about work and unconscious and we are working in a setting which enables everybody as a person and within a group to work on these issues."

Participants in interviews noted that it is a relatively straightforward methodology, where the facilitator is present with the group throughout the process. One termed it "An accessible methodology that doesn't feel too frightening." Another observed,

"You didn't make it too complicated. . . . You just created the space . . . because it was just a space . . . with a task, I suppose, but a creative task . . . What I experienced was enjoying the process . . . like a small child . . . nothing else but sitting in the process . . . .a long space just to sit with it."

At the same time, interviewees recognise that facilitation is important. More than one noted the fun that we had together.

So, in conclusion, from the complications of the original dream material, the dreamer attempts a representation of his/her unconscious. And this representation, this third object, is brought into a group setting, with clear boundaries and a clear task. And then we go to work. For those so far who have participated in this "daring experiment" which is "full of surprises", it seems to have been important, memorable, and meaningful. As one former participant expressed it,

> "This drawing that we have now with the papers I can really see, I experience them, not so actively, but certainly not passive, but as a kind of landmark that you rely on, like the mountain, it's not so close but you know it's there, and it helps you position yourself. That's the place of the sessions in my life and in my work."

References

Bain, A. (2005). The organisation containing and being contained by dream: the organisation as a container for dreams (unpublished manuscript).

Bion, W. R. (1965). Transformations. Reprinted in: *Seven Servants.* New York: Jason Aronson, 1977.

Bion, W. R. (1988). The psychoanalytical study of thinking. In: E. B. Spillius (Ed.) *Melanie Klein Today. Developments in Theory and Practice. Vol. I, Mainly Theory* (pp.178–186). London: Routledge.

Bollas, C. (1987). *The Shadow of the Object: Psychoanalysis of the Unthought Known.* New York: Columbia University Press.

Brakel, L. A. (1993). Shall drawing become part of free association? Proposal for a modification in psychoanalytic technique. *Journal of the American Psychoanalytic Association, 41*: 359–393.

Broussine, M. (2007). Drawings and art. In: *Creative Methods in Organizational Research* (pp. 70–91). London: Sage.

Fisher, C. (1957). A study of the preliminary stages of the constructions of dreams and images. *Journal of the American Psychoanalytic Association, 5*: 5–60.

Freud, S. (1900a). *The Interpretation of Dreams. S.E., 4–5.* London: Hogarth.

Freud, S. (1916–1917). *Introductory Lectures on Psychoanalysis. S.E., 15–16.* London: Hogarth.

Furth, G. M. (1998). *The Secret World of Drawings: Healing Through Art.* Boston, MA: Sigo Press.

Gould, L. J. (1987). A methodology for assessing internal working models of the organization—applications to management and organizational development programs. Paper presented to the Annual Meeting of the International Society for the Psychoanalytic Study of Organizations, New York, 24–25 October.

Hau, S. (2002). Vom Traum zum Traumbild—Über das Zeichnen von Traümen. In: S. Hau, W. Leuschner, & H. Deserno (Eds.), *Traum-Expeditionen* (pp. 183–200). Tübingen: Edition Diskord. 183–200.

Hau, S. (2004). *Über die visuelle Darstellung von Traumbildern.* Tübingen: Edition Diskord.

Lawrence, W. G. (1999a). Thinking refracted in organizations. The finite and the infinite/the conscious and the unconscious. Paper presented to the 1999 Symposium of The International Society for the Psychoanalytic Study of Organizations, Toronto. www.ispso.org/Symposia/Toronto/1999lawrence.htm. Accessed 30 November 2010.

Lawrence, W. G. (1999b). "Won from the void and formless infinite": experiences of social dreaming. In: W. G. Lawrence (Ed.), *Social Dreaming @ Work* (pp. 9–41). London: Karnac.

Mersky, R. (2006). Organizational role analysis by telephone—the client I met only once. In: J. Newton, S. Long, & B. Sievers (Eds.), *Coaching-in-Depth: The Organizational Role Analysis Approach* (pp. 113–125). London: Karnac.

Mersky, R. (2012). Contemporary methodologies to surface and act on unconscious dynamics in organizations: an exploration of design, facilitation capacities, consultant paradigm and ultimate value. *Organisational and Social Dynamics, 12*(1): 19–43.

Michael, T. A. (2007). "You must not be dreaming!": how social dreaming may help us wake up. In: W. G. Lawrence (Ed.), *Infinite Possibilities of Social Dreaming* (pp. 120–130). London: Karnac.

Morgan, G. (1993). *Imaginization: The Art of Creative Management.* Newbury Park, CA: Sage.

Nossal, B. (2003). The use of drawing in socio-analytic exploration. Paper presented to the Scientific Meeting of the Australian Institute of Socio-Analysis.

Nutkevitch, A. (1998). The "container" and its containment: a meeting space for psychoanalytic and open systems theories. Paper presented to the 1998 Symposium of the International Society for the Psychoanalytic Study of Organizations, Jerusalem.

Segal, S. (2007). Personal e-mail communication.

Sievers, B. (2007). "There's nothing more worth fighting for": social dreaming with social democrats in Austria. In: W. G. Lawrence (Ed.), *Infinite Possibilities of Social Dreaming* (pp. 18–28). London: Karnac.

Sievers, B. (2008). "Perhaps it is the role of pictures to get in contact with the uncanny". The social photo-matrix as a method to promote the understanding of the unconscious in organizations. *Organisational and Social Dynamics, 8*(2): 234–254.

Sievers, B., & Beumer, U. (2006). Organisational role analysis and consultation: the organisation as inner object. In: J. Newton, S. Long, & B. Sievers (Eds.), *Coaching-in-Depth: The Organizational Role Analysis Approach* (pp. 65–81). London: Karnac.

Vince, R., & Broussine, M. (1996). Paradox, defense, attachment: accessing and working with emotions and relations underlying organizational change. *Organization Studies, 17*: 1–21.

CHAPTER NINE

OPUS Listening Posts: researching society

Olya Khaleelee and Lionel Stapley

This chapter is written in two parts. The first section, by Olya Khaleelee, a previous Director of OPUS: An Organisation for Promoting Understanding of Society, outlines the early development of the concept and method of the listening post. The second part, by Lionel Stapley, the current OPUS Director, describes the listening post methodology as it is now practised and provides an example of a listening post report. To avoid any misunderstanding, it should be noted that, during its history, the organisational name changed to OPUS: An Organisation for Promoting Understanding in Society, and then changed back again to the above.

Part 1: the early development of OPUS Listening Posts 1980–1989

Olya Khaleelee

Introduction

One prevailing and pervasive motif is of everything falling apart. A university teacher experienced around him a fear of impending dissolution (or was it 'disillusion') and disaster . . . The sense of doom and the inevitability of death is located in an expectation of nuclear war. (Khaleelee & Miller, 1980, p. 7).

This is the first few sentences of the first report of the first Organisation for Promoting the Understanding of Society (OPUS) Listening Post, which conveyed graphically the sense of angst experienced over thirty years ago. The report of that Listening Post goes on to offer a tentative societal hypothesis: "Anxiety about the bomb/doom/destruction is a defence against a deeper fear of anarchy. All may be destroyed (including children=future) but government must survive" (Khaleelee & Miller, 1980, p. 8).

The question was: does fear of anarchy relate to current fragmentation of the social and economic order? Today, we live in a more anarchic society, but that generational angst and the preoccupation of the citizen is now more focused on climate change, rising water levels, and whether it is possible to save the planet. Perhaps each generation has its survival theme. So, might we, as citizens, reflect on whether current anxieties are also defensive and, if so, what function might they serve?

The first Listening Posts consisted of regular, free-floating, associative two-hour discussions in which participants drawn from the associate staff of OPUS were invited to take up the role of citizen and speak of their experiences over the previous weeks and months. A summary of their discussion was then offered to a more diverse group drawn from different walks of life, which we called a Forum. Their role was to respond to the input from the associate staff as a way of testing out their ideas with a group perceived to be more representative of British society. The resulting dialogue and our hypotheses about the state of society from a psychodynamic perspective were then published in a series of Bulletins available for sale to OPUS subscribers and others interested in our reflections.

Twenty-nine OPUS Bulletins reflecting on the state of British society were published, elaborating the societal themes that arose between 1980 and 1989, during and beyond Margaret Thatcher's Britain, in which, as she said,

I think we have gone through a period when too many children and people have been given to understand 'I have a problem, it is the

Government's job to cope with it!' or 'I have a problem, I will go and get a grant to cope with it!' 'I am homeless, the Government must house me!' and so they are casting their problems on society and who is society? There is no such thing! There are individual men and women and there are families and no government can do anything except through people and people look to themselves first. . . . There is no such thing as society. (Thatcher, 1987)

Development of OPUS

OPUS: an Organisation for Promoting the Understanding of Society, had originally been set up in 1975 by Sir Charles Goodeve, a founder of operational research after the Second World War, who wanted to apply a more scientific approach to relations in the workplace (Goodeve, 1975). Sir Charles had witnessed many strikes and disputes in the commercial and industrial spheres and he came to the belief that if employees had a better understanding of the system of which they were a part, and understood some of the underlying forces at work, they would be less likely to walk out on strike.

He believed that the workforce would be more likely to think about what was going on, and how, in their employee roles, they were being caught up in a wider organisational and systemic process. Without being psychoanalytically trained, nevertheless he had an intuitive grasp of systems psychodynamics (Gould, Stapley, & Stein, 2001) and the concept of "citizen of the organisation".

Sir Charles had approached a number of corporations, including Rank Xerox and General Electric, and managed to get some funding. In establishing OPUS as an independent, non-political organisation, with charitable status, Sir Charles was supported and encouraged by Dr Eric Miller at The Tavistock Institute of Human Relations and by John Garnett at the Industrial Society. Miller was interested in the idea of exploring conflict as an aspect of societal dynamics. He invented the acronym of the OPUS name and was the Policy Adviser. Later, he also became the Research Adviser.

The concept of the Listening Post was also Miller's innovation, having developed from earlier organisational consultancy in which employees were encouraged to take up the role of "citizen of the organization" (Miller, 1977). In addition, anthropological enquiry, such as that carried out during the 1930s on mass observation had intrigued him (Madge & Harrison, 1938). The publication of this work contained an essay by fellow anthropologist Bronislaw Malinowsky, entitled "A nation-wide intelligence service", which was a source for thinking about the development of the Listening Post concept.

The Industrial Society actively supported the formation of OPUS by seconding one of its staff members, Jeremy Leathers, now the Chairman of the OPUS Management Committee, to be its first Secretary, and also provided free meeting space for the initial phase. It was recognised that the study and promotion of a better understanding of society (how it works, how the individual relates to it), with a particular emphasis on conflict, formed a distinctive field of endeavour, which could most effectively be tackled from an autonomous base. In its overall aim, therefore, and in particular in its focus on helping the individual to act with authority and responsibility in his role as citizen, OPUS was not seen as duplicating the work of other bodies.

OPUS was distinctive in the mix of interlocking activities through which it set out to perform its task. The operational programmes that were developed during the early 1980s included educational and training activities, and research and advisory services. Through working in these ways, OPUS reached specific sets of people, such as client organisations and community groups, and the experience so gained led to the fourth and crucial task of dissemination to the public at large and to selected audiences. This was the most difficult of all its tasks.

Within its education and training function, OPUS ran a workshop and several talks on the theme of managing stress, held a round table of managers and union officials on workplace relations in the 1980s, ran a conference on psychotherapy and society, and was planning study days on issues of current concern.

The advisory services provided consultancy on organisational strategy, organisation development projects designed to create new and more appropriate relationships of employees to the organisation, and a pilot project for unemployed people, to enable them to find usefulness and meaning in alternative roles.

During these early years, the research function included a small-scale study of the effect of society's attitude to prisons on organisation and relationships within a prison. A book was being considered with the title, "The Unconscious Society", to be edited by Gordon Lawrence, and negotiations had taken place with possible publishers. Finally, the concept of Listening Post had been developed further and emerged as one element of the research programme. The idea was to have a number of groups in different regions and varying in composition as a means of tapping into current preoccupations in society. This was reflected in the mission statement of OPUS: ("A restatement of policy and objectives 14 June 1982"). Such an approach also enabled and compelled OPUS to be responsive to the changing demands and needs of its environment. Indeed, given the high unemployment at that time and little prospect of a return to full employment, OPUS's task of helping individuals to re-examine their roles and ways they related to society took on a special relevance.

The final, but most important, element was to disseminate the understanding of societal processes from all these activities. First, to generate a greater public awareness and understanding of processes in society and of ways in which the individual relates to society; second, to help and encourage the individual citizen to identify his scope for exercising authority and for taking responsible action in his various roles; third, to establish the credibility and status of OPUS as a socially relevant but impartial organisation.

In order to fulfil its mission, fourteen associate staff had been gathered from a wide range of skills and backgrounds. Associate staff of OPUS in this first phase included Tony Berry, John Broadbent, Tim Dartington, Alan Day, Brendan Duddy, Peter Goold, Bob Gosling, Robin Hall, David Hay, Joan Hutten, Gordon Lawrence, Denis Pym, Esmee Roberts, and Irene Young. Later, Miranda Feuchtwang and Sheila Ramsay joined the staff.

While some were academics and practitioners from the social sciences, others represented a broader spread of professions and disciplines, including architecture, medicine, the church, business, industry, and psychotherapy. All had a specific interest and training in the analysis of group and organisational behaviour, conscious and unconscious. They came together non-hierarchically in varying configurations and roles to carry out their work within the different task areas.

The background to the Listening Post

A precursor of the Listening Post was an experimental intervention in a manufacturing company from 1976–1979, which, as a result of a takeover and merger with a competitor, had suffered fragmentation at all levels, so that individuals had fallen back on their individual boundaries in a culture of survival (Khaleelee & Miller, 1985). The architect of this programme was a colleague, Andrew Szmidla, who provided many original ideas and who was associated with the project from 1973 to 1977. The author's involvement was as research officer 1973–1974 and internal consultant 1975–1979. Eric Miller was external consultant 1975–1979.

The diagnosis of the consultants to the organisation was that it had lost its identity and needed to be reconstructed at the three levels of relationships between individuals, between groups, and between the organisation and the outside world. An applied model of the Leicester Conference structure was used to begin the process of reconstruction of this organisation's identity, through establishment of the "People Programme". This included small and intergroup work as well as the institution of a "large group", which met weekly for three years. Here, employees attended in their roles as citizens of the organisation, that is to say, standing aside from their usual managerial roles and thinking about the state of the organisation as a whole. The successful development of this programme involved the whole of management and later cascaded into the rest of the workforce.

One technical issue that arose at the systemic level was how to offer an interpretation to the organisation as a whole, comprising 1,000 people on two sites 150 miles apart. In 1976, this led to the formation of a Consulting Resource Group (CRG), comprising initially the three consultants in the programme and, later, the addition of seconded employees. The CRG was a quasi-independent body that met weekly and conceived of itself as a satellite orbiting the organisational "planet". As well as providing internal consultancy as needed, the CRG also endeavoured to say something about the organisation as a whole and tried to interpret that to the organisation. Its primary task was

> the creation of opportunities for learning, which, if taken by the organization, will lead to a progressive and cumulative gain within the organization in terms of relations between individuals in their various roles at work, between groups, and between the organization and the outside world. (Miller, 1977, p. 57)

This involved new ways of working and thinking. The CRG had a two-part weekly meeting. During the first half they worked together but "in public", reflecting on how the organisation had related to them individually and collectively during the preceding week. During the second part they were available to engage with whoever had come to listen to their earlier exchange and wanted to discuss matters further. This was, to some extent, like an applied version of a Leicester Conference Institutional Event.

The CRG, by locating itself conceptually outside the organisation, aimed to help the organisation understand itself better in relation to its environment. Therefore, CRG members, in their interactions within the organisation, not only regarded these contacts as being with members of a particular department or sub-group, but regarded the nature of that contact as transferential at the organisational level. Therefore, individual employees were also perceived as representing an aspect of the organisation as a whole, an organisation in which they had their "citizen-of-the-organisation" role as well as the specific function for which they had been recruited. Engagement with individuals in this setting, therefore, had utilised a different level of systemic thinking which affected what was communicated or interpreted to the individual as representative of the organisation. Herein lay the kernel of the concept of the individual as citizen of the organisation, a concept that Sir Charles Goodeve had also implicitly recognised and which had underpinned the creation of OPUS.

In 1979, this work came to an end. The People Programme had succeeded in rebuilding the identity of the organisation and, indeed, it had become profitable within the division. This had an impact on the performance of the other subsidiary companies, so that pressure on top management of the holding company led to the cessation of the programme and the redundancy of the consultants. Despite this very disappointing outcome, conceptually this was nevertheless an exciting intervention. This way of working at the interface between the organisation and the outside world was then transposed into the early thinking about the Listening Posts.

The concept of the Listening Post

The Listening Post took this idea of a body that could reflect on organisational dynamics in relation to the external world out into society, initially with

> OPUS staff . . . formulating a role of "consultant" in relation to society as client and from this position to identify and interpret societal dynamics. This seemed to be a natural extension from the analyst/consultant working at the transference in the analytic pair, the small group and the large group, and from the role of the Consulting Resource Group in our manufacturing company. (Khaleelee & Miller, 1985, p. 369)

The aim was to extend OPUS's capability to develop and disseminate understanding of societal processes.

As we thought about it in 1980, the arrangement was that associate staff of OPUS would have a one-day meeting every three months in order to review their experience and perceptions derived from working in their OPUS roles and also in their other institutional roles. Emerging hypotheses were to be reviewed and developed further in meetings with another group, a Forum, and then publicised, initially through issues of a Bulletin (*OPUS Bulletin No. 1*, pp. 1–2, Khaleelee & Miller, 1980). Discussion of ideas and hypotheses by the general public was to be encouraged through wider media coverage.

Although it was thought that this process could generate useful insights, there were several difficulties associated with the idea. For example, at that point in the development of OPUS, it would have taken some time before significant numbers of associate staff would be involved in OPUS projects and even then they would be engaged with only limited and specialised segments of society. It was also felt that the Forum, which was then slowly being recruited, had inevitable limitations. The thinking was that the ideal body had to include committed members from a wide diversity of backgrounds, while, at the same time, it had to be compact enough to be able to work as a group. Related to these difficulties, the hypotheses and ideas that OPUS disseminated ran the risk of being dismissed as too theoretical, unrepresentative, and insufficiently grounded in realities.

To broaden the database, one idea was to run a one-off series of discussion groups, drawn from different social backgrounds and held in different parts of the country. The aim was to elicit people's current preoccupations and some understanding of how they relate to society at both the conscious and unconscious levels.

A proposal for a set of standing groups, or Listening Posts, which would meet at regular intervals, was developed. Apart from serving in a general way as a source of data to those associate staff members who would be meeting with them, and, thus, to OPUS as a whole, they would act as extensions of the Forum in allowing OPUS to test more specific hypotheses as they emerged. This would give a much firmer base to OPUS's public statements and would also keep the organisation more directly in touch with different preoccupations and views in society.

The associate staff of OPUS was physically distributed all round the UK. Accordingly, two Listening Posts were set up in each of several different locations: Basingstoke, Bath/Bristol, Nottingham, Greater Manchester, Norfolk, Edinburgh, Glasgow, Belfast/Londonderry, and four in London, with one staff member with primary responsibility for two locally based Listening Posts.

The idea was to recruit eleven to twelve members per group and to expect an attendance of eight to nine at each meeting.

While it was recognised that OPUS would be unable to achieve a stratified random sample of the UK population with a panel of 200 people, nevertheless it aimed to encompass people from a number of dimensions, such as socio-economic class, gender, age, race, urban/rural, employed/unemployed. At the same time, it was mooted that each group should be relatively homogeneous so as to facilitate disclosure and discussion. Hence, there might be a female group in one location, a group with persons of colour in a second location, an unemployed group in a third location, and so on.

It was thought possible to assemble a few of the groups through personal contacts of staff or negotiation with such bodies as the Townswomen's Guilds or Workers' Education Associations. The rest were to be recruited through market research agencies. It was hoped that the groups themselves, once formed, would recruit substitutes for drop-outs.

Optimally, there would be four sessions a year, each lasting two hours. It was hoped that this would give each group a sufficient feeling of identity and continuity and help it to develop a way of working that would enrich two-way learning. This would also fit with the quarterly pattern of associate staff and Forum meetings.

The method envisaged was that two staff members would run each group meeting, one primarily the group "taker" and the other the "recorder". The locally based staff member would be one of these and was to be the continuity figure, responsible for convening the group meetings.

Even at this early stage there was an awareness of the technical difficulties of running such groups, as the concern was to elicit both overt and covert preoccupations, constructs, and ways of looking at the world, and that this would be a learning process for OPUS staff. It was proposed that in order to develop the method, it would be useful to form a small central nucleus of staff. During the initial phase, the second staff member in every group would also be a member of this nucleus. Members of the nucleus would subsequently meet quite often to share their varied experiences from each having attended a number of groups. At the end of each round of Listening Post meetings, one member of the nucleus would also take the responsibility of trying to distil themes from the whole set of transcripts/summaries for presentation at the quarterly associate staff meeting.

After this developmental phase, the proposal was that the nucleus would disband and the geographically nearest available staff member might take on the second role in the local group. The responsibility for producing themes from the discussions would then also pass to other individual associate staff members.

In the event, it proved not possible to implement the Listening Posts as originally envisaged because OPUS's research budget at this point was only sufficient to pilot the methodology with a few discussion groups during 1980–1981. Further development of the scheme depended on being able to get external funding, and this was extremely difficult for a task that was primarily to do with reflection.

Nevertheless, a regular pattern of quarterly meetings of associate staff and the Forum was developed and maintained during the first five years, forming the core of the Listening Post concept. By 1981, OPUS had set up Listening Posts of clergy in Nottingham, a mixed middle-class group in Manchester, another professional group in Basingstoke, along with a group of unemployed people, and, finally, a group of adolescent school-children in Edinburgh with particular reference to their experience of the educational system (OPUS Bulletin 2, January 1981, p. 8, Khaleelee & Miller,).

In November 1983, responding to various requests for more ways of participating in OPUS and responding to the Listening Post discussions, subscribers' meetings were set up. A further Listening Post was set up in Slough, which met regularly from its formation in 1982. Lack of finance was making it difficult to take the idea further, particularly as an inherent problem was the intangibility of the Listening Post information. In 1986, associate staff had realised that there was no necessity for a testing process for their hypotheses against another group because society, in the mind of the citizen, was always present, even when not consciously mobilised. Therefore, the Forum decided to become the North West London Listening Post. It met regularly, as did the Slough Listening Post, which met in September and December 1986. A third Listening Post was being considered for Bristol. By 1988, a new Listening Post had been set up in Scotland. At the same time, regular study days had been instituted as well as one- and two-day conferences on relevant societal themes, such as "Them and Us in British Society", held in Glasgow in 1987, and "It's Not Fair! Outside and Inside in British Society", held in London the same year. These study days also incorporated a Listening Post event and are described in more detail elsewhere (Dartington, 2001).

Listening Post themes

In 1981, the Forum, commenting on the views of the associate staff, said that there was a tendency

> to see the sweep of change over the last 25 years as having been brutal and destructive. . . . One hypothesis is that in a time of transition I have to find somewhere to put my negative feelings and my anxiety, so 'changing society' becomes a good receptacle.

This idea that parts of society could become unconscious projective receptacles in the same way as individuals and groups are for each other became a useful way of thinking about society from a systems psychodynamic or socioanalytic perspective.

Bulletin No. 3 suggested that "we project our inhumanity into institutions like prisons, hospitals and bureaucracies in order to remain human ourselves" (p. 12). The suggestion was that these institutions enact those disowned and split-off feelings on our behalf. At a societal level, the theme of failed dependency was also explored. This phenomenon has been explored in depth, on the theme of psychic withdrawal from organisation and the experience of societal betrayal (Miller, 1986). Part of this theme was a shift that we hypothesised was taking place in society from 1982. "What came through . . . was the sense that no known structure could accommodate and control the diversity, the individual fragmentation, the 'psychotic-ness' of what's going on in society at present" (OPUS Bulletin No. 6, January 1982, p. 8).

Failed dependency was an ongoing theme, generated by big organisations letting go of their employees. "Many employees feel orphaned" (OPUS Bulletin No. 6, January 1982, p. 15). The Forum, offered another perspective: "there is an opportunity now for creative leadership" (OPUS Bulletin No. 6, January 1982, p. 19). This was seen to be linked with "the dependent wish for magnificent men who'll lead us out of the mess we're in; and alongside that, at the other extreme, the drive for individual survival, every man for himself" (OPUS Bulletin No. 6, January 1982, p. 21).

Bulletin No 8 (July 1982) considered the Falklands Islands' War "Perhaps we need to acknowledge the suicidal potency that comes out of the rage of impotence; it came out in the riots and it was coming out in the Falkland Islands" (OPUS Bulletin No 8, p. 26). But, by Bulletin No 9, it seemed as though projections into the wider society, represented by Argentina, were now beginning to be taken back, leading to some confusion about where to place them. There was also an acknowledgement of the defence mechanism of displacement:

> ... it is illegitimate for 'us liberals' to feel aggressive against the Argentinians; so we let Thatcher do it for us and vent our anger on her. One gets caught up in the simple win-lose mentality that she offers. There's the temptation to believe that if you tidy up the outside world, you can be safe in your own little enclave; but the more we do that, the more precarious the enclave becomes. (OPUS Bulletin No. 9, p. 19)

1983 brought a more positive frame of mind, despite people still having their heads down in order to survive high levels of unemployment. Alongside retreat to the family (see Jones, 1957) there was room for innovation, initiative, and the active search for alternative roles. This coincided with a search for meaning and spirituality.

There was considerable debate about the nature of aggression in society in this post Falklands War phase:

> Our aggression and fear make us behave so that the outcome is aggression on all sides and widening splits. The irony is that in fact you lose nothing by co-operating with the other; you don't have to

sacrifice, yet it's not done. So our behaviour has not kept up with technology. We can do all kinds of things mechanically and with the
microchip but our instincts are still in the primaeval swamp and there
we flounder. (Opus Bulletin No. 11, 1983, p. 14)

This perspective seems highly relevant today, thirty years later, in
the global context of the so-called "Arab Spring" and, at the time of
writing, the Syrian government's suppression of its own citizens.
Furthermore, today the available projective receptacles have widened,
so that we do not just project into institutions and categories of people
in UK society, but globally.

In 1983, OPUS Listening Posts were preoccupied with different
kinds of leaders :"Why do we need them? Leadership for what? And
comparisons between different leaders: Hitler, the Queen, Reagan,
Kennedy, Arafat, and last, but by no means least, Thatcher" (OPUS
Bulletin No. 12, July 1983, p. 27). But there was great anxiety about
power being put into the hands of one individual. Further thoughts
were that "in times of frustration and impotence people become more
infantile and dependent . . ." Might this also be to do with female leadership that keeps individuals in a child-like position? The anxiety was
articulated thus:

> And Thatcher offers a fantasy of a meaning – some sense of integration
> in a world of fragmentation. But the other side of the wish for contain-
> ment is a fear that, in our desperate search for security, we will end up
> creating a dictatorship with a deceptively clear ideology. (p. 18)

It was interesting, in view of anxieties about regression, that
Bulletin No. 14 1984 was concerned about men and women, mothers
and their sons, and with babies, both as a receptacle for hope for the
future and as a group in society to be envied. Violent attacks on young
people were seen to be on the increase. "If we can't have hope, we
can't bear that the next generation should have it" (p. 13). Anxiety
about a nuclear holocaust was still high:

> The holocaust is an expiation. We are to be punished for the mess
> we've made and there's no way to reverse it. So society has to be
> destroyed before it can be rebuilt. . . . Change through mutation.
> People are huddling together in small 'safe' groups in pubs and clubs
> – enclaves, bunkers. (p. 16)

Male–female relations and mutual projections were part of this theme, with violence being projected into men who were perceived as the architects of the bomb. This nuclear anxiety was hypothesised to be a defence against the pace of change and the possibility of creativity.

By the end of 1984, unemployment was still very high. The year was marked by the miners' strike and was an interesting example from our perspective of how rage and aggression, if not channelled externally, as in the Falklands War, is reintrojected and enacted internally. This was another kind of war. But it was also noted that

> many people are not merely surviving but leading satisfying (and sometimes lucrative) lives outside employment [which] is calling into question the work ethic – which is really the employment ethic. Even for some of those still in employment, this is beginning to open up a sense of real choice: if the organisation offers them what they want – be it money or job satisfaction – they stay; if not, they feel able to quit. So their relationship with the organisation is more genuinely instrumental. This is partly a consequence of being treated in an instrumental way by the organisation – asked to be an object, a commodity. (OPUS Bulletin No. 17, October 1984, pp. 11–12)

It was also noted that the relationship of the citizen to the church was changing and that dependency needs in society were changing (OPUS Bulletin No.19, p. 17). Self-help groups were burgeoning, independence was valued (OPUS Bulletin No. 20–21, Winter 1985, p. 16).

By 1986, it was recognised that "Britain was shifting towards a 'post dependent society' in which individuals are more autonomous, more questioning of hierarchical structures based on status and more instrumental in relation to their employing organisations" (OPUS Bulletin No. 24–25, Winter 1986, Part I, p. 27). Drawing on the work of OPUS over the previous six years, Miller described how, following a phase of "failed dependency", the post-dependent society was just beginning to emerge, and how individuals were renegotiating their identity on a new basis.

Conceptual development

One of the preoccupations during this early phase of the development of the Listening Posts was the question of whether it was possible to regard society as an intelligible field of study when we who were studying it were doing so in our roles as citizens. Was there a risk that the phenomena observed were a function of the measuring instrument used? (Khaleelee & Miller, 1985, p. 369). Was it possible to have a stance of "consultant to society" while having a citizen role? Could society be an intelligible field of study? Our orientation to these questions drew from psychoanalysis, including Freud's views on group life.

In *Group Psychology and the Analysis of the Ego* (1921c), Freud had expounded on the bonds that unite members of a group, whether a temporary group such as a crowd and a more lasting institution such as a church, army, or nation. He made a link between the family dynamic and what the individual carried with him into the group, and stressed the importance of the leader. Freud also commented on how the strong instinct of aggressive cruelty in man needs to be kept in check. "Civilized society is perpetually menaced with disintegration through this primary hostility of men towards each other" (Jones, 1957, p. 341).

Bion's propositions about unconscious behaviour in groups and his theory of proto-mental phenomena are also highly relevant. His ideas about large group phenomena included the societal level. He cited the phase in ancient Egyptian history when the country was manifestly exhausted by the building of the pyramids for the Pharaohs. He saw this as "a group movement to allay the anxiety state of the leader of the group. The nature of that anxiety . . . appears to be centred on the death of the leader and the need to deny its reality" (Bion, 1961, p. 120). However, apart from elaborating the basic assumptions in relation to certain institutions, he did not take this further into society as a whole. Although he had linked the basic assumptions of dependency, fight/flight, and pairing with the institutions of the church, army, and the aristocracy, he pointed out that these were specialised sub-groups. He did not develop these ideas on society further.

His work was, however, taken into the Group Relations Training Programme at the Tavistock Institute and the development of the Leicester Conferences, which fostered system psychodynamic thinking by analysing unconscious processes in larger groups such as the institution as a whole (Gould, Stapley, & Stein, 2001). Turquet (1975) took it further in his work on large groups, as did others: for example,

Brown and Jaques (1965), Kreeger (1971), de Maré (1971), Hopper (2002), and Menzies Lyth (1989).

One observation was that it was not primarily group size that affected the dynamics, because "groups that are small in size may express phenomena that do not belong to the small group in itself but are manifestations of the large group, or even of society" (Khaleelee & Miller, 1985, p. 367). This had been very noticeable in the organisational case study described above, and also had been noted by other colleagues, for example, those conducting therapy groups where sometimes they might be working with very depleted groups, yet the absent group-in-the-mind had a profound influence on the dynamics of the interaction, even if only one person was present. Thus, the larger group is always present in the small group.

Concluding comments

By the time the final OPUS bulletin of the 1980s (Nos. 28–29, Winter 1988–1989) was published, the organisation had extended its activities and formed two wings: OPUS Education and Research (OER), under the leadership of Miranda Feuchtwang, and OPUS Consultancy Services (OCS), led by Tim Dartington. Listening Posts were meeting regularly and the first phase of development had come to an end.

In the mid-1990s, Lionel Stapley assumed the role of Director and had begun to take the organisation into its next phase of development, which, over the following years, saw the spread of Listening Posts worldwide. Listening Posts now operate globally and reports from their meetings are available on the OPUS website, www.opus.org.uk. Reports are also regularly published in its international journal, *Organisational and Social Dynamics*. A description of these developments can be found in the next section of this chapter.

Returning to the first phase of development, the OPUS Listening Posts during the 1980s aimed to tap into people's preoccupations at a societal level, and in all our meetings "society" was a significant feature in that people had a picture in their minds of an entity beyond themselves, beyond institutions and organisations. It was clear that the notion of "society" was used as a projective container, so that parts of the self are projected into parts of society, which is an inescapable group even for a hermit. The evidence from this early phase of development was that, by inviting the individual to take up their roles as citizens, it was possible "to evoke, experience and observe societal dynamics in a group of 10–12. Society is present in the group; society and the group are present in the individual" (Khaleelee & Miller, 1985, pp. 381–382).

Looking back at that statement almost thirty years later, it is possible to see how that process of projecting into our own society is clearly seen as a global phenomenon where we project aspects of our selves and of our society into other countries around the world.

Part 2

Lionel Stapley

Introduction

Since OPUS was founded in 1975, we have worked on the development and application of adapting our psychosocial, reflective approach to gaining an understanding of society through a unique process called OPUS Listening Posts. Over the years, there have been several versions of OPUS Listening Posts, the most recent of which was developed in 2000, and this introduced a form of standardisation of the process which made available a greater degree of comparison across time and location.

Since 2000, Listening Posts have been convened on a quarterly basis in London, at less regular intervals at various regional locations throughout the UK, and annually through the International Listening Post Project. We have always found the results to be highly significant and valuable, but now that we have the added benefit of easy comparison, they become even more interesting.

The International Listening Post Project is convened on an annual basis (Stapley & Collie, 2004, 2005; Stapley & Cave, 2006, 2007; Stapley & Rickman, 2008, 2009, 2010, 2011, 2012) to coincide with the London New Year Listening Post. The Project was first convened in fifteen countries in January 2004 and there are now up to thirty-seven countries involved in the Project. On or about an agreed date in January of each year, under the guidance and co-ordination of OPUS, Listening Posts aimed at providing a snapshot of the societal dynamics of each country at the dawn of the specific year are held in the different countries around the world. These are all reported in a similar format, researched and analysed by OPUS personnel, to produce a Global Report. (For Global Reports 2004–2012 see *Organisational and Social Dynamics*).

Now that there are several years of Reports to compare, it is becoming valuable data that do not appear to be available from other sources. The Project seems to be developing a greater degree of importance, as this period of world history truly is one of formative changes in the structure of the world economy, the shape of societies, and the framework of world governance.

Listening Post methodology

Listening Posts are exemplars of the application of the OPUS stated methodology. They are a psychosocial process which encourages the reflective citizen. The Listening Post process is not limited to social evidence gathering. The process goes beyond this simpler process of talking to people. The distinct and vital difference is that Listening Posts employ a much more rigorous methodology that provides analyses and hypotheses regarding what is happening in society.

Put another way, whereas social evidence gathering is solely concerned with, and stops at, the social level, Listening Posts go much deeper through analysing the social and working to develop a further understanding at the psychological level. The way we provide explanations for what is happening is to develop hypotheses. That is, we develop theories to account for whatever it is that we do not understand.

What is a Listening Post?

Listening Posts provide a "snapshot" of a society at a particular moment in time. They are regular meetings of eight to fifteen people that provide opportunities for participants to think about the society they are part of.

The concept of a Listening Post is based on the notion that a group of people meeting together to study the behaviour of the society, as a society, allows the unconscious expression of some characteristics of the wider social system, and the experience of the Listening Post is itself, therefore, relevant to an understanding of society beyond individual and personal preoccupations.

The aim of the Listening Post is to enable participants as individual citizens to reflect on their own relatedness to society and to try to develop an understanding of what is happening in society at any given moment.

Listening Posts provide an opportunity for participants to share their preoccupations in relation to the various societal roles they may have. Collectively, they are invited to try to identify the underlying dynamics, both conscious and unconscious, that might be predominant at any given time.

The dynamics of the group might be such that even a small group may, nevertheless, act as if it is a microcosm of the large group that is society, so that the themes that emerge through associative dialogue may legitimately be analysed for their societal content. Themes that emerge are the work of participants taking up their citizen roles.

Listening Post process

The Listening Post process is divided into three distinct parts.

Part 1. The sharing of preoccupations and experiences

Here, participants are invited to identify, contribute, and explore their experience in their various social roles, be these in work, unemployed, or retired, as members of religious, political, neighbourhood, or voluntary or leisure organisations, or as members of families and communities: what might be called the "social" or "external" world of participants.

In this Part, the group discussion is unstructured—no agenda is set or issue identified beforehand. The aim is to obtain an authentic representation of society at the given time. The process enables participants to speak of their preoccupations and experiences of society from their various societal roles in a free-flowing and unhindered manner.

Part 2. Identification of major themes

In this Part, participants collectively try to identify the major themes emerging from Part 1. This Part acts as a sort of transitional space, and enables the members to put a boundary around the material from Part 1, which will be the subject of analysis in Part 3.

Part 3. Analysis and hypothesis formation

In this Part, working with the information resulting from Parts 1 and 2, participants collectively try to identify the underlying dynamics, both conscious and unconscious, that might be predominant at the given time, and to develop hypotheses as to why they might be occurring at this moment.

In this Part, members are working more with what might be called their "psycho" or "internal" worlds: the collective ideas and ways of thinking that both determine how they perceive the external realities and shape their actions towards them.

The role of the members is to analyse the material from Part 1 and to work at providing psychological explanations that can be developed into hypotheses that are theories assumed to account for something not understood.

Listening Posts are based on the notion that a group of people meeting together to work in the way described below allows the unconscious expression of some characteristics of the wider social system and the experience of the Listening Post is itself, therefore, relevant to an understanding of society beyond individual and personal preoccupations. The aim of the Listening Post is to enable participants as individual citizens to reflect on their own relatedness to society and to try to develop an understanding of what is happening in society at this moment.

The Listening Post will provide an opportunity for participants to share their preoccupations in relation to the various societal roles they might have. Collectively, they are invited to try to identify the underlying dynamics, both conscious and unconscious, that might be predominant at this time.

Britain and the world at the dawn of 2003

Report of a New Year's Listening Post on Wednesday 8th January 2003 from 7.00 p.m. to 9.30 p.m. at College Hall, University of London, Malet Street, London WC1E.

Report

Part 1. The sharing of preoccupations and experiences

In this part of the Listening Post, participants were invited to identify, contribute, and explore their experience in their various social roles, be those in work, unemployed or retired, as members of religious, political, neighbourhood, or voluntary or leisure organisations, or as members of families and communities. This part was largely concerned with what might be called, "the stuff of people's everyday lives", that relating to the "socio" or "external" world of participants.

Part 2. Identification of major themes

In Part 2, the aim was collectively to identify the major themes emerging from Part 1. On this occasion, themes were difficult to name, but can be drawn together as the following three interrelated statements.

- The world is currently experienced as highly complicated and complex; it seems clear that we are moving (have moved) from a reasonably predictable environment to a situation where we just cannot begin to make sense of what is happening. It really is experienced as a paradigm change. Of the factors that can be identified as contributing to this situation, it seems that the tension between global and national economies and politics is highly significant. It is the view that a global economy results in serious weakening of the national (known) system.
- There were frequent references to death and to insecurity. It seems likely that this is a resultant effect of the theme developed above. The world was viewed as a frightening place, both locally and globally, and the death "of a way of life" was seen to pose a great challenge. There is a struggle around the very concept of democracy. The problem faced was how we defend against a fear of death in all its manifestations. It seemed that, at the personal and social levels, we were being overwhelmed by the complexity, and were feeling quite helpless and retreating from the problem. We did not even seem to have the language to discuss some of the issues faced by society. As one person put it, "It's like a search for the Holy Grail."

- There was also a feeling that we were living through an illusion, or that we were being manipulated or "conned", or facing some sort of dishonesty. Allied to this theme, there were allusions to fairy stories and a view that the media were adopting a role as the spokespeople for the societal unconscious.

Part 3. Analysis and hypothesis formation

In this part of the Listening Post, the members were working with the information resulting from Parts 1 and 2, with a view to identifying collectively the underlying dynamics, both conscious and unconscious, that might be predominant at the time, and developing hypotheses as to why they might be occurring at that moment. Here, the members were working more with what might be called their "psycho" or "internal" world: their collective ideas and ways of thinking that both determine how they perceive the external realities and shape their actions towards them. Again, there was a lack of clear, easily identifiable issues, but there was, none the less, a lively and vigorous struggle to make sense of the Listening Post experience. This analysis has been distilled into the following three interrelated hypotheses.

Analysis and hypothesis 1

Analysis

It was the view that society being faced with an array of complicated, new, and diverse issues (at a global and local level), we are left with a strong experience and feeling of not knowing, of not having the knowledge to meet the challenges. This raises the problem of how we can live without knowing. The truth is that we really do not know what to do. This leads to us not trusting and being fearful, and this is expressed, on the one hand, as rage (fight) and, on the other hand, as helplessness (flight).

Hypothesis

The complicated and changing dynamics arising from the tension between global and national economies and politics is such that members of society are left with an inability and inadequacy of knowledge to meet the challenges presented. They react, on the one hand, with rage (fight), and, on the other hand, with helplessness (flight).

Analysis and hypothesis 2

Analysis

The members reflected on the election of New Labour and likened it to an idealised marriage (between government and citizens) where we would all live happily ever after without any consideration of the realities of marriage. It was felt that the expectancy was not real, but was largely based on phantasy. It was a state of hope based on fantastical notions that we projected into the incoming government in general, and into Tony Blair in particular. We were well aware that we had previously created a bad object, which had resulted in negative and hostile projections being laid at the door of anything behind the Iron Curtain, and were aware of the demonising effects that these projections had on those concerned. Having been placed in a situation where we have had to take back our projections, it seems that we seek to locate them elsewhere, for example, in Saddam Hussein. We now came to realise that this extreme and exaggerated idealisation of Tony Blair had created a good object that was equally dangerous. We have projected into Tony Blair all our fantasies about our hopes of a perfect world and beliefs that everything is possible and inevitably to be achieved; this has helped to create an omnipotent being. It is hard to acknowledge our part in this dynamic, as the origins lie in our very hopes and dreams. We also experience guilt and find it hard to accept our part in creating this omnipotent being, a quality we complain about. We asked, "What have we done?", "What is our responsibility?" There was now a realisation that a marriage is the beginning and not an end in itself. We need to take back our idealised projections. Or, as one member said, "We need a divorce."

Hypothesis

The current government was elected at a time of great hope and with many fantasising that their dreams had come true. The result was a continuous and powerful stream of positive projections into what was seen as an idealised good object. These projections, predominantly based on omnipotent thinking and seldom on reality, had the effect of helping to create a Prime Minister who acted as if he were omnipotent. Initially, we attack this omnipotent being, but realising, grudgingly, our part in this process, we are able to take back our projections and begin to work with reality.

Analysis and hypothesis 3

Analysis

Part of the work in this part concerned a struggle to be hopeful. It was considered that hope resides in individuals, in what we referred to as "The power of ONE". It was also clear that the process of the Listening Post had started to clarify issues and to enable members to begin to think about how they might use the power of one. It was realised that change meant giving up some previously strongly held values and beliefs: the question raised was whether we were willing to give up what we have. There was an acknowledgement that the old has died and that there was an inevitability about the possibility of social change at the national level. As one member said, "We can't continue to have what we had before." An example was the welfare state, which took care of people but also created dependency. It was also realised that there was currently a major reorganisation of capitalism occurring, and that there will be a restructuring, even though the results are not obvious at this time. The question was also asked, "Do we not know?" Yes, there is, of course, a fear of what is round the corner, but there was also a strong feeling that we might, in fact, know, but that we do not want to know; we cannot face the future. Members drew hope from analysing the dynamics. The realisation of death was felt to bring with it a responsibility for knowing. The realisation that we are vulnerable, that no one will help us, reminded us that we need to take responsibility for knowing more.

Hypothesis

Albeit that the quality of change at this time makes it exceptionally difficult to understand, part of "not knowing" is a result of denial that things are changing and that they have to change. Faced with the realisation that death (of a way of life) is inevitable, this brings with it a responsibility for knowing: a movement away from denial to facing up to reality. In doing so, it enables us to hold on to the notion of hope.

References

Bion, W. (1961). *Experiences in Groups*. London: Tavistock.

Brown, W., & Jaques, E. (1965). *Glacier Project Papers*. London: Heinemann.

Dartington, T. (2001). The preoccupations of the citizen: reflections from the OPUS Listening Posts. *Organisational and Social Dynamics*, 1(1): 94–112.

De Maré, P. (1990). The development of the median group. *Group Analysis*, 23: 113–127.

Freud, S. (1921c). *Group Psychology and the Analysis of the Ego*. S.E., 18: 67–143. London: Institute of Psychoanalysis and the Hogarth Press.

Goodeve, C. (1975). *How Society Works: The Need for Wider Understanding*. London: OPUS.

Gould, L., Stapley, L. F., & Stein, M. (2001). *The Systems Psychodynamics of Organizations*. London: Karnac.

Hopper, E. (2002). *The Social Unconscious: Selected Papers*. London: Jessica Kingsley.

Jones, E. (1957). *The Life and Work of Sigmund Freud, Volume 3*. New York: Basic Books.

Khaleelee, O., & Miller, E. (1980). *Bulletin No.1, October 1980*. London: OPUS.

Khaleelee, O., & Miller, E. (1980–1989). *OPUS Bulletins 1–29 from October 1980–Winter 1988/9*. London: OPUS.

Khaleelee, O., & Miller, E. (1985). Beyond the small group: society as an intelligible field of study. In: M. Pines (Ed.), *Bion and Group Psychotherapy* (pp. 354–385). London: Routledge and Kegan Paul.

Kreeger, L. (Ed.) (1971). *The Large Group*. London: Constable.

Madge, C., & Harrison, T. (Eds.) (1938). *First Year's Work 1937–38 by Mass Observation*. London: Lindsay Drummond.

Menzies Lyth, I. (1989). *The Dynamics of the Social* (Vol. II). London: Free Association Books.

Miller, E. (1986). Making room for individual autonomy. In: S. Srivastava and Associates (Eds.), *Executive Power* (pp. 257–288). London: Jossey-Bass.

Miller, E. J. (1977). Organizational development and industrial democracy: a current case study. In: C. Cooper (Ed.), *Organizational Development in the UK and USA: A Joint Evaluation* (pp. 31–63). London: Macmillan.

OPUS (1982). A restatement of policy and objectives 14 June 1982. Unpublished OPUS Internal document.

Stapley, L. & Cave, C. (2006). Global dynamics at the dawn of 2006. *Organisational and Social Dynamics, 6*(1): 111–132.

Stapley, L., & Cave, C. (2007). Global dynamics at the dawn of 2007. *Organisational and Social Dynamics, 7*(1): 73–110.

Stapley, L., & Collie, A. (2004). Global dynamics at the dawn of 2004. *Organisational and Social Dynamics, 4*(1): 116–131.

Stapley, L., & Collie, A. (2005). Global dynamics at the dawn of 2005. *Organisational and Social Dynamics, 5*(1): 111–133.

Stapley, L., & Rickman, C. (2008). Global dynamics at the dawn of 2008. *Organisational and Social Dynamics, 8*(1): 73–110.

Stapley, L., & Rickman, C. (2009). Global dynamics at the dawn of 2009. *Organisational and Social Dynamics, 9*(1): 109–137.

Stapley, L., & Rickman, C. (2010). Global dynamics at the dawn of 2010. *Organisational and Social Dynamics, 10*(1): 118–141

Stapley, L., & Rickman, C. (2011). Global dynamics at the dawn of 2011. *Organisational and Social Dynamics, 11*(1): 93–119.

Stapley, L., & Rickman, C. (2012). Global dynamics at the dawn of 2012. *Organisational and Social Dynamics, 12*(1): 81–105.

Thatcher, M. (1987). Interview in *Woman's Own*, 31 October.

Turquet, P. (1975). Threats to identity in the large group. In: L. Kreeger (Ed.), *The Large Group: Dynamics and Therapy* (pp. 87–144). London: Constable [reprinted London: Karnac, 1994].

CHAPTER TEN

Organisational role analysis

John Newton

Beginning in role

We are all born into existing social systems. Whatever the circumstances of our birth, we arrive to encounter the expectations of others. These expectations include the fantasies about us held by those who anticipate our arrival, such as parents, extended family, friends of our family, doctors and midwives, plus the expectations held by these and others in our community of how we will be behave. Such expectations exist not only in the minds of our immediate human contacts, but also in the collected form of guidelines and textbooks on parenting and childhood development that shape parenting and educational and health practices directed towards us. Our gender, birth order, and the ethnic, religious, political, economic, and geographical circumstances of our inherited social context will also contribute to our formation. The dynamics of this formation, the push and pull between external expectations and the emergent characteristics and drives of the individual, can be analysed in terms of the roles that the individual accepts and/or creates in the process of forming an identity and determining a life course. Role, in this sense, is the pattern of attitude, meaning, feeling, and behaviour that characterises an individual's way of living and working within the various systems of activity, such as a family, work organisation, professional association, social clubs. etc., through which a life is led.

Some roles have pre-existing titles and scripts, such as "son"; others attract labels shaped by the collective meaning given to the contribution an individual's behaviour, or way of being, makes to the group or community. For instance, "mummy's boy", "little devil", "real little lady", "whizz kid", "second mother to her siblings" are labels attached to roles that emerge within the social system of the family and its context. Similarly, when we join a work organisation, our designated position will have a title, but the nature of our role will be determined by the interplay of forces between what we bring, individually, and the expectations of the "system", a constellation of existing role-holders. This interplay of forces has been called the dynamic of "the role as taken and the role as given" (Krantz & Maltz, 1997).

The "drama" of our role taking

The term "role" has dramaturgical origins referring to the part a character will play in the invented narrative of a story. A piece of theatre succeeds, at least for the audience, when they can identify to some extent with the roles portrayed on stage or screen and can engage in an imaginative interplay between their own role experience and the role performances they are witnessing. A powerful theatrical performance might stay with you, be internalised and revisited in future, but there is a degree of comfort in knowing that there is a boundary between a temporary fiction and the more permanent reality of one's own role experiences in the groups and organisations to which one is attached.

If, as Shakespeare famously wrote, "All the world's a stage, and all the men and women merely players", we can draw from his metaphor to examine the ways in which our experiences in role are similar to being on stage or not. The themes that Shakespeare explored, such as power, authority, rivalry, greed, envy, jealousy, madness, and tragic love have a timeless, human quality that can be experienced in role relations today. We live our lives through our roles, and, in work, the challenge is to negotiate a shared reality with those other role holders who have a stake in the task.

Role as taken and role as given

When one is born into the role of "daughter" or "son", it does not take long to discover that others have expectations of how you should take up this role. There is a script to learn, mostly unconsciously. Sometimes, powerful elders will try to impose a clear set of rules, but the "rules" often come from multiple sources and might be implicit and hidden rather than overt. For instance, children speak with others and discover similarities and differences in expectation of the roles of daughter and son, both within and between families. Whose expectations should you pay most attention to; what are the consequences of not meeting expectations; how helpful and/or limiting are such expectations for our individual strivings and development? How do others' ideas about our role performance affect our potential to grow through our experience of taking up the role? How do they affect our relations with the holders of similar and different roles? Are role expectations negotiable? When, how, with whom?

Harnessing for "work" what we already know about role taking

From birth, we learn about the dynamics of role-taking within a social system. Some of it we remember readily, other aspects we repress, preferring to forget. All this experience, remembered and forgotten, we take with us to work. And, into each new position, we take with us the accumulated experience of past roles. Our challenge is to clarify just how our *current* role is best shaped to contribute to the shared task of *this* organisation, and to harness what we can bring appropriately from our past experience to fill out *this* role. For example, we might have to disentangle experiences in our family system from those in our work system, and this might be made more difficult when managers use family metaphors, or we actually work in a family business. We might need assistance to clarify the essential differences between different sorts of systems and, hence, the different implications for how we shape our role in the current system. For instance, we might need to be reminded that we need not get trapped in the eternal power of the family metaphor: while it is not possible to resign from our family, it is possible to resign from our work organisation; that we experienced the power of our parents long before we could conceptualise the notion of their authority and how they exercised it, and, hence, this might affect how we are responding to the dynamics of power and authority at work, perhaps infusing and confusing these concepts on the basis of earlier experiences. And, while we are trying to clarify our own work role experience, we have to be mindful that the other role-holders in the work system are grappling, too, with their role histories. It can get very complicated, particularly if expectations cannot be openly discussed and performance anxiety pushes individuals to default to role performances that derive from other settings. If that happens, the creative opportunities for role-taking in the current setting are diminished. Organisations achieve their outputs and outcomes through the way in which staff take up their work roles. If organisations are to be productive, innovative, flexible, reliable, trustworthy, and ethical, then staff must have confidence in bringing these capacities and values to their role performance. Since this does not always happen as a matter of course, for the reasons alluded to above, the methodology of organisational role analysis (ORA) was developed.

A conceptual basis for organisational role analysis

Organisational role analysis is a process for assisting individuals and organisations to clarify and support effective role performance in achieving the aim of their organisation. The thinking behind this specific method began in the 1960s (see Rice, 1969; Miller, 1976) and has continued to evolve as working life, organisations, and environmental conditions have changed.

Seminal contributions to the conceptualisation and practice of ORA have been explained by Borwick, Lawrence, Reed, and Bazalgette (Newton, Long, & Sievers, 2006). The idea of ORA sprang from the involvement of these originators in the experiential methods for learning about group and organisational dynamics pioneered by the Tavistock Institute of Human Relations (Miller, 1990). The design of these Learning for Leadership conferences begun at Leicester University in 1957 (Rice, 1965) was grounded in the object relations stream of psychoanalysis (Bion, 1961; Klein, 1959, 1975), open systems theory (Katz & Kahn, 1966; Miller & Rice, 1967; Von Bertalanffy, 1968), and socio-technical theory (Trist & Murray, 1993). More recently, this expanding theory base has been termed "systems psychodynamics" (Gould, Stapley, & Stein, 2001), or socioanalysis (Bain, 1999). These conferences, now more generally referred to internationally as group relations conferences, provide opportunities for participants to learn in the "here and now" about the operation of unconscious processes, their own and that of other participants, as these affect the mobilisation of leadership to achieve an agreed task, within a context that is open to internal and external influences. This approach to learning about organisation dynamics and the exercise of authority assumes, unlike mainstream, rationalist management theory (Jaques, 1990; Newton, 1998), that humans are motivated to defend themselves against the anxiety which derives from the need to collaborate in open-ended problem solving. Such anxieties can derive from past, often repressed, feelings of dependency, shame, envy, rivalry, guilt, and aggression, as well as from the nature of the work itself, which might involve responsibility for decisions that carry the risk of inflicting hurt or damage on individuals, relationships, or the environment (Hirschhorn, 1988; Krantz, Chapter Two of this book; Menzies Lyth, 1988).

Group relations conferences are very effective in helping participants gain insight into the unconscious social defences that distort communication and role performance in the workplace when excessive anxiety is not contained by appropriate leadership and clear task and role boundaries. However, early conference designs paid insufficient attention to helping participants transfer their insights to the actual workplace when they returned there without the support of a conference culture and staff consultants. Across the years, there have been various developments to address the "transfer to work" of group relations learning (Bridger, 1990; Long, 2004) but the first initiatives were to use systems psychodynamic concepts as the basis for "one on one" consultation to individual managers. This approach became known as organisational role analysis, and its aim was to help an individual manager to explore his/her internal picture of their work role and its organisational context, and to test this against the expectations of other role-holders.

The first publications describing a method of organisational role analysis (Mant, 1976; Reed, 1976) were by members of the Grubb Institute of Behavioural Studies, London, who had links to the Tavistock. In these and subsequent publications (Armstrong, 2005; Hutton,

Bazalgette, & Reed, 1997; Reed, 2001), members of the Grubb began to formulate specific concepts to guide the analysis and transformation of the lived experience of an organisational role holder. The *content analysis* was predicated on the premise that an organisation has a valid "primary task" (Miller & Rice, 1967) that it must achieve if it is to "survive" (that is, maintain the support of its primary stakeholders to continue its work). Accordingly, a manager's "role idea" must effectively link that individual's efforts to the primary task, and this effort will be influenced by the individual's internalised image of the workplace, his/her "organisation-in-the mind". The aim of the ORA is to recognise the forces, individual and organisational, which would prevent the client from working fully in role and on task. Recognition is given to the effort taken to reach a sound understanding of one's work role and how to best use one's energy and talent, particularly if new to the role and/or the context of the role is characterised by rapid change or instability. Three phases of individual development in role were identified: finding the role, making the role, and taking the role (Quine & Hutton, 1992). Each phase attends to data gathering and activity that would build a robust correspondence between the individual's internal picture of their role and the actual reality of what was needed to achieve the primary task. A primary aspect of this internal picture is clarity about the boundaries that define the client's role, its responsibilities and accountabilities, and its relatedness to other roles in contributing jointly to the primary task of the organisation.

The *process* of the ORA involves the consultant negotiating an appropriate number of time-limited sessions to work with the client to analyse his/her work role experience. The spaces between these sessions are opportunities for the client to test out new thoughts in the workplace and, in effect, collaborate with the consultant in an action learning modality to discover the most effective way for this client to be *in-role and on-task in this organisation, now*. The structure of the process also enables a psychoanalytically informed consultant to experience the unconscious dynamics which distort the client's grasp of what their role requires, whether the origin of these dynamics are within the individual or the organisation. As in a clinical setting, the consultant has the opportunity to experience transference and countertransference phenomena, but the requirement is to work with these feelings within the frame of a workplace: initially, the workplace of the ORA setting.

The ORA "workplace" has the fundamental elements of a work organisation in that it has a primary task (to analyse the client's work role experience), has the differentiated roles of consultant and client, the necessity for those role-holders to maintain their relatedness and collaborate in the work, and the resource constraint which has been negotiated in terms of time, territory, and payment. The consultant is responsible for the management of the setting, for staying on the task of the ORA, and remaining in the role of ORA consultant. The client needs to take up the role of ORA client and collaborate in an analysis of their lived work role experience if the work of the ORA is to proceed effectively.

This "frame" provides a boundary to the focus of the work and distinguishes ORA from personal therapy. This is a clear conceptual distinction, but, as in the workplace, it is a matter of judgement about what personal knowledge contributes to the furtherance of the ORA task and what remains private and out of scope. If the consultant is also a therapist or psychoanalyst, then this boundary can be more contested and require more thoughtful negotiation (Gould, 2006; White, 1996).

A brief example might illustrate the potential of this "workplace" frame for ORA.

Case 1: The "new" manager

I was invited to conduct an ORA with a recently appointed manager (F), within the office of a corporate regulator. (To provide anonymity, significant features of this and other clients have been altered.) The invitation was initiated by the human resource manager and supported by the new manager's director. They regarded this young man (twenty-nine years of age) as a potential "star" and were prepared to invest in his development. His director, like me, was male and in his early fifties at the time.

F agreed to five fortnightly sessions of ninety minutes duration, to take place in my office at the university.

F was ten minutes late for our first session and made what felt to me like an insincere apology. At the outset, I invited F to tell me about his work role: what it entailed, how it contributed to the organisation's primary task, and any uncertainties or difficulties he had experienced so far.

The first thing F told me was his new salary level. My spontaneous reaction was to mentally label him "a cocky little upstart". (He was more than twenty years younger than me and already he was earning a higher salary.) Was my emotional reaction just envy of the younger male or was this an unconscious communication from the client about how he viewed himself in his work role? I could not recall any other ORA client ever telling me their salary as the leading detail about their role. As I struggled with the significance of this exchange, I became aware of how shabby my office seemed compared to my client's corporate lodgings. F proceeded to tell me that he was a technical, legal specialist and he had been promoted because of his outstanding achievements in investigating possible breaches of corporate regulations by listed companies. He was not at all inclined to discuss any difficulties he was experiencing in his new role, even though he had never previously held a management role, or had any management training. He did not want to criticise his director, but he implied that he was a bit annoyed that his director should think he needed this sort of support. He used a lot of technical jargon in describing his work and I struggled to get a clear picture of his role. I often had to ask him to explain what he was talking about. For the next session, I asked him to prepare a work role drawing (Nossal, 2010, and Chapter Four of this book). My instruction was to draw a picture of himself in his work role and to include all the relationships that were important to his work; to convey how he spent his time and the "pushes and pulls" he experienced as he performed his role. He could use colour if this helped to convey his experience at work.

Between sessions, I digested my negative reaction to F and became more curious about what he was unconsciously communicating to me about his work role experience. I could accept that I was a little envious of his self-assurance and career achievement, and resolved to be a reliable recipient of any other tacit messages.

For the second session, F was again late and this time offered no apology. I pointed this out and asked if the starting time, which he had requested and which was early morning, was still appropriate. He said it was, because he lived less than ten minutes walk away. I began to feel as if my time was of no importance and that we would work on his terms unless I somehow proved "worthy" of his respect.

His monochrome work role drawing featured a "head" that represented F, surrounded by boxes that represented positions—a scant organisational chart. In explaining his work role drawing, he offered a fairly lengthy iteration of the tasks, duties, and legal processes men-

tioned in the previous session. I then asked if these boxes also represented actual people, since he had not mentioned any individuals. Yes,
he had seven direct reports. I wondered, out loud, why other people
did not appear in his drawing. His answer was aggressively simple:
"Because you did not tell me to put them in."

I felt provoked again, as if my directions were not good enough,
and I was challenged by the prospect of developing a collaborative
working relations ship with F. I asked him to tell me about his direct
reports. "What do you want to know?" "Perhaps we could start with
their first names." F managed to remember the names of five of his
direct reports. He excused himself on the basis that they worked from
remote locations and they mainly interacted via telephone conferences. It soon emerged that he was having great difficulty managing
this team. He said he asked for their input to problem solving but all
they offered were progress reports and awkward silences. When they
did meet face to face, it was no different. He comforted himself with
a self-report that he had been promoted because he was brighter than
all of them and he could come up with the best solutions anyway. I
began to understand why he had begun the first session by telling me
his salary, and the nature of his work role drawing. I told F then how
the manner of his lateness to sessions left me feeling as if my input
was not being sought, and I wondered how it would feel to be
managed by someone who could not remember my name. Would he
care to think about how he was relating to people, me included, and
not just the content of the work?

F responded well to this confrontation. I felt some risk in making
the intervention, but I was supported by the data he had offered me,
albeit unconsciously. We discussed the possibility that his promotion
caused his former peers to envy him, hence they were reluctant to
contribute to his success in his team leader role, and he defended
himself by pretending he did not need them.

We went on to discover that a similar dynamic existed between F
and his director as between F and his team. He experienced his director as always knowing the answer before he asked the question, and
so F was caught in a game of guessing what the director wanted, so
that F could be a "star" and give it to him. By telling F what was on
my mind, I helped differentiate myself from his director and so did
not play into their game. This "game", it transpired, was linked to
another problem for F and the director. A new strategy of "community

engagement" had been announced by the CEO and F was not sure how his director would want this enacted. In fact, he thought the director himself was unsure, but, given the current "game", he did not want to press him. One version of the new strategy was that the regulator was to shift from being a policing agency that "caught out" violators of company law to a more proactive educator of corporate citizens. Such a shift would have major implications for F's "role idea" of managing within the corporate regulator.

As F got a glimmer of the necessary shift from a "legal/policing" mindset to the "managerial" mindset required by his new role, he became more able to offer data about his lived experience. He was an only son, the eldest of four children, and, in his father's eyes, the only high achiever of the brood. (A "star" in the family!) He was a new father himself and not sure about what sort of authority figure he wanted to be as father to his daughter. In fact, his only association to the concept of authority was to statutory authorities. Our collaboration developed sufficiently for him to invite me, after our last session, to join him in conversation with his director about the individual and systemic challenges they faced together, and the further development F would need if he were to become a competent manager. It was an acceptance by F that he needed some help in working with authority, within himself, within his role, and within the authority structure of his organisation. Psychodynamically speaking, he was reaching toward a "depressive position" (Krantz, 1998), acceptance of a dependence on others for his growth as a manager. Grasping the systemic nature of role, F knew it would not be possible for him to build on his insights without he and his director changing the current "game" between them.

This case example illustrates the basic method of ORA as a bounded process with a focus on the client's lived experience of performing their work role, conceptualising the enquiry in terms of an individual in a role, in a system, which strives to achieve its primary task in a context of variable stability. The process assumes that some of the challenges facing the client will stem from unconscious avoidance, whether by the client or those who hold expectations of the client's role, of anxieties provoked by past associations, by the work itself, and by contextual uncertainties. The role of the consultant is to manage the setting; to be available to receive evidence of such unconscious dynamics within the "workplace" of the ORA, and to assist the client to connect this evidence to work role dynamics within their organisation.

The evolution of ORA

Across the decades, during which ORA has become part of an inter-national community of practice, the very concepts from which it was originally formed have themselves been critiqued and extended. Organisational analysis has moved beyond open system formulations to include approaches such as enactment/sensemaking (Weick, 1995), metaphoric analysis/imaginization (Morgan, 1993, 2006), and com-plex adaptive systems (Stacey, 2007) to name but a few approaches. Alongside such theoretical developments, the world of work has also been changing with the turbulent field forecast by Emery and Trist (1965) now everywhere manifest in the tight, global intersections of profit-making activity, the explosive feedback loops enabled by digi-tal communication, rapid technological innovation, contested rela-tions between gender, work, and home, and the endemic conflict between economic and spiritual values. To listen attentively to a client's work role experience is to risk being exposed to myriad competing forces that are present *in* the client but are not necessarily *of* the client (Armstrong, 2010).

It is not easy to calculate the implications for the ORA method of developments such as these, and yet there are threads of consistency in published accounts of practice that provide some sense of evolu-tion. One might summarise a general implication of these changes by declaring that the model of an expert consultant, taking a position as "objective" outsider to the system in order to make an independent diagnosis, which then determines a corrective intervention, is now barely relevant. In complex adaptive systems, there is no "objective" outside position and an interpretation offered by a consultant is not intended as a solution, but, rather, as an invitation to collaborative meaning making and shared testing. This is a move from "salvation to revelation" (Lawrence, 2000).

To infinity and beyond

"Mysticism is just tomorrow's science dreamed today" (McLuhan, 1969).

This line of development is most evident in the work of Lawrence (2000), who, over more than three decades, has developed the idea of what it means to "manage oneself in role", enlarging the possibilities of ORA greatly from an immediate focus on organisational function-ality to a force for "Social change, which implies an inspection of social realities, (and) starts from the individual considering his or her authority for being in a role in institutions in society" (p. 42).

Lawrence, inspired by Bion, emphasises a shift of perspective from Oedipus, the classic psychoanalytic attention to repressed wishes related to pairing and sexuality, to Sphinx, which represents the ques-tioning attitude and the associated dread of discovering what reality might be in actuality. Sphinx represents learning from experience, including the tragic dimension of human existence that raises ques-tions of individual, group, and organisational survival in a turbulent environment (Lawrence, 1999). Sphinx draws forth the "associative unconscious" (Long, Introduction and Chapter One of this book) that finds creative possibility in what has been sensed, intuited, felt, or dreamt, but not yet articulated or been available for thinking and social sense making. The possibilities of a finite world of prediction and control are giving way to the formless infinite (Lawrence, 1999) and ORA is a method with the potential to assist institutional role-holders to examine their experience without retreating into psychotic defences such as the "totalitarian state-of-mind" (Lawrence, 1995) or perverse cultures (Long, 2008).

One impetus for Lawrence's reversal of perspective from "narcis-sism to social-ism" (Lawrence, 2003) is the almost universal change of medium from a visual environment to an acoustic environment, largely as a result of rapid developments in information technology. Lawrence (personal communication) draws from McLuhan's (1969) use of the term "'acoustic environment" to mean a non-linear experi-ence in which each sense interacts with others; when one sense is extended, the ratio of the others senses is also affected. Acoustic space demands that you apprehend figure and ground simultaneously, that the senses work together. Acoustic space lends itself to an oral culture in which narrative intersubjectivity enables new meaning, and, hence, new possibilities for relatedness to emerge: seeing and valuing a detached, linear analysis of the environment becomes less relevant than listening for, intuiting and sensing, multi-faceted possibilities in real time. At the unconscious level, this is the interplay of "container and contained" (Bion, 1970) which, in harmony, pro-motes psychic growth and, when mismatched, produces the nameless dread of meaninglessness and psychosis. A tragedy in the making.

The importance of this re-centring of social-ism, following the narcissistic, consumption-driven, global financial crisis of 2008–2009, has been noted in a cogent critique of business education in the USA. Pointing to the notable absence of "Reflective exploration of meaning" in the business curriculum, the report states, "It is by imagining the stance of others that reflection on narrative stirs new insights along with a greater awareness of one's own stance, something that, until that time, may have remained entirely unconscious" (Colby, Erlich, Sullivan, & Dolle, 2011, p. 66).

It is about mutual interpretation, and explicit questioning of orientation and purpose.

Armstrong (2010), with an acute and nuanced sense of the object of ORA, emphasises that

> the boundary of engagement is not simply that of the couple, nor indeed that of the group, but rather that of the organisation as a whole: that is of the organisation as a bounded psycho social field . . . a kind of third party in the wings of the exchanges between consultant and client, however personal or interpersonal these exchanges may at first appear. (p. 102)

The consultant must keep in mind the possibility that what passes between consultant and client represents something of the client's internal organisation of his/her emotional experience of the work organisation, including his/her role. Armstrong extends, too, the concept of "interpretation" from one of a straightforward, verbal explanation of experience to include the "rhythm of (their) work together" (p. 109) as consultant and client engage across time, shared meaning emerging from the intentionality of their efforts as they become more collaborative.

The following case example illustrates some of these concepts.

Case 2: Pressure at the top

H was referred to me by one of his business advisers (A), a woman with whom I had worked in a different setting some years before. I was surprised by the referral, since this woman had been wary then of the ORA method and afraid to examine closely the extreme tensions she was feeling between her first CEO role and her family responsibilities. Now she was referring H, a first time CEO with a young family, to ORA. I was reminded, again, that I cannot foreknow what and when a client will learn through this method.

H's presenting issues were "stress", for which he was seeing a psychologist, and some recent negative feedback from his staff about the aggressive manner in which he made demands of staff. He was concerned that he might be charged with "bullying".

We contracted for five sessions, and then H negotiated for two more sessions, then two more sessions, and then another two sessions.

H was an experienced engineer and project manager, mainly in the private sector. He was forty years of age and ambitious. His latest appointment was as CEO of a temporary organisation, formed under a public–private partnership, to undertake a huge infrastructure project. He was responsible for an enormous budget, his political context was particularly sensitive following a change of government, and the project's range of stakeholders was highly varied and conflicted. H's worry about possibly being experienced as a bully had to be viewed within his role shift from being a project manager to CEO, having to report directly to a board, and having to manage relations with government ministers and senior public servants across a variety of departments, plus private contractors and unions.

From the outset, the pressure on me as consultant to dive into all this complexity was very strong. H arrived at the first session having "done his homework" (even though I had not set any homework), armed with charts and diagrams which he tried to explain to me at a furious pace. At some point the look on my face must have communicated that I was not finding this helpful, for he stopped suddenly and said that he did not know what else to talk about. I asked him what was really on his mind and he blurted out, "I am afraid this job will kill me."

This unexpected admission proved to be my real invitation to work with H, but in a strangely elusive way. We spent the remainder of Session One exploring H's fear of the job killing him and I expected this weighty theme to continue. However, in Session Two, the time was taken by a pressing new problem and then, in Session Three, H was surprised when I reminded him of what he had said in Session One. (Later in our work, when he was requesting more sessions, H said it was the fact that I reminded him of what he forgot that was becoming valuable to him.)

Session Two had been filled with his distress at the political pressure he was being put under to sack one of his staff who had displeased a government minister. He felt "sick in the guts" about it and had lost a lot of sleep over the matter. When he broached the matter with her, the staff member had a "stress reaction and collapsed" and had to be helped from the room. He protested loudly to his Chair about "due process", but knew he did not have the power to save this staff member's job. In Session Three, I made the connection between his fear of the job killing him and the political pressure he was put under "to kill a staff member's career". His back stiffened and he outlined to me the steps he had taken to deal with what he felt was an impossible position. A skilful, courageous, and empathic strategy allowed the staff member to leave with some dignity, mitigated the reputational effects on her career, and compensated her financially. He refused to blame others and publicly took responsibility for the decision to replace her.

I was impressed by H's personal integrity and his willingness to put himself in the firing line by daring the Minister to challenge his care of the departing staff member. This did not seem to me like the behaviour of a bully. He was educating me about the sheer competence and effort it took to perform his job while maintaining his own values. I soon realised that he did not need much from me in terms of the actual work task. He was intelligent and a quick learner. His lingering concern was about the toll it might take. Important people in his life had died around the age of forty, but his medical reports indicated no physical concerns for his health. He was working long hours and absorbing huge amounts of detail in his quest to ensure the viability of the project. He struggled to balance his own ego needs and his desire to guarantee the financial security of his family. I was struggling to find the balance between his personal quest and the dynamics of his role. I felt in danger of becoming a life coach rather than a consultant to his work role.

As I pondered this dilemma, H voiced his rising concern, as the project moved closer to the construction phase, that fatal accidents might occur. He was justly proud that so far in his career no worker had ever died on a project he managed. He had a total commitment to workplace safety but now had to face the fact that on this project he was depending on five project managers to enact this commitment. Already he had fantasies of being cross-examined by a coroner after a fatality. He was facing the possibility that his "luck" might run out and he would have to live with the inevitability of the death of a worker on his watch. A tragic dimension of his profession was emerging in his consciousness.

During this time, we had been examining the way in which H managed his direct reports and how he went about delegating. He preferred a tight regime of weekly progress reports and problem identification, meeting with his project managers both individually and as a group. This seemed appropriate, given the risks they were carrying, but he worried if this close accountability was "over the top". He did not believe himself to be a bully, but acknowledged that he could be blunt. One of his direct reports, who had complained about H's style, resigned to take a management position with a large private company. Within weeks he had recanted and informed H that he himself was following the reporting structure H used because "you need to demand accountability".

H and I began to form a working hypothesis that his "demand" for accountability (and the risk of being experienced as a bully) was linked to his fear for the safety of his staff. What he needed was to link "accountability" to a shared "organisation-in-the-mind" with his direct reports so that their role performance was felt to includethe safety of frontline workers. With this accountability–safety link in mind, H could more confidently discuss the meaning of accountability with his direct reports rather than just forcefully insist.

This breakthrough in understanding between us came after a shift in the ORA structure. During the first five sessions, I had insisted that we meet away from H's office and I had taken up my role as consultant with care to maintain our role relatedness as consultant and client who had come together to analyse his work role experience. My experience of H in this setting was that he was collaborative, attentive to my comments, although not shy to disagree, willing to be challenged about sticking to the task, without always knowing what data would be relevant to the task. Because of his attitude, I was willing to continue our work on his terms after our five sessions. He wanted to meet in his office, ostensibly to save time, and to contract for just two more sessions because he felt unfinished but did not want an open-ended commitment.

H kept his end of the contract and managed his office space without interruption. I had the experience of sitting in his office and getting the feel of his day at work. Without realising it at first, I became more open about myself, freely answering his questions about my family obligations, my age, sporting interests, etc. I think I felt free to be more personal because he was respecting the ORA task and contributing to the management of the setting. I found it instructive to be in his office where every square centimetre of wall and table space was covered in GANT charts, site maps, timelines, etc. The symbols of the work pressure he experienced were all around us.

I formed a private working hypothesis that F was now exploring my "humanity" inside his workplace as a way of trying to internalise a sustainable reminder of his own human values. For instance, he discovered that I was twenty years older than him, had the same number of children, and was still married to my first wife. This was important to him as he struggled with his ambition and his concern for his family. If he succeeded in this job, his market value as a CEO would skyrocket, but that probably meant a geographical shift and more pressure on his family. He did not want to "kill his marriage", but he did want professional recognition. He was driven to provide materially for his family, unlike his father, and only gradually could he consider his psychological presence to his family as a valuable provision. This applied, too, to his way of being with his staff. Perhaps they would not find him so "aggressive" if he allowed space for what they valued beyond work.

Before I felt able to share my private hypothesis, H told me of the "adjustments" he was making: (i) he had moved A from her business adviser position into his management team. "She will keep us honest." A had previously foregone her CEO role to find a more conducive work–family balance when she accepted a position on this project. She would be the only woman in his regular team meetings; (ii) H removed all the charts from his office walls. He said they were evidence of his "comfort" as a project manager and he now wanted to be more the CEO; (iii) he also dropped his weekly "one on one" meetings with his project managers and would rely on them to report to each other in team meetings, and to him "by exception". This felt very risky for H, but he admitted he could never take a break if he did not actually delegate. It was now a matter of managing the Minister's anxiety if H could not answer every question immediately; (iv) with more time to think, he realised that he had not developed an adequate culture among his staff of listening to community stakeholder concerns about the impact of construction on their day-to-day existence. Many held fears about loss of amenity, and if a grass-roots political campaign got media coverage, then all his achievement so far could be undone. He was intending to lead by example.

H was moving from "doing" the project to "tending" the project. He already knew how to build things; the ORA process challenged and supported him in learning how to grow things, such as relationships. In doing so, however, he had to face the knowledge that growth risks death.

Other forms of ORA

The examples above are of "one on one consultations". There are published examples of other ORA configurations where the focus is on the role relations between functions (Long, Newton, & Chapman, 2006), between professional disciplines (Biran, 2006), between team members (Newton, 2005), as part of performance management (Long, Dalton, Faris, & Newton, 2010), and as a vehicle for organisational change (French & Simpson, 1997). Practitioners can provide many more examples of variations in the method, particularly as it might form part of a wider programme of organisation development. Brunning (2006) includes many examples of the intersection of coaching with the systems-psychodynamics of organisational role.

Developing the skills and capacity to conduct ORA

The essential focus of ORA is on the connection between work role performance and the sanctioned task of organisation. Role is a system construct because you cannot change role without influencing the role network of the system. An ORA consultant needs a systems framework to analyse the multi-faceted pressures that shape a role and the implications for renegotiating a role. In addition, human beings bring to their work desires that might conflict with, or not find, realisation within those systems. These desires are often unconscious to the individual and/or the collective of role-holders within the system. In order to engage with the dynamics of unconscious desires, the ORA consultant must have a disciplined, experiential, and conceptual training in recognising the interplay of his/her own unconscious desires with those to whom they consult.

Currently, the body of theory relevant to this work is referred to as systems-psychodynamics, or sometimes as socioanalytic, and most institutes which offer an education in this field would acknowledge a historical link to the work of the Tavistock Institute of Human Relations. There is no governing body for the accreditation of ORA practice and ORA consultants generally come to the method through participating in group relations conferences and professional programmes aimed at coaching, organisational consultation, or organisation dynamics. Typically, these programmes attract clinicians who wish to extend their work to organisations and managers who wish to understand more about the unconscious dynamics that bedevil their rational work plans. ORA stands at the juncture of the "socio" and "technical" in organisations and it requires knowledge and skill in both domains.

In England, the Grubb Institute has most consistently put ORA at the forefront of its work and now offers an MA in Organisational Analysis. The Tavistock has an Advanced Coaching Programme which features role consultation. In Australia, the National Institute for Organisation Dynamics Australia (NIODA) offers training in ORA and education in managing oneself in role. More generally, practitioners are usually connected to institutes that offer training in group relations, since that practice is the genesis of the method.

References

Armstrong, D. (2005). *Organization In The Mind*. London: Karnac.

Armstrong, D. (2010). Meaning found and meaning lost: on the boundaries of a psychoanalytic study of organisations. *Organisational and Social Dynamics*, 10(1): 99–117.

Bain, A. (1999). On socioanalysis. *Socioanalysis*, 1(1): 1–17.

Bion, W. R. (1961). *Experiences in Groups*. London: Tavistock.

Bion, W. R. (1970). Container and contained. In: *Attention and Interpretation* (pp. 72–82). London: Jason Aronson, 1983.

Biran, H. (2006). Organizational role analysis: using Bion's binocular vision. In: J. Newton, S. Long, & B. Sievers (Eds.) *Coaching In Depth. The Organisational Role Analysis Approach*. London: Karnac.

Bridger, H. (1990). Courses and working conferences as transitional learning institutions. In: E. Trist & H. Murray (Eds.), *The Social Engagement of Social Science, Vol. 1, The Socio-Psychological Perspective* (pp. 221–245). London: Free Association Books.

Brunning, H. (Ed.) (2006). *Executive Coaching. Systems-Psychodynamic Perspective.* London: Karnac.

Colby, A., Erlich, T., Sullivan, W., & Dolle, J. (2011). *Rethinking Undergraduate Business Education.* The Carnegie Foundation for the Advancement of Teaching. San Francisco, CA: Jossey-Bass.

Emery, F., & Trist, E. L. (1965). The causal texture of organizational environments. *Human Relations, 18*: 21–32.

French, R., & Simpson, P. (1997). A systemic approach to organizational role and the management of change. In: F. A. Stowell, R. L. Ison, R. Armson, J. Holloway, S. Jackson, & S. McRobb (Eds.), *Systems for Sustainability: People, Organisations and Environments* (pp. 709–713). London: Plenum.

Gould, L. (2006). Coaching senior executives: personal/work conflicts, mortality and legacy. In: J. Newton, S. Long, & B. Sievers (Eds.), *Coaching In Depth. The Organisational Role Analysis Approach* (pp. 145–158). London: Karnac.

Gould, L., Stapley, L. F., & Stein, M. (Eds.) (2001). *The Systems Psychodynamics of Organizations.* London: Karnac.

Hirschhorn, L. (1988). *The Workplace Within.* MA: MIT Press.

Hutton, J., Bazalgette, J., & Reed, B. (1997). Organization-in-the-mind: a tool for leadership and management of institutions. In: J. E. Neumann, K. Kellner, & A. Dawson-Shepherd (Eds.), *Developing Organizational Consultancy* (pp. 113–126). London: Routledge.

Jaques, E. (1990). Learning for uncertainty. In: *Creativity and Work* (pp. 149–170). Madison, CT: International Universities Press.

Katz, D., & Kahn, R. L. (1966). *The Social Psychology of Organizations.* New York: John Wiley.

Klein, M. (1959). Our adult world and its roots in infancy. *Human Relations, 12*: 291–303.

Klein, M. (1975). *The Writings of Melanie Klein.* London: Hogarth Press.

Krantz, J. (1998). Anxiety and the new order. In: E. Klein, F. Gabelnick, & P. Herr (Eds.), *The Psychodynamics of Leadership* (pp. 77–107). Madison, CT: Psychosocial Press.

Krantz, J., & Maltz, M. (1997). A framework for consulting to organizational role. *Consulting Psychology Journal: Practice and Research, 49*(2): 137–151.

Lawrence, W. G. (1995). The seductiveness of totalitarian states of mind. *Journal of Health Care Chaplaincy, 7*(October): 11–22.

Lawrence, W. G. (1999). Centring of the Sphinx for the psychoanalytic study of organisations. *Socio-Analysis, 1*(2): 99–126.

Lawrence, W. G. (2000). The politics of salvation and revelation in the practice of consultancy. In: *Tongued With Fire* (Chapter 8). London: Karnac.

Lawrence, W. G. (2003). Narcissism versus social-ism governing thinking is social systems. In: R. M. Lipgar & M. Pines (Eds.), *Building on Bion: Branches* (pp. 204–228). London: Jessica Kingsley.

Long, S. (2004). Building an institution for experiential learning. In: L. J. Gould, L. F. Stapley, & M. Stein (Eds.), *Experiential Learning In Organizations. Applications of the Tavistock Group Relations Approach* (pp. 101–136). London: Karnac.

Long, S. (2008). *The Perverse Organisation and Its Deadly Sins.* London: Karnac.

Long, S., Dalton, D., Faris, M., & Newton, J. (2010). Me and my job. *Socio-Analysis, 12*: 39–56.

Long, S., Newton, J., & Chapman, J. (2006). Role dialogue: organizational role analysis with pairs from the same organization. In: J. Newton, S. Long, & B. Sievers (Eds.) *Coaching In Depth. The Organizational Role Analysis Approach* (pp. 95–112). London: Karnac.

Mant, A. (1976). How to analyse management. *Management Today, October*: 62–65.

McLuhan, M. (1969). Marshall McLuhan. The Playboy Interview. *Playboy Magazine*, March 1969.

Menzies Lyth, I. (1988). *Containing Anxiety in Institutions. Volume 1.* London: Free Association Books.

Miller, E. J. (1976). Introductory essay: role perspectives and the understanding of organizational behaviour. In: E. J. Miller (Ed.), *Task and Organization* (pp. 1–16). London: John Wiley.

Miller, E. J. (1990). Experiential learning in groups: the development of the Leicester Model. In: E. L. Trist & H. Murray (Eds.), *The Social Engagement of Social Science. A Tavistock Anthology. Vol. 1: The Socio-Psychological Perspective* (pp. 165–185). London: Free Association.

Miller, E. J., & Rice, A. K. (1967). *Systems of Organization.* London: Tavistock.

Morgan, G. (1993). *Imaginization.* London: Sage.

Morgan, G. (2006). *Images of Organization.* London: Sage.

Newton, J. F. (1998). Learning from the experience in management education. A psychodynamic perspective. Unpublished PhD thesis. Department of Psychological Medicine, Monash University.

Newton, J. (2005). "I've never thought of that before": organisational role analysis and systems development. *Socio-Analysis*, 7: 67–79.

Newton, J., Long, S., & Sievers, B. (Eds.) (2006). *Coaching In Depth. The Organisational Role Analysis Approach*. London: Karnac.

Nossal, B. (2010). The use of drawing in socio-analytic exploration. *Socio-Analysis*, 12: 77–92.

Quine, C., & Hutton, J. (1992). Finding, making and taking the role of head: a Grubb Institute perspective on mentoring for headteachers. Unpublished manuscript. The Grubb Institute, London.

Reed, B. (1976). Organizational role analysis. In: C. L. Cooper (Ed.), *Developing Social Skills in Managers. Advances in Group Training* (pp. 89–102). London: Macmillan.

Reed, B. (2001). *An Exploration of Role as Used in the Grubb Institute*. London: The Grubb Institute.

Rice, A. K. (1965). *Learning for Leadership*. London: Tavistock.

Rice, A. K. (1969). Individual, group and intergroup processes. *Human Relations*, 22: 565–584.

Stacey, R. (2007). *Strategic Management and Organisational Dynamics: The Challenge of Complexity to Ways of Thinking about Organisations* (fifth edn). London: Prentice Hall.

Trist, E. L., & Murray, H. (Eds.) (1993). *The Social Engagement of Social Science. A Tavistock Anthology. Vol. 11: The Socio-Technical Perspective*. Philadelphia, PA: University of Pennsylvania Press.

Von Bertalanffy, I. (1968). *General Systems Theory*. New York: George Braziller.

Weick, K. (1995). *Sensemaking in Organizations*. Thousand Oaks, CA: Sage

White, K. (1996). Reflections from practice: the interface of psychoanalysis and organizational role consultation. Paper presented to the 13th Annual Meeting of the International Society for the Psychoanalytic Study of Organizations, New York, ISPSO.

CHAPTER ELEVEN

Role biography, role history, and the reflection group

Susan Long

Role biography

Role biography is a term used to describe a biography of the *person-in-role* as described through the various work roles that they have taken up throughout their lives (Long, 2006). This is distinguished from "role history", which is a history of a particular organisational role, shaped over time by its various incumbents, especially the original or foundation role-holder (Chapman & Long, 2009). Both role biography and role history, taken together, give the current role-holder a strong sense of how the past might be unconsciously influencing their current behaviour in role. This can be added to the exploration of their role in its current system.

Role biography provides a method for understanding the impact of work roles taken throughout life on the client's current work role. This can give the role-holder a better sense of his or her uniqueness in role. It can also give a fuller understanding of where valencies in role have their origins. New roles are not taken up in a vacuum. The person has a history of role taking. In contrast to a personal biography tracing the development of a personality over time, the role biography stresses how past roles affect current roles. The emphasis is on the current role and how the past might be unconsciously driving behaviour in the role.

Since first writing about role biography, I have used the method, as have numerous of my students, in teaching, in organisational consultancies, and in one-on-one coaching sessions. Linked closely to organisational role analysis (see Chapter Ten) and organisational drawing (see Chapter Four), it is a method that speedily taps the unconscious. Although mostly used with drawings in order to symbolically and visually capture the roles taken up at different ages and stages of the life journey, a role biography can be taken through a discussion with the client.

To recapitulate the method more fully discussed in Long (2006), I provide here an outline of the major points. (See Long 2006 for case studies using the method.)

- The client is asked to draw the work roles that they have taken up throughout their life. The drawing is to be done as a journey of mini-drawings, starting with roles taken at age six (ages given can be approximate, not exact). Later stages of the journey are roles taken at ages sixteen, twenty-six, thirty-six, and so on until the current role. Each mini-drawing should be a symbolic representation of the role taken. Drawing ability is not relevant.

- Importantly, the client chooses which roles they wish to explore and, thus, is in charge of what they feel comfortable in revealing. This is not designed as "psychotherapy", even though results are sometimes therapeutic. Of course, the client may wish to work "more deeply" if they are in a situation that they trust and that has been demonstrably trustworthy in the past.

- The ages I choose are arbitrary and can change with the client. They represent early childhood (with childhood chores as work in the family), adolescence (perhaps with the first work outside the family—in a shop, for a neighbour, etc.), in the twenties (perhaps the first established and "serious" job), in the thirties (when career is established), in forties, fifties, etc., according to the client's age and life stage. The client can choose the ages they wish to focus on within these general categories. The idea is not to be rigid, but to capture some of the work roles that are important to the individual's biography. The last mini-drawing is of the current work role.

- I emphasise *work* role, explaining that work occurs for the child in the family. Very often clients consider that their "emotional roles" within the family were the most important roles they took up. For example, "I was the oldest and took on the role of carer for the younger children", or, "I was responsible for feeding the pets. That meant that I developed a closer bond to them and took on the role of protecting them from other children. This made me appear to be the bossy one".

- I explain that this is not an exercise in capturing all the work roles that taken up throughout life, just a sample of the most important ones. Often, a first "real job" is significant. But the client should choose.

- When the drawing is completed, the consultant works with the client to explore the biography. The consultant takes a supportive role, asking first what each of the drawings mean and allowing the client to express what she sees as important. As each mini-drawing is described, the important questions following the description are: "What do you think you learned in that role?" "How do you think you carry that learning into your current role?" If the client has done a current work role drawing it is useful to have that on hand. In any case, the last mini-drawing in the role biography journey should be the current role. If drawings are not used, the narrative exploration should ask these questions at each stage of the biography.

- During the exploration, some socioanalytic concepts might be helpful. For example, the exploration of role is enhanced by looking at "the institution-in-the-mind" (Armstrong, 1997) or the "organisation-in-experience" (Long, Newton, & Dalgleish, 2000) of each of the roles. The "role idea" (Reed, 1976) is another useful such concept. For further ideas about role exploration, see Chapter Ten of this book.

- The client is encouraged to look over the whole drawing or think through the whole narrative of their work roles. In particular, themes and recurrent motifs and patterns are noted and explored.

- The consultant does not make "interpretations" of the material, but may suggest associations that are evoked. The client might or might not accept these associations as useful.

The role exploration is sometimes quite startling for the client. Patterns that had not been noted previously might come into focus.

Or, if they had been noted, they are given new emphasis and meaning. When conducted one-on-one with a consultant, the role biography can be an important part of a coaching process (Newton, Long, & Sievers, 2006). However, role biographies can also be used to understand how persons take up roles in relation to how others take up their roles. A work team is a system where each role works closely with each of the other roles and where intersubjective meanings are co-created by the role-holders in the team (Long, 2002). Such co-creations are affected by role biographies and role histories.

In this context, the role biography can be used to explore role relations in a team or work group. A reflection group process is useful in this regard.

The reflection group

The reflection group is a group of people trained and able to use observation and reflective practices to draw out and amplify the implicate (Bohm, 1980), perhaps hidden, meanings in material presented by a client or that are in an interview or activity: in this case, meanings within the role biography.

Most often, the reflection group comprises members of a training course or programme where each member is working with their own role biography. Or the group could be colleagues within a work group wanting to understand more about their roles, or even participants in collaborative action research projects, or organisational change projects. It is essential that the group works in a contained space with a trained consultant and where trust has been developed and confidentiality kept. That participants (clients and reflection group members) are willing and not under any form of coercion should go without saying.

The reflection group members freely associate to the material, saying whatever comes into their heads and expressing the feelings that the material evokes. It is made clear that the reflections are not about the "reality" of the biography, but are the responses of the people in the reflection group. The working hypothesis here is that through free association the reflections transform the "implicate" into the "explicate". The reflections provide a way to access the associative unconscious (see Chapter One of this book) and so to expand upon or amplify the meanings within the biography—meanings that, while important to the individual, are also linked to the broader culture of the group, organisation, or society.

The client refrains from joining with the reflection group, but quietly listens to their associations and reflections. During this time, reflection group members are asked not to question the client or interact with them. This leaves a mental space for the client to hear the associations and amplifications without having to respond or defend their own way of understanding the material. This is made clear to all the participants. The client can "take it or leave it", according to how helpful they find the reflections of others. This is not a process whereby clients are pushed to see beyond what they want to see, or to explore their own repressed material. It is a method where, through the material of one of the participants, the associative unconscious of the broader system may be accessed. This is then available for learning and thinking. The client is given a short time to have a "final say" following the reflection group.

The reflection group can open up new meanings for the social systems that they are part of, especially if all members of the group are able to share their role biographies. In this way, the process bears similarities to the associative work done in the Listening Post (Chapter Nine), the social dreaming matrix (see Chapter Six), the social photo-matrix (see Chapter Seven), and the social dream-drawing process (see Chapter Eight).

None the less, it is a highly personal process and should be treated with the respect and confidentiality ethically accorded to clients, students, research participants, or trainees. The new meanings discovered might be of intense personal importance.

The way the method works

The client presenter

In this role, a client or team member works on their role biography with a consultant. During the reflection group process, the client presenter listens in silence.

The consultant

Consultants have the role of facilitating and engaging a collaborative conversation about the role biography. Concepts such as "primary task of the organisation", "role idea" of the client presenter and other players, the "system, institution or organisation-in-the-mind" of different players, leadership and authority, organisation dynamics, and the presenter's experience of the situation are kept in mind (Newton, Long, & Sievers, 2006).

The observers

Observers silently observe the consultation and then become members in a reflection group.

The reflection group

The reflection group members explore their observation, paying attention to what they have seen, heard, and (especially) thought and felt during the consultation. Members may offer associations to the material and may formulate a hypothesis around role or system, although this is neither necessary nor should it be forced. Reflection group members should not directly engage or question the presenter. This allows the presenter to observe the reflections without the "pull" of having to respond to the group.

Guidelines

The following provide guidelines for the process.

- The consultant and the client presenter *work collaboratively* to explore the role. This is not a one-way "interview". The tone best worked toward is one of mutual curiosity.
- The exploration is of *persons in role in a system*, not of *personality*.
- Associations and connections are made from the observers' experiences of the presentation. Interpretations are avoided. This is not *feedback* to the client presenter or consultant about their performance in role or in the session.
- Working hypotheses about *roles in the system* or other *system dynamics* might emerge.
- All work is in confidence.
- Links may be made between the material in the presentation and the here and now of the team.

Reflective practice

Reflective practice involves group members in observing and examining:

- their own involvement in the group/meeting/encounter;
- how roles and tasks develop;
- what aids or interferes with the work of the group.

There are four broad types of observations. Reflections might emerge from each of these areas of observation.

1. *Content*: What is occurring and what is said. This is the content of the meeting, interview, or encounter, the issues raised, the arguments put forward, and the decisions made, what is included and what is left out;
2. *Climate*: What is the "climate of the meeting" and the observer's involvement in this? The climate refers to the general movement of "mood in the group" and how people interact together. What members are feeling. The emotions of group members are as important as their thoughts because these give a clear indication about the group dynamics, levels of trust, success of communications, members motivations, and, hence, the capacity for effective collaboration.
3. *Process*: Who interacts with whom, how the meeting/encounter is organised and proceeds, how leadership and other roles are taken up;
4. *Self observation*: What is it that the observer is thinking and feeling? This forms a clue or working hypothesis to what others might be thinking or feeling but are not able to express.

Each of these types of observation forms the basis for working hypotheses to be developed as described in Chapter One. The major work of the role biography is to find patterns in the various roles taken up by the client presenter. The working hypotheses will refer to these patterns rather than to any interpretation about the client and her personality. This must be stressed, because any "wild analysis" can be destructive rather than helpful. In the end, it is for the client to decide what patterns really do exist and how their articulation is helpful.

Role history

A role does not sit alone. It is influenced by, and influences, all other roles within an organisational system. Moreover, roles have histories that are built up through the various ways that previous incumbents have worked (Chapman & Long, 2009). Role histories include the expectations that others have had. The roles of Prime Minister and Governor, for example, have each changed due to the ways in which various players have enacted the role and how others have reacted to their use of authority in the role, some of these changes becoming institutionalised through informal and formal means. Even the roles that children take up in the playground and in their games bear the imprint of those children who came before and played the same games (Opie & Opie, 2001).

Many authors have considered the ways that roles are affected by their incumbents and how, when joining an organisation, new role-holders go through a process of finding, making, and taking roles (Bazalgette & Reed, 2006). First, new role-holders conceptualise and make sense for themselves the nature of the system they are entering; then they shape the role within that understanding and according to their own dispositions and valencies (Bion, 1961), and, finally, take up the authority and discretion available to that role. In this process, roles are moulded by persons to fit with their experience and what they think will be expected of them. We expect new employees to bring their own ideas to their roles.

In contrast, how does the role shape and affect the person? Just as newcomers bring their own personal attributes and qualities to roles, so roles, too, have an impact on their incumbents, usually at the less-than-conscious level. The position of roles within the organisation, their status, and the expectations of others all affect the incumbent through processes of identification. While high status roles might readily lead the new role-holder to consciously accept all associations that come with that role, in identifying or being identified with any role, the joys and burdens of its history also are introjected unconsciously. An employee might easily say to a newcomer, "Ron used to do it that way", referring to a past incumbent and revealing their expectations about the role. My colleague, Jane Chapman, and I (Chapman & Long, 2009) discuss a situation where a new CEO finds it difficult to exercise his authority because of the way the previous CEO worked in the role. It was as if he, the current CEO, was de-authorised from the past.

In working with role biography, it is useful also to work with role history, aiding the client to explore how the role was situated systemically prior to their engagement. The current role is a coming together of its history with the role biography of the incumbent, the place where two streams meet. Again, a reflection group may be used as part of this exploration. The client presenter may explore the role history and the reflection group may associate to what has been discovered.

Role biography and role history-taking are two methods that together aid in exploring the background context to current roles and social systems.

References

Armstrong, D. (1997). The 'institution-in-the-mind': reflections on the relation of psycho-analysis to work with institutions. *Free Associations*, 7(41): 1–14.

Bazalgette, J., & Reed, B. (2006). Organisational role analysis at the Grubb Institute of Behavioural Studies: origins and development In: J. Newton, S. Long, & B. Sievers (Eds.), *Coaching in Depth: The Organisational Role Analysis Method* (pp. 43–62). London: Karnac.

Bion, W. R. (1961). *Experiences in Groups.* London: Tavistock.

Bohm, D. (1980). *Wholeness and the Implicate Order.* London: Routledge and Kegan Paul.

Chapman, J., & Long, S. D. (2009). Role contamination: is the poison in the person or in the bottle? *Organisations and People: Toxic Leadership*, 15(3): 40–48. Revised and reprinted in *Socio-Analysis: the Journal of the Australian Institute of Socio-Analysis*, 11: 53–66.

Long, S. D. (2002). The internal team: a discussion of the socio-emotional dynamics of team (work). In: R. Weisner & B. Millett (Eds.), *Human Resource Management: Contemporary Challenges and Future Direction.* An interactive digital book on CD Rom. Wiley. www.johnwiley.com.au

Long, S. D. (2006). Drawing from role biography in organisational role analysis. In: J. Newton, S. Long, & B. Sievers (Eds.), *Coaching in Depth: The Organisational Role Analysis Method.* (pp. 127–144). London: Karnac.

Long, S. D., Newton, J., & Dalgleish, J. (2000). In the presence of the other: developing working relations for organisational learning. In: E. Klein, F. Gablenick, & P. Herr (Eds.), *Dynamic Consultation in a Changing Workplace* (pp. 161–192). Madison: Psycho-Social Press.

Newton, J., Long, S., & Sievers, B. (Eds.) (2006). *Coaching in Depth: The Organisational Role Analysis Method*. London: Karnac.

Opie I., & Opie P. (2001). *The Lore and Language of Schoolchildren* (new edn). New York: The New York Review of Books.

Reed, B. (1976). Organizational role analysis. In: C. L. Cooper (Ed.), *Developing Social Skills in Managers. Advances in Group Training* (pp. 89–102). London: Macmillan.

CHAPTER TWELVE

Diagnosing organisational work cultures: a socioanalytic approach

Jinette de Gooijer

S urveying the health of workplace culture is contemporary practice in many organisations. There are many instruments in the marketplace that offer to evaluate and measure employee satisfaction, to map culture against various characteristics of employee behaviour and business performance, or to compare "espoused culture" with "culture-in-use" (Argyris & Schön, 1974). The fantasy is that a work culture is an asset that can be managed and thereby controlled.

What can a socioanalytic approach offer to understand work cultures and organisational change? Primarily, socioanalytic methods seek to engage people in a collaborative task of analysis, interpretation, shared insight, and active choices. Unlike the more commonplace culture survey, a socioanalytic approach to assessing work culture is neither done to people, nor presumes to be objective in the usual sense. Rather, it engages with people as subjects, acknowledges their subjective experiences as valid reality, and considers work culture as the product of a dynamic social system. To understand a work culture with a socioanalytic mind is to see, feel, listen, and experience the organisation as a living system of people working in roles at purposeful tasks. That, at times, this system of working together might not function well, or be experienced as completely dysfunctional, is not unusual. Organisations are social constructs. They exist within an external reality of a society and its communities, the marketplace, and physical environment. But the internal reality holds a mental world of emotions, beliefs, fantasies, and assumptions that sit below the surface of people visibly going about their work. This mental world is what socioanalysis refers to as the psychic reality of the organisation, discernible through the felt experiences of its members.

In this chapter, I describe socioanalytic principles and practices for assessing organisational work cultures. The techniques described are used by me and my colleagues in our consultancy work with clients. They have their origins in the work of the Tavistock Institute for understanding groups, and in ongoing developments in the field of systems psychodynamics. Fraher's history of group relations and psychodynamic institutions is a useful account of the formation of these ideas and their subsequent development (Fraher, 2004). Levinson's work (Levinson, 1972, 2002) on the principles and techniques for dianosing the health of organisations also informs contemporary practices. He emphasises comprehensive processes for analysing organisations and paying attention to the nature of the psychological relationship between consultants and clients (Diamond, 2003), both of which are important to the socioanalytic approach.

I describe the conceptual underpinnings of a socioanalytic approach to work culture diagnosis, followed by how these concepts can be put into practice, drawing on case material from my consulting work to illustrate the techniques in practice.

What is organisational culture?

An organisation's culture is made up of key aspects of its history, the meanings people make of the work they do, the roles they perform, others with whom they interact, the pressures and environmental factors which impinge on individual and business performance, and of individuals' felt experiences of the organisation and its work.

A common metaphor for describing organisational culture is to say it is like an iceberg. On the surface are the things easily observed: physical workplace, the way people dress, the language used, who interacts with whom, what gets said and what does not get said, office

rituals; these and other symbols communicate the visible manifestations of organisational culture. They can be described and talked
about with relative ease. These visible phenomena include organisational statements (such as vision, mission, values, goals, strategies),
and the technical systems (plans, policies, structures, processes, services, products, and technologies) for executing the primary task of
the organisation.

However, the deeper aspects of organisational culture are below
the surface, the assumptions, beliefs, and values that influence
people's behaviour and their responses to stresses and anxieties in the
workplace. Feelings and beliefs are much harder to articulate; they
might derive from unconscious processes, and explorations of these
aspects rely on subjective methods of diagnosis.

Another way of thinking about this interplay of visible and invisible phenomena is to consider the visible aspects as symbolic evidence
of a culture, and that below the surface is the psychic reality of the
organisation, in which emotional drivers and mental models influence
all that sits above.

The social context of an organisation is also significant to its
culture. An organisation exists within a social domain containing
other organisations like itself. This domain may be characterised by
similar services, or stakeholders, or by being part of a social institution, such as "The Law", or "Health Services". An organisation's primary task performs a social function as much as it achieves the
specific goals of its enterprise.

By thinking of organisations as social systems, we can consider
work cultures as a product of their social context, primary task and the
way it is performed, and the lived experiences of the people who work
at the task.

What is a socioanalytic work culture diagnostic?

Conceptually, socioanalysis is concerned with understanding aspects
of an organisation's psychic reality through the lived experience of its
individual members and the groups they belong to. People's experiences provide vivid data on real phenomena, help reveal the human
dimension of work, and all the complexities of working co-opera-
tively. Engaging with the lived experiences of the organisation also

helps leaders and managers get in touch with underlying issues in the tacit environment of a work culture that are often not explored as a normal part of doing business.

A consultant working in a socioanalytic frame will be concerned with engaging their client in a collaborative process for discerning the organisation's psychic reality and its influence upon the work culture. What measure of understanding and insight that flows from this process is intended to free thinking in the client system so that role-holders can exercise a wider repertoire of choice in performing their roles.

An essential element of organisational culture is the unconscious assumptions, attitudes, and beliefs about the work performed in service of the primary task of the enterprise (Skogstad, 2004). Shared unconscious fantasies are part of an organisation's system. Revealing individuals' and groups' "organisation-in-the-mind" is a means to discern such fantasies (Armstrong, 2005; Hutton, 2000). Collaborative discernment of the "organisation-in-the-mind" between consultant and client enables meaning and awareness of unconscious processes to be co-created. It also encourages active participation in improvements to an organisation's functioning.

Underpinning a socioanalytic approach is a complex set of assumptions about lived experience and unconscious processes (de Gooijer, 2009, pp. 233–234). These assumptions frame the design and implementation of work culture assessment. They are that:

1. Individuals experience both conscious and unconscious states of mind.
2. Individuals have an inner world of subjective experience distinct from an external world of action. This inner world is affected by, and is the product of, conscious and unconscious states of mind.
3. Individuals in a group both generate and are affected by conscious and unconscious processes of relating among members of the group.
4. The psychic reality of a group is discernible in the interactions between members and individuals' felt experiences.
5. Humans are social animals. Individuals derive a sense of self and their own "being-in-the-world" from relationships with others.
6. Unconscious processes of relating (between self and others, or among group members) are not discernible as objective facts. The

sources of data for discerning unconscious processes are feelings and emotions, that is, *subjective* facts.

7. Unconscious processes of relating can be hypothesised and tested in the social reality of individuals concerned. They are working hypotheses and subject to change in response to the dynamics of human interaction.

8. Reality can be distinguished from fantasy. Reality may be concrete, as in physical experiences of the world, or social, derived from agreement about human actions, or symbolic, as in the representations of reality through images, language, symbols, and artefacts.

9. Unconscious processes of relating among members of a group, or between groups and within an enterprise, strongly influence organisational actions. Yet, it is difficult to link such processes and actions in simple cause–effect relationships. When the possible *meaning* of action/s is reflected upon, links may be discerned between unconscious processes and human action.

10. Environmental context is a key influence upon the psychodynamic processes experienced by organisational members. Context includes primary task of the enterprise, the external environment in which it operates (e.g., social, political, geographic, industry, economic), and internal operating structure.

A socioanalysis of work culture relies on direct observation and rich description (Geertz, 1993) of what is both observed and experienced. Feelings, thoughts, fantasies, dreams and observable actions are sources for revealing and interpreting unconscious processes. Self-reflexivity on the part of the consultant is a vital capacity to bring to this process.

Creating data about subjective experiences is never clear-cut, and especially when the intention is to create data about large group cultures. As Hollway and Jefferson (2000) note, humans are defended subjects who might not know why they experience or feel things the way they do, and are motivated to disguise the meaning of some of their feelings in an effort to protect certain vulnerabilities. Socio-analytic consultancy makes room for the emergent, intersubjective entity to be studied. Interpretation is conducted through construction of working hypotheses as feedback to client groups on emergent themes. They are tentative interpretations and one way for validating experiences of organisation members. The authority and legitimacy of interpretations rest in the data. In other words, interpretations are grounded in evidence and validated by organisation members.

Investigative techniques which can be employed for interpretive culture assessment include reflexivity, workplace observation, drawings, interviews, critical review of organisation documents, narratives, experiential workshops, participant–observer activities, and collaborative action research.

"Reflexivity" is an essential element of studying relationships and relatedness at individual and group levels, especially when unconscious processes such as transference are to be discerned. It is the ability to reflect on one's internal state and responses to what is going on in immediate experiences. Importantly, the utilisation of countertransference enables the consultant to create data that would otherwise be inaccessible (Sher, 1999).

Workplace observation derives from infant observation techniques within psychoanalytic training methods. It aims to connect the observer/consultant with the feelings and experiences of those working in an organisation (Hinshelwood & Skogstad, 2000; Willshire, 2001; Chapter Three of this book). The method requires the consultant to quietly observe a situation for an hour or so at a regular time each week over several weeks, with the aim of engaging countertransference processes within the consultant.

How a consultant believes she or he is *being made to feel* is important data about unconscious feelings which might be present in that part of the organisation (a team, business unit, or whole organisation) (Bain, 1999). Feelings aroused within the consultant help to form questions or working hypotheses to be used in later discussions or interviews with organisational members. This ensures that what was experienced during observation is tested with organisational members' own experiences. For this reason, a work culture assessment will frequently begin with observation; the consultant is usually fresh to the situation, more easily able to suspend memory and desire (Bion, 1984), and is immediately thrust into the raw emotional experience of being inside the organisation. By keeping silent (in the main), the consultant is more able to connect with fantasies and feelings about the work, to be surprised, and to form naïve questions. The capacity to remain open to "not knowing" is an important one for the consultant to maintain. This is referred to as "negative capability", following the idea propounded by the poet Keats (French, 2000). Since it is not possible to reproduce observations, validity and reliability of observations are enhanced by collaborative interpretation, separating observations from interpretations, and combining with other techniques (such as interviews).

The aim of *interviews* is to follow up initial impressions and presenting issues with in-depth perspectives on experiences of being a member in the group observed and other organisational groups. In theory, every work group is a "part" of an organisation and potentially relates to the organisational system as a "part-object" (Klein, 1975). Group members in turn might project their part- or partial-connectedness into the organisation as a whole. Interviews create data that might reveal some of these potential dynamics, or objects of projective identification. They are best conducted face-to-face wherever possible, so that data on intersubjective dynamics can be created, and for the opportunity to invite interviewees to create visual pictures of their experiences in role (their personal or collective "organisation-in-the-mind"). (See Chapter Five of this book for more detail about socioanalytic interviewing.)

Depending on the size and characteristics of the organisation or unit involved in the culture assessment, interviews might be a mix of individual and focus group discussions. The selection is negotiated and discussed with the client. Typically, leadership roles and members of intact work teams are individually interviewed, but, in the case of multiple teams within a large business unit, the intact work teams are frequently interviewed in a group workshop-like setting, or focus group.

All interviews are interactional events and, therefore, the "knowledge" generated is inevitably co-created—a narrative or dialogue in which both parties contribute to making sense of events and experiences (Holstein & Gubrium, 1995). An interviewer influences the creation of the emergent story by offering pertinent ways of conceptualising issues and making connections through the design of the questions and the conceptual framework in which they sit. In practice, interpretative data analysis is embedded in the interview process.

The stance of the interviewer is important: suspending judgement and allowing the speaker to respond to comments freely enables the interviewer to freely associate to the material presented by respondents, and to provide space for selected facts to emerge (Bion, 1984; Freud, 1912e).

Drawing is the third and other vital technique in the assessment of a work culture. In Chapter Four of this book, Brigid Nossal elaborates on the utility, application, and value of drawings as a socioanalytic method. The essential purpose of using drawings is to bring to the surface less conscious thoughts and feelings about working in the organisation and provides an immediate and vibrant image of the mental models people hold about their workplace. Drawings also help to encapsulate key emotional experiences that are more difficult to express in words, or are otherwise rationalised. They have the potential to reveal remarkable data about roles and role relatedness and connections between the individual and the organisation, within groups and across organisational boundaries.

When to introduce drawings is a matter of overall design. When the task of the consultancy is solely focused on understanding a presenting issue in the work culture, or there are many participants involved in the assessment, drawings may usefully be part of the interview encounter, when there is sufficient time to associate to the drawing. These pictures would be included in the later feedback process. In the case of a long-term culture change programme, drawings might be more usefully introduced in a workshop setting as part of a collaborative data creation and analysis activity.

In the first instance, issues of anonymity and confidentiality come into play. Consultants need to be aware of anxieties about revelation, and how the "defended subject" might use anonymity as an attack upon the organisation. The initial group sanction of the consultancy helps to surface some of these anxieties, but naturally cannot reveal or work through all: that "everything is potential data" is apposite.

A successful technique my colleagues and I have used for working with maintaining anonymity of individuals is to seek agreement that the drawing can be displayed in a "gallery showing" along with all the other drawings, as part of the feedback workshop. As an early activity in the workshop, it presents a powerful image of the collective organisation-in-the-mind and engages all in association, data analysis, and hypothesis formation. Individuals may choose to identify their own pictures, and some do so. That of itself can be an indicator of the level of trust and vulnerability within the group.

When drawings are created within a workshop, the task of association, data analysis, and hypothesis formation remains the same,
while the problem of anonymity is removed. As a consequence, the
group usually experiences more directly the value of meaning making
through drawings, and with greater ownership of the results (both the
process and emergent interpretations). A shared understanding is
more likely to be created, and to be more alive in the group.

Sometimes, instead of a drawing, we ask interviewees to describe
their experiences with a work culture metaphor. For example, they are
invited to imagine: "If this organisation/group/unit were an animal,
what kind of animal would that be? Where does this animal live?
What does it eat? How does it reproduce?" This technique is a softer
approach, often experienced as playful, and can help those unfamiliar
with reflective practices or socioanalytic approaches to engage with
non-rational data. The results can be surprisingly revealing about the
multiplicity of perspectives and experiences in a group, or also of the
commonalities. One group with whom we used this technique identified many animals that were not real—either extinct, mythical, or
stuffed toys. It presented a potent symbol of an organisational environment where the meaning of the work no longer felt alive.

The initial intensive phase of a work culture assessment usually
culminates in a "working note" (Miller, 1995) for the client group to
discuss. As we describe it to our clients, the purpose of a working note
is to present the results of our analysis of individual interviews, group
discussions, review of organisational documents, and the felt experiences of our interactions with the culture of the organisation. The aim
is to generate discussion and develop deeper understanding of the
situation under examination. It is always an incomplete picture. The
working note is a distillation of initial interpretations for open examination with the group. From that exploration, we can begin to build
a collective view of current reality and possibilities for change.

As Miller (1995, p. 28) describes it, the working note is written for
the client system, and is based on a range of data from interviews and
observations recorded in field notes and organisational documents. It
is not a report, but a work-in-progress. Often, it is a presentation of the
consultants' interpretations and working hypotheses about discrepancies between stated and existential aspects of the organisational work
environment. While its purpose is always to generate dialogue with
and within the client system, this is not without substantial risks. The

potential is there for the consultant to be experienced as an expert who pronounces interpretations. When meaning making rests with the consultant alone, the client is made into a disengaged party. Armstrong (2010) notes that when consultants create hypotheses and interpretations on their own, meaning becomes lost. Such an approach privileges the consultant's understanding. Meaning made from the data created becomes too much the property of the consultant and not enough of the working with the client in a lived engagement. If there is too little exchange between consultant and client, then co-creation of meaning is unlikely to occur.

Returning to Miller (1995, p. 29), he notes,

> . . . the principle of being the enabler rather than the expert remains valid. Our ordinary everyday experience teaches us that even if we have a clear idea of what troubled people ought to do, telling them has little or no effect: they need to discover and own the solution for themselves . . . The essential point is that we are engaged in a collaborative relationship, working together to undertake the diagnosis and arrive at possible actions.

The "feedback workshop" is often where the diagnostic data are first analysed by the group as a whole.

"If culture is co-created by the members of an organisation, it is they who should jointly inquire into it" (Seel, 2001, p. 2).

The feedback of data to all participants is a vital step in validating data created by consultants, and to test the legitimacy of interpretations and other material presented in the working note. A workshop setting is most useful for this. While the consultants will offer their hunches and initial hypotheses in the working note, the design of the feedback workshop is to facilitate collaborative analysis, elaboration, and amplification of themes. As with other socioanalytic methods, such as social dreaming and the social photo-matrix, participants are engaged in the task of amplifying associations to the data and themes, "so as to make links, find connections and to discover new thinking and thoughts and thus hidden meanings of what in an organization usually remains unseen and unnoticed" (Sievers, 2008, p. 1).

The complexity of subjective data created during a work culture diagnostic needs proper time to digest. In my experience, this cannot be done in a few hours, and is best done over a whole day. Participants need time and space to engage with what might feel highly unfamiliar, deliberately invokes emotional responses, and asks them to think in depth about their and others' experiences of working together. The workshop will create new data at the same time as feedback on previously created data is presented. Hence, the design of the feedback workshop will incorporate both experiential and analytic activities. A typical structure is depicted below.

Feedback Workshop

Opening: Plenary
Session 1. Drawing activity
Session 2. Presentation of working note
Session 3. Themes and hypothesis formation
Session 4. Organisational responses and strategies
Closing: Plenary, and next steps

It is helpful to begin the workshop with an experiential activity, such as drawings. Participants immediately become active collaborators in creating data and the task of associative analysis. It prepares them for Session Two, the presentation of the working note. Their reception of the material in the working note is influenced by the work they have already done themselves. Not unexpectedly, links and connections between the "data in the room" and the "data in the working note" are often made.

There are many variations on how a feedback workshop might be designed and structured. What is given here is a simple example of the essential elements to be covered in a workshop.

Socioanalytic work culture diagnosis in practice

In this section, I describe two consultancy projects that used a socioanalytic approach to work culture diagnosis. While the techniques and processes were similar in each project, the outcomes were different. The first describes a work culture audit that used socioanalytic methodology, but which was isolated from any organisational change process. The second describes a case in which the work culture assessment formed part of a long-term process of organisational change.

A work culture audit of a legal service

Some years ago, we were invited to conduct a culture audit of a small public agency. The client, a statutory legal office, wanted a "health check" of the organisation's work culture, in order to understand what would make the organisation a happier workplace. Staff had identified the need for a "culture audit" in response to a "Quality Improvement Self-assessment" survey. They hoped to achieve a reality check of the organisation's statement of values, and whether the culture of the organisation aligned to these values. The organisation employed about fifty staff, most of whom were lawyers or legal administrators. The agency was in transition from a publicly funded service to a commercially competitive service, competing with private sector legal firms for government business. However, the agency remained a statutory authority, beholden to public sector obligations.

The use of the term "culture audit" by the client suggested they thought of culture as something that could be measured within a rational framework of benchmarks. By researching people's experience of working at the organisation as it was currently experienced, our study was based in real-time and real events. It meant, at times, that we were present at meetings or general workplace activity. What we observed of day-to-day styles of interaction, how we were interacted with, and what we felt alerted us to emotional currents flowing through people's transactions and relationships with each other. We asked people to "draw" their mental image of the organisation—in pictures and metaphor—to bring to the surface non-rational perspectives. And we paid close attention to what was said, as much as to what was not said. The methodology we employed involved:

- seven hours of workplace observation over two sites, in which we focused on emotional resonances and countertransference experiences;
- two two-hour focus groups involving eleven staff, in which we asked participants to create a picture of their experiences of working in the organisation, explore associations and themes with the group, and to relate these to the organisation's Statement of Values;
- seven individual interviews with senior legal advisers (members of a senior management team), who were invited to describe their

role and role relationships, experiences, and expectations of themselves and others as managers and leaders, the work culture, and what metaphor (animal) best described this culture and its values-in-use;

- a review of key organisational documents, such as the "Statement of Values" and "Self-Assessment Report";
- two "working notes" and a "final report" presented in an iterative cycle of feedback meetings.

What we discerned about the culture

Our workplace visits left us with an initial impression of a friendly atmosphere, of a pleasant surface to interactions, of competent staff working in extremely crowded conditions, and of a "paperwork factory". The emotional tone of the workplace felt subdued, even somewhat depressed, which made us wonder about the expression of emotional experiences in this organisation, that is, who gave expression to them? How? Where? Our hypothesis at this stage was that there was a "rational legal system" and a "non-rational human system" operating separately, side-by-side.

In discussions with senior management, we discerned that the pressure to achieve eighty per cent billable hours was at the expense of collegial interaction, peer advice, and supervision, and the strength of professional independence was weakened by experiences of isolation from everyday human interactions. In contrast to this, legal administrators experienced their jobs as boring and routine, and were seen by the lawyers to be emotionally volatile individuals. That said, neither management, lawyers, nor administrators felt that "people issues", that is, interpersonal relations, were managed well in the organisation. Instead, people issues had become codified into a list of fourteen Organisational Values covering two pages of text. The wish for the work culture to be "civilised" had created a deep split between rational (legal) processes, and the non-rational (human behaviour).

However, the insights gained by the client, real and powerful as they were at the time, did not generate any impetus for change. This was because the purpose of "the culture audit" was not linked to a desire or vision for cultural change; what meanings that were found through our diagnostic process became lost. There was no container for change as such. The transformative value of a culture diagnostic ultimately could not be realised.

Turning around the work culture of a health service

The second case I discuss presents a situation in which a culture diagnostic formed a key role in a culture change programme.

The CEO of a health service engaged us to assist with effecting a major shift in work culture values and practices. Many changes in personnel and clinical practices were already under way, with the CEO having a vision for the organisation of modernised business practices, increased accountability and responsibility throughout all management levels, and service excellence. She recognised that this demanded an entirely different work culture ethic and performance than one based on hierarchy and dependency in authority relations.

The work culture diagnostic in this case was designed to be a tool in a long-term process of organisational change. It would be led by the executives and next level managers. The diagnostic was not thought of as a one-off process, but designed within a programme of staged activities, in which ongoing assessment of the work culture would occur. The primary task of the consultancy was defined as "to examine the work culture at the health service through working with the executives and senior managers. The work will assist in identifying possible areas for development and improvement and in designing the most appropriate consulting intervention". The initial task was undertaken through a two-stage process and inclusive of a number of activities.

The design of the consultancy process was strongly embedded in the socioanalytic principles of engagement, collaboration, and mutual accountability. Task, roles, and responsibilities formed a strong container for the work; they were articulated, reviewed, and continually held in mind. The following outlines the major elements of the framework we employed.

1. *Establishment of a Project Directorate to oversee the consultancy.* This was a small representative group with responsibility and authority for the governance of the project for its duration. Members of this group comprised the executive group of four, with the CEO as Project Sponsor, plus two consultants. The group

collaboratively developed the cultural change programme, identified business areas for particular attention, and authorised consultancy activities. It met regularly to reflect upon results and current experiences of the culture.

2. *Group sanction.* This involved an initial meeting with the leadership group at which we introduced ourselves, the consultancy task and process, and held an open discussion on people's hopes and concerns for the group's development. Because the work sought to get at what was below the surface of working relationships, and invited people to reflect on their personal experiences of working at the health service, we sought agreement from all involved to be willing to participate in the process. It was an important ethical step as well as a statement of in-principle commitment from the group. We would only proceed with the culture diagnosis once we had gained the group's sanction.

An important message is also communicated with this step: that of representative authorisation. It is by no means intended as a pseudo-democratic process of majority vote, or a process of consensus by which each and every member of the group (whether present at the meeting or not) must agree before anything can proceed. Rather, it is an engagement in real-time, with those present deemed to be an authorised group to make decisions on behalf of all members. Dissent is examined and openly explored, and changes are made to the process in response to realistic concerns and suggestions. Role modelling the very process we say we will engage in—such as examining felt experiences, observations of group dynamics, and reflecting on here and now experiences—demonstrates the value a socioanalytic approach places on authenticity in working relationships.

3. *Data creation activities.* We conducted individual interviews with all fourteen members of the senior leadership group. The purpose of these was to provide each manager with an opportunity to speak freely and in confidence about their experiences of their role and working at the service. Each interview was of one to one and a half hours duration. The interviews were semi-structured narratives, as shown below.

   Culture diagnostic interview structure and process.
   • What is your role, history of working at the organisation, and relationship with other roles?

- Tell me about your experience of being in this role.
- What is your experience of the senior leadership group?
- How would you describe the culture of the group?
- What does the group need?
- Thinking about the broader organisational culture, how would you describe it?
- If that culture were an animal, what sort of animal is it? Where does it live? What does it eat? How does it reproduce?
- Are there any other comments you would like to make about the work culture here?

Note that the questions were very broad in scope. The intention was to stimulate feelings, thoughts, associations, and not be too directive.

On completion of each interview, the interviewer noted in a consultancy journal her or his own reactions during the interview, the atmosphere of the encounter, and any other impressions formed from the experience. The aim was to capture an account of the countertransference feelings. The interview was then written up more completely from the handwritten notes taken during the discussion and initial themes identified. We did not tape-record the interviews, preferring to take handwritten notes that were visible to the interviewee. We also used whiteboards or large sheets of paper to collaboratively create data.

Data creation activities also included a tour of the site, and four hours of observing the group at its regular management meetings. Since this was the only time that the group actually got together as a working group, it provided the best opportunity to see group interactions and experience dynamic processes.

Data analysis involved an examination of our notes and experiences for themes "bothering the group". By this, I mean the preoccupations discernible in people's stories and narratives about their role experiences. At this stage, we were concerned about articulating initial hunches about the dynamics in the work culture, and their impact upon the service and the functioning of the senior leadership group. The animal metaphors helped us access symbolic data about the culture.

4. *Working note.* Themes and interpretations of the matters raised in interviews and observations were then documented in a working

note for discussion with the whole group. It documented our initial diagnosis of the situation. A half-day discussion on the working note continued the data analysis. With the group, our interpretations and diagnosis were elaborated and checked for their validity. The group was also encouraged to think about appropriate strategies for working through the matters raised in the working note. Any strategies were then taken up in the next step.

5.   *Design of Stage 2 Interventions and implementation of strategies.* The Project Directorate considered the results of the initial work culture to design a programme of interventions, which included organisational role analysis (ORA) with individuals or groups, action learning projects, whole of system reflections, and staff retreats.

What we discerned from the culture diagnostic

We learnt that the organisation was in a state of immense change: high turnover of staff in key management roles, the leadership group in a constant state of forming and transition, and pockets of resistance to changes were said to exist in certain units. "Old" and "new" seemed to be in collision. Ambivalence and splitting were prevalent dynamics. Such dynamics related directly to people not knowing each other well and of feeling they were in the role of "learner".

What the work culture diagnostic achieved, among other things, was to bring individual anxieties, fears, and projections into an open group forum for the first time. It legitimised these feelings, and offered the group hope for change. The socioanalytic focus on experiences of roles, role relatedness, and the group as a whole provided a new way of thinking for the group, one that could begin to free people from feeling caught in interpersonal dynamics.

Because the diagnostic was an opening activity to a programme of long-term change, there was a substantial holding environment for the working note and group reflection on its contents. The importance of this containment of purpose and application cannot be underestimated.

Ongoing effects

What has distinguished this programme of work culture change at the health service, which has now been ongoing for several years, is the process for examining the work culture as a constant aspect of the Project Directorate's work, and that of the leadership group dialogues. Action learning projects within particular service units usually begin with a culture diagnostic process. In other consultancy activities, such as group consultation and ORA, reflection has developed as an embedded practice for assessing the shifts in the work culture. As the programme of cultural change has progressed, we can discern an interweaving of interventions with reflective diagnosis of the work culture. As people became more attuned to thinking through the dynamics of role and organisational system, so their capacity to assess the psychodynamics in their work culture has grown.

Conclusion

A socioanalytic approach to work culture diagnostic is a process of collaborative enquiry into the lived experience of performing one's role in the organisation for the purpose of gaining insight to unconscious processes influencing the organisational reality. This chapter has described some of the techniques that can be used for conducting a socioanalytic work culture diagnostic, and given practical examples of application in real-life consulting assignments. The examples demonstrate that, when coupled with a programme of organisational change, the work culture diagnostic is a meaningful tool for the transformation of insight into action. The chapter argues that a culture diagnostic needs a purposeful container in order for it to be meaningful and capable of transformative change in the organisation.

References

Argyris, C., & Schön, D. A. (1974). *Theory in Practice: Increasing Professional Effectiveness*. San Francisco, CA: Jossey-Bass.

Armstrong, D. (2005). *Organization in the Mind: Psychoanalysis, Group Relations, and Organizational Consultancy. Occasional Papers 1989–2003*. London: Karnac.

Armstrong, D. (2010). Meaning found and meaning lost: on the boundaries of a psychoanalytic study of organisations. *Organisational & Social Dynamics*, 10(1): 99–117.

Bain, A. (1999). On socio-analysis. *Socio-Analysis*, 1(1): 1–17.

Bion, W. R. (1984). *Attention and Interpretation* (reprinted edn). London: Karnac.

De Gooijer, J. (2009). *The Murder in Merger: A Systems Psychodynamic Exploration of a Corporate Merger*. London: Karnac.

Diamond, M. A. (2003). Organizational immersion and diagnosis: the work of Harry Levinson. *Organisational & Social Dynamics*, 3(1): 1–18.

Fraher, A. L. (2004). *A History of Group Study and Psychodynamic Organizations*. London: Free Association Books.

French, R. (2000). "Negative capability", dispersal and the containment of emotion. Paper presented to the International Society for the Psychoanalytic Study of Organisations Symposium, London.

Freud, S. (1912e). Recommendations to physicians practising psychoanalysis. *S.E., 12*: 109–120). London: Hogarth.

Geertz, C. (1993). Thick description: towards an interpretive theory of culture. In: *The Interpretation of Cultures* (pp. 3–30). London: Fontana.

Hinshelwood, R. D., & Skogstad, W. (2000). The method of observing organisations. In: R. D. Hinshelwood & W. Skogstad (Eds.), *Observing Organisations: Anxiety, Defence and Culture in Health Care* (pp. 17–26). London: Routledge.

Hollway, W., & Jefferson, T. (2000). *Doing Qualitative Research Differently: Free Association, Narrative and the Interview Method*. London: Sage.

Holstein, J., & Gubrium, J. F. (1995). *The Active Interviewer*. Thousand Oaks, CA: Sage.

Hutton, J. (2000). Working with the concept of organisation-in-the-mind. www.grubb.org.uk/html/body_orgmind.html. Accessed 24 June 2003.

Klein, M. (1975). Our adult world and its roots in infancy. In: *The Writings of Melanie Klein: Vol. 3 Envy and Gratitude and Other Works, 1946-1963* (pp. 247–263). London: Hogarth.

Levinson, H. (1972). *Organizational Diagnosis*. Cambridge, MA: Harvard University Press.

Levinson, H. (2002). *Organizational Assessment: A Step-by-Step Guide to Effective Consulting*. Washington, DC: American Psychological Society.

Miller, E. J. (1995). Dialogue with the client system: use of the 'working note' in organizational consultancy. *Journal of Managerial Psychology*, 10(6): 27–31.

Seel, R. (2001). Describing culture: from diagnosis to inquiry. Accessed at: www.new-paradigm.co.uk

Sher, M. (1999). Transference, counter-transference, and organisational change: a study of the relationship between organisation and consultant. Paper presented to the International Society for the Psycho-analytic Study of Organizations Symposium, Toronto.

Sievers, B. (2008). Hosting a social photo-matrix (unpublished notes).

Skogstad, W. (2004). Psychoanalytic observation: the mind as research instrument. *Organisational & Social Dynamics*, 4(1): 67–87.

Willshire, L. (2001). To know or not know: a management and educational dilemma. Unpublished manuscript, Melbourne.

CHAPTER THIRTEEN

Group relations conferences

Eliat Aram and Mannie Sher

G ordon Lawrence (2000, p. 51) writes that

> ... [group relations] is the most potent of methodologies because it enables one to distinguish between phantasy and reality. It also enables one, among other things, to judge between truth and the lie; to come to grips between projection and introjection, transference and countertransference, which are the basic "stuff" of human relations.

Group relations (GR) is a method of study and training in the way people perform their roles in groups and systems. These can be work groups, teams, or organisations, or less formal social groups such as faiths, race, and gender groups. A group might be said to be two or more people interacting to achieve a common task. GR theory views groups as tending to move in and out of focusing on their task and adopting a number of different defensive positions based on unarticulated group phantasy.

There are certain features of GR work that are held in common and are probably subscribed to by most practitioners of this craft. These include working with transference and countertransference phenomena, skill in interpreting group unconscious dynamics, working within the boundaries of space and time as well as within psychological boundaries, being clear about working within role and task, working with group-as-a-whole, not individual, phenomena, and having the capability of generating working hypotheses about group and organisational functioning.

What is group relations?

Group relations was the phrase coined in the late 1950s by staff working at the Tavistock Institute of Human Relations to refer to the laboratory method of studying relationships in and between groups. This laboratory method had been developed at Bethel, Maine, from 1947 by the National Training Laboratory, based on ideas of Kurt Lewin on intensive experiential learning. Lewin's group theories strongly influenced the thinking of the early Tavistock staff. This early group of Tavistock pioneers were social scientists and psychodynamically orientated psychiatrists who had been using group approaches to tackle practical wartime problems, such as officer selection. They later applied their group-based experiences and approaches to post-war social reconstruction. They drew on many sources: the work of sociologists Gustave le Bon (1895) and William McDougall (1920), psychoanalysts Sigmund Freud (1915c, 1921c, 192h) and Melanie Klein (1932, 1957, 1959), and social scientists Mary Parker Follett (1920, 1973), Elton Mayo (1933), and Kurt Lewin (1947).

Group relations is the study in real time of relationship and relatedness, where relationship is about actual relationships and relatedness concerns systemic relationships, say, as between parliamentarian and voter. It is the accelerated study of the connections and discontinuities of person and role, of role and group, of group and group, of group and organisation, of organisation and environment, and, therefore, benefits from drawing on other theoretical frameworks such as anthropology, architecture, existential and phenomenological philosophies, and philosophies of practice and spirituality such as body work, Yoga, and psychotherapy.

Lewin's field theory provided a way in which the tension between the individual and the group could be studied: "the group to which an individual belongs is the ground for his perceptions, his feelings and his actions" (Allport, 1948, p. viii). Lewin considered groups to have properties that are different from their subgroups or their individual members. This finding, and the experiential workshop method of training which Lewin developed, influenced staff at the Tavistock Institute that ultimately led to the development of the first group relations conferences in the 1950s.

Klein's object relations theory was another important influence, which built upon Freud's theories, in particular, that people learn from early childhood to cope with unpleasant emotions by relying on the psychological defences of splitting and projective identification. The psychoanalyst Bion influenced models of group work and group behaviour. In his work at the Tavistock Clinic, and later at the Tavistock Institute, he established that groups operate on two levels: the work level, where concern is for completing the task, and the level of basic assumptions that are meant to ease anxieties and avoid the painful emotions that membership of groups might evoke. Bion identifies three types of basic assumption: dependency, pairing, and fight/flight. He reported his work in a series of articles for the Tavistock Institute's journal *Human Relations*, that later appeared as the book *Experiences in Groups* (Bion, 1961).

Since the first group relations conference in 1957 at the University of Leicester, there have been developments in group relations by Ken Rice, Isobel Menzies Lyth, Harold Bridger, Pierre Turquet, Robert Gosling, Eric Miller, Mary Barker, and Gordon Lawrence. In addition to the contributions made by these pioneers, there have been significant influences on the development of group relations made by group relations institutions around the world.

By the mid-1950s, the basic design of the Tavistock GR conferences had been established by the early pioneers (Bridger & Higgin, 1964; Miller, 1990a,b; Rice, 1958, 1963, 1965, 1969; Turquet, 1975, 1985) and later workers such as Lawrence (1993, 2000), Gosling (1979, 1981), Armstrong (1992, 1997), and Gould, Stapley, and Stein (2001, 2004). Despite numerous adaptations and innovations to GR conference design, the Tavistock Institute's GR programme continued to be criticised for being intellectual, authoritarian, and anachronistic—a reference to the Northfields military setting in which Bion's and Bridger's work originated (Harrison & Clarke, 1992). Nevertheless, GR conference work has continued to provide opportunities for learning about the dynamics of roles, groups, leadership, and organisations. The role of Director of the Group Relations Programme is variously described as "preserving the tradition" and "innovating for change". Despite regular changes in conference theme and design, the perception remained of a Tavistock fixed in old paradigms (Wasdell, 1997). The persistence of this projection was explained by Tim Dartington in a personal communication that the next generation of GR practitioners seems to need to retain an image of an "old Tavistock" so that their own innovations and efforts at growth can be progressed without experiencing the feelings of guilt that often accompany altering or abandoning a tradition. Therefore, the Tavistock's vigorous engagement in continuing leadership in the field (Aram, 2010, 2011, in Aram, Baxter, & Nutkevitch, 2012; Aram, Baxter, & Nutkevitch, 2009; Brunner, Nutkevitch, & Sher, 2006), its vitality and innovation in GR conferences, is often challenged. In this chapter, we demonstrate how GR is relevant in role clarification, leadership development, organisational and environmental transformation and its impact on social issues, its influence in the research and evaluation, in clinical work, and in educational and professional development (Brunner, Perini, & Vera, 2009; Huffington, Armstrong, Halton, Hoyle, & Pooley, 2004; Hupkens, 2006; Jager & Sher 2009; Lahav, 2009; Litvin & Bonwitt, 2006; Nutkevitch & Sher, 2003, 2009; Viswanath, 2009).

Bion's (1952) interest in pushing further into the primitive of the group was extended by his colleagues at the Tavistock Institute, working in particular on the challenge to memory and desire, to the very human wish that everything should revert to the *status quo ante* (Bion, 1961, 1970, 1985a,b). Elaborating and working through the obstacles to group and organisational learning formed the basis of much of the work of the Tavistock Institute (Miller, 1959, 1976, 1983, 1995, 1997; Miller & Rice, 1967; Rice, 1958, 1963, 1965, 1969). Rediscovering Bion's thinking in relation to the life of contemporary institutions, and specifically the impact of Bion's ideas, lie at the heart of Tavistock GR conference work.

We believe that Tavistock–Leicester GR conferences worldwide share in the guardianship of Tavistock Bion–Kleinian orientations in which the constructs of transference, countertransference, splitting, projection, and projective identification, the group unconscious, Oedipal conflicts, leadership, and authority are especially relevant. We realise the significance of this view when we observe the potentially destabilising unconscious dynamics in intragroup and intergroup relations, where group members' feelings and emotions are sometimes overwhelmed in relation to both the group's task and the individual's desire for security and safety. Group relations conference design provides a robust framework for experiential learning and studying the behaviour of groups as they happen in real time, often referred to as the "here-and-now". Group relations conference thinking can be useful also in working with groups outside conference work, where Bion's constructs of the work group and basic assumption group apply to the interplay between conscious and unconscious dynamics in organisations. Directors and staff aim to develop and extend understanding of intragroup here-and-now experience and intergroup interactions between sub-systems and authority issues of the individual and the group (Lawrence, 1986, 1996, 1997). An example of this type of understanding is illustrated in the post-conference evaluation of a participant:

"My most important recollections from the last conference are: (i) the large study group would leave me feeling like a child in kindergarten; (ii) the small group, where I took the role of 'mother' to other members whose families had had similar experiences to my own—children separated from their parents; (iii) the application groups, and the atmosphere of sincerity that prevailed there.

"The Tavistock Leicester method was a huge lesson for me in experimenting with different the forms of relating—listening, sharing, seeing connections, gaining insights—and welcoming everyone into this process. I have followed up my conference experience by applying this method in my work and in my personal life—the experience and knowledge I gained from taking part in the conference has also been experienced in my personal life. Altogether I feel less alone now in my country where this kind of thinking is not common. Sometimes feel alien in my job and in my studies because a sense of cooperation between individuals and organisations is often lacking. As a member of the conference, I learned that the 'problem' lies both in me and in my surroundings and that I need to take responsibility for my own efforts at cooperation. When I did this, people supported me in choosing roles, assuming authority and taking responsibility for facilitating change. Decided to pursue a thesis on the role of HR managers in organisations in my country and explore the problem from a feminist perspective. People around me—my professor, teachers and other students—were interested in the topic. However, it is still hard for me to stick with my ideas and say 'no' to authority. For example, I was advised by my supervisor to do the research from a classical perspective and I automatically agreed. The result is I am bored and unmotivated and the most annoying thing is that, during the research interviews, HR managers are telling me about the problems connected with gender stereotypes! I feel ashamed for not daring to challenge my supervisor and say 'no'. I felt like a schoolgirl again. Instead of arguing, I started my research using a classical model, while secretly I kept on reading group relations literature that is more interesting for me. When I finally revealed my true aspirations to my supervisor he did not like the idea, but he eventually acceded to my request. The saying of my grandmother to her granddaughter (me) came to mind: 'be lower than the grass'.

"Taking part in the group relations conference was an opportunity for me to experience a different way of relating, especially as a woman from a country where women automatically defer to men. Instead of conforming, we had opportunities for hearing different thoughts; we could hesitate, have doubts or simply reflect in the face of authority (male and female) in real life. So, during the next conference, I need to explore my fears and try different behaviours that will foster collaboration in me and encourage it in others."

We believe that what differentiates GR conference work from other group constructed events is its solid theoretical underpinning: certain structural and design elements, including elements of the primary task, that the staff of GR conferences adopt consultative stances, and that conferences extend over a period of days.

Theoretical underpinning

The theoretical underpinning of GR conferences derives from the adaptation of concepts from at least two bodies of knowledge:

From *psychoanalytic theory* we derive knowledge of conscious and unconscious processes, consciousness being the presence of feelings, emotions, desires, or the absences of these, and a reasonable degree of awareness of their reasons and their consequences. Conversely, and in parallel, we understand that unconsciousness is the presence of feelings, emotions, desires, or lack of these, and their reasons and their consequences are outside of awareness, that is, individuals and groups do not have access to their dynamics, or the ability to understand them, and, therefore, are unable to take action based on that understanding.

People working as staff in GR conferences have had training in, and manifest understanding of, the concepts of transference and countertransference. Transference is defined as the attribution of feelings, emotions, behaviour, attitudes, fear, love, eroticism, envy, jealousy, competition, rejection, attachment, etc., to figures of authority in the present that have their origins in relationships with previous earlier figures of authority, for example, parents, teachers, doctors, bosses. Countertransference would be the feelings, emotions, attitudes, behaviour, etc., aroused in the figure of authority, for example, the teacher, therapist, consultant, boss, political leader.

Projection is part of a normal process of interpreting sense data of the perceptual system. It is based on instinctual impulse to take into the self or one's group all that is good and eject from the self or one's group all that is bad. It is defined as the attribution of certain states of mind to someone else or to another group, where internal conflict is projected into the external world. Projective identification is used to avoid having to experience negative feelings, for example, unwelcome anger, in oneself or in one's group. Projective identification is usually regarded as projection that results in the "other" actually changing against their will, that is, getting caught up uncontrollably in someone else's or another group's drama.

In a large study group, a member says,

> "Individuals have no value in this group; we're always defined as part of something else—nation, gender, race or faith. My individuality is being killed off. I'm looking for my small study group; I can't find it and the consultants do nothing to help with my fears."

Resentment and the wish for revenge arises in the large study group that feels injured and wronged. Often, what begins as a demand for fairness (protection) becomes inflamed into a hatred, as other motives, such as envy, recruited to create a hatred and a quest for revenge, cannot be restrained and everything feels likely to be destroyed. Such unopposed destructiveness is terrifying and, in most cases, restraining forces are mobilised to protect the group, the learning, and the self from the devastating effects of the violence. Consequently, wishful revenge may be denied or bottled up and is expressed as grievance. Instead of being directly acted on, destructiveness is controlled and expressed in indirect and often hidden ways. This is affirmed by a member of the Leicester conference:

"The group relations conference experience is a whole cycle of life and death. Boundaries of time, around events, structures and roles, named and unnamed, enable underlying assumptions in the person, between persons and in the system, to be explored.

"I learned that to experience membership of an organisation involves managing feelings like fear, anger and joy; tolerating changes in the system; taking up many membership roles, involvement in relationships and relatedness; understanding systems; group and inter-group behaviour. Topics explored cover relationship between men and women; parent–child roles; sexuality, cultures, nationalities, language; service; respect and desire, race, faith, technology and dynamics; espionage and counterespionage (especially relevant to me as a German); mourning and joy; hate and love; silence; communication; integration and disintegration; creativity and chaos; positive energy and waste.

"The conference introduced me to the concept of 'projection': to feel them, name them and then work with them. I never before understood what they meant. Everybody learned how we use projections and why understanding them is so important in organisational and social environments. This importance is underlined because projections can be so destructive, particularly in the globalisation of everything."

Defences are paradoxical in that they are an essential part of human developmental activity; they can foster development or they can hinder it. Projection and introjection are the mechanisms involved in building up the internal world and are the basis of all cognitive and emotional activity, exploration, knowledge, and symbol formation. Klein (1932) views defences as directed specifically against the death instinct, and the introduction of her theory of the paranoid–schizoid and depressive positions led to the understanding that defences in the paranoid–schizoid are directed against anxieties of annihilation, and defences of the depressive position are directed against feelings of loss and guilt about damage to the "object". Defences are steps taken to preserve the *status quo*, or a state of equilibrium, or to prevent being overwhelmed by anxiety, for example, rigid hierarchies in situations of life and death, such as in medicine and the military. This idea is supported by the experiences of a member who wrote in his evaluation:

"I have never learned as much about organisations as whole systems as I did at the Leicester conference. I learned that if I want things to happen in my organisation I have to take responsibility for my feelings and actions. Additionally, I never realized how easily and how strongly groups set up defences to avoid the painful realities about their task, their relationships with other groups and their performance. Despite my ten years of university studies in psychology and business, leadership & strategy, attendance at many courses and much working experience, my participation in group relations conferences has been the most powerful learning experience ever.

"It is difficult to specify key learning moments, but what stands out are the opportunities for reflection of emotions and frustrations. I cannot imagine working life now without using the paradigm of cycles of action, feedback, reflection, planning, second-level actions, feedback on those, more reflection and planning and so on. Creating designs and interventions in every aspect of my working life is strongly inspired by my group relations experiences and learning. The combination of psychodynamic thinking and the Tavistock open systems approach is the most powerful tool I have ever come across and used. I would be a poorer and less qualified organisational consultant without my group relations learning experiences."

A key concept borrowed from open systems theory is *primary task*—the single most required thing that groups or organisations have to do in order to survive. Rice (1958) and Miller (1993a,b) wrote that each system or sub-system at any given time has one function, which may be defined as its primary task—the task which it is created to perform. In making judgements about any organisation, two questions have priority over all others: what is the primary task? How well is it being performed? Rice compared his definition of "primary task" with Bion's definition of "sophisticated task" as the specific task for which the work group meets (1958, p. 229). The primary task is essentially a heuristic concept that allows the ordering of multiple activities. It is possible to construct and compare different organisational models based on the different definitions of its primary task, and to compare the organisations of different enterprises with the same or different primary tasks. The definition of the primary task determines the dominant import–conversion–export system. Lawrence (1985 [1977] p. 236, 1982; Lawrence & Miller, 1976; Lawrence & Robinson, 1975) added clarifications by expanding the definition of primary task to include its explicit distinctions:

> The *normative* primary task—the task that people in an organisation *ought to* pursue.
> The *existential* primary task—the task that people believe they are carrying out.
> The *phenomenal* primary task—the task which is hypothesised that they are engaged in and of which they may not be consciously aware.

Boundary, a key concept derived from open systems theory, forms a significant part of our understanding of GR conferences. In Western society, a high value is placed on individuals developing maturity in controlling the boundary between their inner worlds and the realities of their external environments (Miller & Rice, 1967, p. 269). This idea is central to the concept of open systems in which all living organisms exist in relation to their environments by engaging in continuous transactions with it; individuals and groups, each has a boundary region exercising a regulatory function mediating between the inner world and the environmental systems with which it interacts. Hence, a boundary is not necessarily a line; it could be a region, as an accident and emergency unit is to a hospital, or an intake committee is to a university.

Roles are sets of expected behaviours, rights, and obligations as conceptualised in boundary situations that are concerned with mediating relations between inside and outside. It is commonly understood that the normative primary task of the group requires of people their contribution of activities, their roles. The roles that individuals bring to the task belong inside the boundary of the enterprise; the individuals who provide the roles belong outside. This implies, therefore, that there is a relationship between the enterprise and the individuals who supply roles within it. Role taking involves a relationship between the enterprise as a system and individuals and groups of individuals as systems.

The primary task of *leadership* is to manage relations between an institution and its environment so as to permit optimal performance of the primary task of the institution. At an unconscious level, the leader expresses on behalf of the group the emotions associated with the basic assumption: that is, the primitive unconscious emotions with which groups identify and which might undermine the group and prevent it from working effectively.

Authority is the claim of legitimacy, the justification and right to exercise power and the ability to influence others to do something that they would not have done. Authority is the capacity or a relationship, innate or acquired, for exercising ascendancy over others. It is sanctioned, institutionalised power.

Sociotechnical systems (STS) is an approach to complex organisational "work design" that recognises the interaction between "people" and "technology" in workplaces. The term refers to the interaction between society's complex infrastructures and human behaviour, in so far as society itself, and most of its substructures, are complex sociotechnical systems. The term *sociotechnical systems* was coined in the 1960s by Trist (1981), Trist and Bamforth (1951), and Emery (1959). Sociotechnical systems theory is concerned with the social aspects of people and society and technical aspects of organisational structure and processes. Sociotechnical refers to the interrelatedness of *social* and *technical* aspects of an organisation that seeks *joint optimisation*, a shared emphasis on achievement of both excellence in technical performance and quality in people's work lives through designing different kinds of organisation in which relationships between sociological and technical elements lead to the emergence of productivity and well-being.

Environment is a later extension to the theory of individuals and groups as systems. Socio-ecological theory includes the evolution of the environment and the consequences of this evolution for the constituent systems that involves going beyond the concept of motivation and the question of sufficient conditions of behaviour. The theory of socio-ecology asserts that the conditions of motivation and sufficient conditions of behaviour are in continuous flux between the individual and the social field. Sometimes, the individual freely chooses goals, purposes, and ideals and the means to pursue them, at other times, individuals choose the means and the ends because the social fabric has left them little choice. The system and its environment have their own identities, but are mutually determinative and, hence, are changing each other's identities. In GR, we are concerned with the conditions conducive to creativity and the micro-climate required to develop and nurture creative minds.

Representation/delegation, that is, exercising authority on behalf of others, lies at the heart of the democratic process and is the assignment of authority and responsibility to another person or group to represent views or carry out specific activities. The person or group that delegates remains accountable for the outcome of the delegated work. Delegation empowers the person or group delegate to make decisions, that is, shift decision-making authority from one organisational level to a lower one. Delegation is regarded as good, saves effort, helps in building skills, and motivates people.

Structure and design elements of group relations conferences

Over the years, group relations conferences in their design have comprised some or all of the following elements: small study groups, groups of up to twelve people and a consultant, studying the behaviour of small groups as it happens; large study groups, groups comprising the whole membership of a conference that might range between thirty and seventy people working with three or four consultants whose purpose is to study the behaviour of large groups as it happens; intergroup events, events in which the conference membership independently sub-divides into smaller groups to work on themes of their choice and to study the nature of the relationships and relatedness of each of the groups to each other (the intergroup event is sometimes called the visiting exercise, which is designed for exploring intergroup dynamics and issues related to communication between groups); institutional event, an event like the intergroup event in which established independent groups examine their own interrelationships as well as their relationships with the staff groups, thus making the event fully institutional. In recent conferences, this event has been termed the world event, or the sustainable society event.

All GR conferences have review and application groups, which provide members with opportunities for reflecting, first, on the conference experiences and, second, on the application of their conference learning to their back-home organisations. Review and application groups are sometimes called consultation syndicates, in which members give and receive consultancy about their current leadership work in teams, units, and organisations and across organisations. Finally, GR conferences have opening and closing plenaries, and sometimes plenaries at mid-points in the conference. These plenaries allow for the exploration of experiences of entering, joining, and leaving the conference.

Consultative stance

The *consultative stance* of the staff of GR conferences adds an important defining difference to other conferences that are centred on groups. Consultant staff, in the main, work in the transference and countertransference for which an extended training is required; they are skilled in interpreting group unconscious dynamics, mindful always of working within psychological boundaries and within the boundaries of time and space, clear about working within role and task and working with group-as-a-whole, not individual, phenomena. This point differentiates GR from other forms of work with groups: staff are capable of generating working hypotheses in group and organisational contexts, that is, a tentative working hypothesis based on what is known so far, staff are in a position of curiosity and "not knowing", following Bion's advice to eschew "memory and desire" (i.e., not to influence the learning process by imposing one's own agenda), and they would be able to tolerate "negative capability", which is tolerating not knowing or accepting inaction while learning is going on (i.e., giving up the need to have brilliant students, adoring clients, etc.).

Applications and innovations

An analysis of the GR field reveals the presence of several different forms of GR conferences. GR conferences, events, approaches, and elements around the world naturally have altered, reshaped and developed over time. The dynamics evident in conferences depend on where in the world the conference is located (www.grouprelations. com). Whatever is current in the organisational, social, and political contexts comes into the conference and the conference, therefore, informs about the state of the members' own institutions and society and their particular preoccupations. In addition to the contributions made by the early pioneers, there have been significant influences on the development of group relations as a method of investigation that comes from the purposes, cultures, and values of different types of institutions that sponsor group relations work.

Group relations—the experiential study of group and organis-ational processes—has influenced social science research. It offers additional ways of collecting and analysing data and knowledge creation and dissemination. Especially relevant is GR's understanding and working with unconscious processes (e.g., Menzies 1960, Menzies Lyth, 1988, 1989, 1998, and Jaques' 1951, 1955 conceptualisations of social defences against anxiety). "Learning from experience" methods are now applied to many forms of social science investigative pro-cesses (Abraham, 2011; Child, 2009; Hills & Child, 2000). GR work has been introduced to organisations suchas universities, clinics, insti-tutes, and membership organisations, leading to cross-fertilisation of ideas and other mutual beneficial influences. In some cases, these institutions, by sponsoring GR conferences, hope to reshape them and their societies—politically, culturally, economically, and socially.

Group relations as a movement tends to be self-authorising and it has a poor record of critiqued analysis. As a force for change, GR requires more published critical research. It rests on sound investi-gative traditions, but is criticised for its attempts to bring different worlds together—the mystical and the organisational (Tarnas, 1991). Consequently, conversations in the GR network often sound like people talking to themselves, perhaps as a reaction to the general suspiciousness towards it by traditional research investigators.

Conferences focused on the work of GR conferences have been held in Oxford, Spa, Melbourne (twice), Maryland, and in Belgirate, Italy. The first of the Belgirate conferences (2003) was organised by Avi Nutkevitch of OFEK, a GR organisation in Israel, and Mannie Sher of the Tavistock Institute of Human Relations, and continues today to be managed by OFEK, the A. K. Rice Institute, and the Tavistock Institute. The primary task of this conference was to review and explore the theory and design, taking up roles in group relations conferences and the application of learning derived there from. The Belgirate conferences, as they have come to be known, are intended as a space not normally available during group relations conferences themselves to review and explore dilemmas and questions that lie at the heart of group relations work. These conferences have produced three volumes on group relations so far (Aram, Baxter, & Nutkevitch, 2009, 2012; Brunner, Nutkevitch, & Sher, 2006). They attest to the vibrancy of group relations conference work around the world. It is understood that the organisers of Oxford, Spa, Melbourne, Maryland, and now the Belgirate conferences, through their own authority, made the conferences self-authorising, signalling that the authority to act in the arena of world group relations would lie within its network.

Conclusion

Over the years, innovative elements have been introduced into the group relations conference design, notably William Halton's marketplace event, and the resource management event (Halton, 2004, 2010); Gordon Lawrence's social dreaming matrix (SDM) (Lawrence, 1998) (see Chapter Six of this book), and many others which are mostly published in the volumes of the Belgirate conferences book series. These and other innovations underline the importance in the GR method of integrated experiential and action learning approaches to group, organisational, and environmental challenges. They are based on learning derived from here-and-now experience and future-orientated action-based learning that participants implement in their home institutions and societies. GR, as a method, like others, might be prone to processes of institutionalisation, but we hope we have demonstrated here the responsiveness of the GR method to the learning needs of individuals and organisations for new ways of understanding and dealing with uncertainties, anxieties, and attacks on authority of leadership roles and membership roles at work and in society. Traditions have weakened as they have strengthened. The GR method provides opportunities for developing new meaning in changing and paradoxical contexts.

References

Abraham, F. (2011). New inter-organisational forms for UK local government partnership delivery. In: P. Lapointe, J. Pelletier, J., &

F. Vaudreuil (Eds), *Different Perspectives on Work Changes* (pp. 103–109). Quebec: Université Laval.

Allport, G. W. (1948). Foreword. In: K. Lewin (Ed.), *Resolving Social Conflict* (pp. vi–xi). London: Harper & Row.

Aram, E. (2010). The aesthetics of group relations. A talk given at the AK Rice Institute's 40th anniversary symposium, Chicago, Ilinois. Accessed at: www.tavinstitute.org/lectures_and_presentations/podcast/%e2%80%98the-aesthetics-of-group-relations%e2%80%99/.

Aram, E. (2011). Introduction to complexity. A talk given as part of the TIHR lunchtime food for thought series. Accessed at: www.tavinstitute.org/lectures_and_presentations/video/an-introduction-to-complexity-theory/.

Aram, E., Baxter, R. & Nutkevitch, A. (Eds.) (2009). *Adaptation and Innovation: Theory, Design and Role-Taking in Group Relations Conferences and their Applications, Volume II.* Karnac: London.

Aram, E., Baxter, R., & Nutkevitch, A. (Eds.) (2012). *Tradition, Creativity, and Succession in the Global Group Relations Network, Volume III.* London: Karnac.

Armstrong, D. (1992). Names, thoughts and lies: the relevance of Bion's later writing for understanding experience in groups. *Free Associations, 3*(26): 261–282.

Armstrong, D. (1997). The 'institution in the mind': reflections on the relationship of psycho-analysis to work with institutions. *Free Associations,* 7I(41): 1–14.

Bion, W. R. (1948–1951). Experiences in groups, I–VII. *Human Relations, 1*(4). Reprinted in: Bion, W. R. (1961). *Experiences in Groups and Other Papers.* London: Tavistock.

Bion W. R. (1952). Group dynamics: a re-view. *International Journal of Psychoanalysis, 33*: 235–47. Reprinted in: M. Klein. P. Heimann, & R. Money-Kyrle (Eds.), *New Directions in Psychoanalysis* (pp. 220–239). London: Tavistock, 1955.

Bion, W. R. (1961). *Experiences in Groups and Other Papers.* London: Tavistock.

Bion, W. R. (1970). *Attention and Interpretation.* London: Tavistock.

Bion, W. R. (1985a). Container and contained. In: A. D. Colman & M. H. Geller (Eds.), *Group Relations Reader 2* (pp. 127–133). Washington, DC: A. K. Rice Institute.

Bion, W. R. (1985b). *All My Sins Remembered and the Other Side of Genius.* Abingdon: Fleetwood Press.

Bridger, H., & Higgin, G. (1964). The psychodynamics of an inter-group experience. *Human Relations, 17*: 391–446. Also in *Tavistock Pamphlet No. 10.* Tavistock Institute of Human Relations, 1965.

Brunner, L., Nutkevitch, A., & Sher, M. (2006). *Group Relations Conferences: Reviewing and Exploring Theory, Design, Role-Taking and Application. Volume I.* London: Karnac.

Brunner, L. D., Perini, M., & Vera, E. (2009). Italian group relations conferences: between adaptation and innovation. In: E. Aram, R. Baxter, & A. Nutkevitch (Eds.), *Adaptation and Innovation* (pp. 73–88). London: Karnac.

Child, C. (2009). Intervening to support the development of partnership capacity and performance at strategic levels in local governance arenas. Unpublished Thesis.

Emery, F. (1959). *Characteristics of Socio-Technical Systems.* London: Tavistock Institute, Document 527.

Follett, M. P. (1920). *The New State.* London: Longmans, Green.

Follett, M. P. (1973) *Dynamic Administration: the Collected Papers of Mary Parker Follett* (pp. 103–116), Elliott M. Fox & L. Urwick (Eds.). London: Pitman.

Freud, S. (1915c). Instincts and their vicissitudes. *S.E., 14*: 237–258. London: Hogarth.

Freud S. (1921c). *Group Psychology and the Analysis of the Ego. S.E., 18*: 67–143. London: Hogarth.

Freud, S. (1925h). Negation. *S.E., 19*: 235–239. London: Hogarth.

Gosling, R. (1979). Another source of conservatism in groups. In: W. G. Lawrence (Ed.), *Exploring Individual and Organisational Boundaries: A Tavistock Open Systems Approach* (pp. 77–86). London: John Wiley [reprinted London: Karnac, 1999].

Gosling, R. (1981). A study of very small groups. In: J. S. Grotstein (Ed.), *Do I Dare Disturb the Universe? A Memorial to Dr Wilfred Bion* (pp. 633–645). New York. Jason Aronson. Also in: A. D. Colman & M. H. Geller (Eds.) (1985). *Group Relations Reader 2* (pp. 151–161). Washington, DC: A. K. Rice Institute.

Gould, L., Stapley, L., & Stein, M. (2001). *The Systems Psychodynamics of Organisations: Integrating the Group Relations Approach, Psychoanalytic and Open Systems Perspectives.* London: Karnac.

Gould, L, Stapley, L., & Stein, M. (2004). *Experiential Learning in Organizations: Applications the Tavistock Group Relations Approach.* London: Karnac.

Halton, W. (2004). By what authority? Psychoanalytical reflections on creativity and change in relation to organizational life. In: C. Huffington, D. Armstrong, W. Halton, L. Hoyle, & J. Pooley (Eds.), *Working Below the Surface: The Emotional Life of Contemporary Organizations* (pp. 107–122). London: Karnac [reprinted 2005, 2007].

Halton, W. (2010). Group relations: achieving a new difference. *Organisational and Social Dynamics*, *10*(2): 219–237.

Harrison, T. & Clarke, D. (1992). The Northfield experiments. *British Journal of Psychiatry*, *160*: 698–708.

Hills, D., & Child C. (2000). *Leadership in Residential Care, Evaluating Qualification Training*. Chichester: John Wiley.

Huffington, C., Armstrong, D., Halton, W., Hoyle, L., & Pooley, J. (Eds.) (2004). *Working Below the Surface: The Emotional Life of Contemporary Organisations*. London: Karnac.

Hupkens, L. (2006). Applying group relations learning to the daily work of consultants and managers: theorists solve the problems they want to; practitioners solve the problems they have to. In: L. D. Brunner, A. Nutkevitch, & M. Sher (Eds.), *Group Relations Conferences* (pp. 138–150). London: Karnac.

Jager, de W., & Sher, M. (2009). Knowing the price of everything and the value of nothing: the application of group relations to organisational development and change with a financial institution. In: E. Aram, R. Baxter, & A. Nutkevitch (Eds.), *Adaptation and Innovation* (pp. 145–161). London: Karnac.

Jaques, E. (1951). *The Changing Culture of a Factory: A Study of Authority and Participation in an Industrial Setting*. London: Tavistock.

Jaques, E. (1955). Social systems as a defence against persecutory and depressive anxiety. In: M. Klein, P. Heimann & R. E. Money-Kyrle (Eds.), *New Directions in Psychoanalysis*. pp. 478–98. London: Tavistock.

Klein, M. (1932). The psychoanalysis of children. In: *The Writings of Melanie Klein* (Volume 3) (pp. 1–24). London: Hogarth Press.

Klein, M. (1957). *Envy and Gratitude*. London: Tavistock [reprinted in: *The Writings of Melanie Klein* (Volume 3) (pp. 176–235). London: Hogarth Press, 1975.

Klein, M. (1959). Our adult and its roots in infancy. In: M. Klein, *Envy and Gratitude and Other Works (1946–1963)* (pp. 247–263), London: Hogarth Press.

Lawrence, W. G. (1977). Management development: ideals, images and realities. *Journal of European Industrial Training*, *1*(2): 21–25. Also in: A. D. Colman & M. H. Geller (Eds.), *Group Relations Reader 2* (pp. 231–240). Washington, DC: A. K. Rice Institute, 1985.

Lawrence, W. G. (Ed.) (1979). *Exploring Individual and Organisational Boundaries*. Chichester: Wiley [reprinted London: Karnac, 1999].

Lawrence, W. G. (1982). *Some Psychic and Political Dimensions of Work Experience*. London: Tavistock Institute, Occasional Paper No. 2.

Lawrence, W. G. (1986). A psychoanalytic perspective for understanding organisational life. In: G. Chattopadhyay, Z. Gangee, L. Hunt, & W. G. Lawrence (Eds.), *When the Twain Meet* (pp. 78–101). Allahabad: A. H. Wheeler.

Lawrence, W. G. (1993). Signals of transcendence in large groups as systems. *Group*, *17*(4): 254–266.

Lawrence, W. G. (1997). Centering of the Sphinx for the psychoanalytic study of organisations. Lecture given at the ISPSO conference in Philadelphia, USA, 27 June.

Lawrence, W. G. (1998). *Social Dreaming @ Work*. London: Karnac.

Lawrence, W. G. (2000). *Tongued with Fire, Groups in Experience*. London: Karnac.

Lawrence, W. G., & Miller, E. J. (1976). Epilogue. In: E. J. Miller (Ed.), *Task and Organisation* (pp. 361–366). Chichester: John Wiley.

Lawrence, W. G., & Robinson, P. (1975). An innovation and its implementation: issues of evaluation, Document No. CASR 1069, Tavistock Institute of Human Relations (unpublished).

Lahav, Y. (2009). Exploring Jewish identity, belonging and leadership through the lens of group relations: reflections and challenges. In: E. Aram, R. Baxter, & A. Nutkevitch (Eds.), *Adaptation and Innovation* (pp. 163–177). London: Karnac.

Le Bon, G. (1895)[1960]. *The Crowd: A Study of the Popular Mind*. New York: Viking Press.

Lewin, K. (1947). Frontiers in group dynamics: concept, method and reality in social sciences; social equilibria and social change. *Human Relations*, *1*: 5–41.

Litvin, I., & Bonwitt, G. (2006). Sexual abuse: application and adaptation of basic group relations concepts, technique and culture to a specific social issue. In: L. D. Brunner, A. Nutkevitch, & M. Sher (Eds.), *Group Relations Conferences* (pp. 47–60). London: Karnac.

Mayo, E. (1933). *The Human Problems of an Industrial Civilization*. New York: Macmillan, London: Routledge & Kegan Paul.

McDougall, W. (1920). *The Group Mind*. Cambridge: Cambridge University Press.

Menzies, I. (1960). A case study in the functioning of social systems as a defence against anxiety. *Human Relations*, *13*: 95–121. Reprinted as Tavistock Pamphlet No. 3, Tavistock Institute (1961) and in I. Menzies-

Lyth (1988) *Containing Anxiety in Institutions* (pp. 43–85). London: Free Association Books.

Menzies Lyth, I. (1988). *Containing Anxiety In Institutions: Selected Essays.* Volume 1. London: Free Association Books.

Menzies Lyth, I. (1989). *The Dynamics of the Social. Selected Essays.* Volume 2. London: Free Association Books.

Menzies Lyth, I. (1990). A psychoanalytical perspective on social institutions. In: E. Trist & H. Murray (Eds.), *The Social Engagement of Social Science* (Volume I) (pp. 404–464). London: Free Association Books.

Miller, E. J. (1959). Technology, territory and time: the internal differentiation of complex production systems. *Human Relations, 12:* 243–272.

Miller, E. J. (1976). The open system approach to organisational analysis, with special reference to the work of A. K. Rice. In: G. Hofstede, & M. Samikassem (Eds.), *European Contributions to Organisation Theory* (pp. 43–61). ASSEN/Amsterdam: Von Gorchum.

Miller, E. J. (1983). Work and creativity. *Occasional Paper No. 6.* London: Tavistock Institute of Human Relations.

Miller, E. J. (1990a). Experiential learning in groups I: the development of the Leicester Model. In: E. Trist & H. Murray (Eds.), *The Social Engagement of Social Science, Vol. 1. The Socio-Psychological Perspective* (pp. 165–185). London. Free Association Books.

Miller, E. J. (1990b). Experiential learning in groups II: recent developments in dissemination and application. In: E. Trist & H. Murray (Eds.), *The Social Engagement of Social Science, Vol. 1. The Socio-Psychological Perspective* (pp. 186–198). London: Free Association Books.

Miller, E. J. (1993a). *From Dependency to Autonomy: Studies in Organisation & Change.* London: Free Association Books.

Miller, E. J. (1993b). The human dynamic. In: R. Stacey (Ed.), *Strategic Thinking and the Management of Change: International Perspectives on Organisational Dynamics* (pp. 98–116). London: Kogan-Page.

Miller, E. J. (1995). Integrated rural development: a Mexican experiment. From the archives: *Occasional Paper No. 1.* London: Tavistock Institute.

Miller, E. J. (1997). Effecting organisational change in large systems: a collaborative consultancy approach. In: J. Neumann, K. Kellner, & A. Dawson-Shepherd (Eds.), *Developing Organisational Consultancy* (pp. 187–212). London: Routledge.

Miller, E. J. & Rice, A. K. (1967). *Systems of Organisation: Task and Sentient Systems and their Boundary Control.* London: Tavistock.

Nutkevitch, A., & Sher, M. (2004). Group relations conferences: reviewing and exploring theory, design, role-taking and application. *Organisational and Social Dynamics, 4*(1): 107–115.

Rice, A. K. (1958). *Productivity and Social Organisation: The Ahmadabad Experiment*. London: Tavistock [reprinted New York: Garland, 1987].

Rice, A. K. (1963). *The Enterprise and its Environment*. London: Tavistock.

Rice, A. K. (1965). *Learning for Leadership: Interpersonal and Intergroup Relations*. London: Tavistock[reprinted London: Karnac, 1999].

Rice, A. K. (1969). Individual, group and inter-group processes. *Human Relations*, 22: 565–584.

Sher, M. (2003). From groups to group relations: Bion's contribution to the Tavistock–'Leicester' Conferences. In: R. M. Lipgar & M. Pines (Eds.), *Building on Bion: Branches. Contemporary Developments and Applications of Bion's Contributions to Theory and Practice* (pp. 109–144). London: Jessica Kingsley.

Sher, M. (2009). Splits, extrusion and integration: the impact of 'potential space' for group relations and sponsoring institutions. *Organisational and Social Dynamics*, 9(1): 138–154.

Tarnas, R. (1991). *The Passion of the Western Mind*. Reading: Pimlico.

Trist, E. (1981). The evolution of socio-technical systems: a conceptual framework and an action research programme. In: A. van de Ven & W. Joy (Eds.), *Perspectives on Organisational Design and Behaviour* (pp. 1–67). New York: Wiley Interscience.

Trist, E., & Bamforth, K. (1951). Some social and psychological consequences of the longwall method of coal-getting. *Human Relations*, 4: 3–38.

Turquet, P. (1975). Threats to indentity in the large group. In: L. Kreeger (Ed.), *The Large Group: Dynamics and Therapy* (pp. 85–144). London. Constable [reprinted London: Karnac, 1994].

Turquet, P. (1985). Leadership: the individual and the group. In: A. Colman & M. Geller (Eds.), *Group Relations Reader 2* (pp. 71–87). Washington, DC: A. K. Rice Institute.

Viswanath, R. (2009). Identity, leadership and authority: experiences in application of group relations concepts for Dalit empowerment in India. In: E. Aram, R. Baxter, & A. Nutkevitch (Eds.), *Adaptation and Innovation* (pp. 179–195). London: Karnac.

Wasdell, D. (1997). Tavistock Review. Self and society. *Journal of the Association for Humanistic Psychology, May*: 1–6.

Socioanalytic dialogue

Bruno Boccara

Motivation

Policy failures and discontent

P olicy makers worldwide seem to be increasingly confronted
with popular protests, whose intensity and suddenness they
often fail to anticipate. Widely divergent explanations as to the
causes suggest that they might also be failing to sufficiently grasp all
the underlying issues behind these protests. Simultaneously, citizens
appear dismayed and repulsed by the political tension and policy
paralysis often gripping their societies. Examples include the dramatic
increase in polarisation in countries such as Chile, Israel, and Nigeria,
citizens' fears and despair in response to the debt crisis and resulting
fiscal tightening in Europe, and the erosion of trust between youth-led
democratisation advocates and Islam-based political groups in North
Africa. These developments point towards the need for a better understanding of the underlying psychosocial dynamics as a prerequisite to
being able to successfully and collectively address them.

The examples above highlight a worrisome level of discontent
with policies. Furthermore, they suggest a high level of anxieties.
These are mostly a consequence of the profound changes induced by

a rapidly evolving social and economic landscape. These anxieties matter because increasingly regressed social defences are likely to be mobilised in response. As manifestation of large group unconscious dynamics, social defences are likely to be poorly assessed and understood. As such, their impact is likely to be significant precisely when policy makers are at a loss understanding resistance to change and disaffection with policies.

Policies "hijacked" as social defences in Argentina

We now turn to motivating the idea that policies can be used as social defences.

Argentina used to be one of the most advanced economies. The memory of this golden age left the nation with a "country romance" of being European-like. In light of traumatic recent political and economic circumstances (e.g., hyperinflation, "Dirty War", the Falklands War), the idealised representation of being European-like meant the existence of a country-level grandiose fantasy. As such, following hyperinflation and the collapse of the military dictatorship, the adoption of a Currency Board in 1989 as a mechanism to restore macroeconomic stability also became a way of rescuing the grandiose fantasy. Societies, like organisations, function at both conscious and unconscious levels. As soon as the Currency Board was established, the guaranteed convertibility of the Argentine peso—at equal parity to the US dollar—enabled an artificially high standard of living, with, for example, the middle class once again able to afford shopping trips to Europe. This instantly enabled the country to regain its pride by reversing a series of recent narcissistic injuries.

However, the Currency Board was a huge gamble at the time, since the central bank did not have sufficient international reserves to guarantee convertibility. Thus, when the policy was initially implemented, the authorities took a huge bet on the faith of the Argentine population in its sustainability. But with the adoption of a living standard commensurate with their country romance, fears of collective narcissistic injuries receded as, once again, Argentina could bask in the glory of its idealised mental representation. This time period is remembered as *la plata dulce*, or easy money.

Unsurprisingly, fiscal issues resurfaced, ultimately leading to the largest sovereign default in history. Identification with wealthier countries probably impeded the adjustment process. Abandoning the Currency Board, thus devaluing the currency, was resisted, and, therefore, delayed. This was not only because it resulted in a painful adjustment in relative prices, but also because it meant abandoning a social defence, which played an essential role in the ability to maintain a grandiose fantasy and avoid a collective narcissistic injury. The Minister of Finance during this time period, D. Cavallo, who, as the original architect of the Currency Board, had been brought back by President de la Rua to "rescue" the economy, instinctively must have felt this. Seemingly perplexed at having failed to anticipate the vigorous resistance to the devaluation, he stated, "Argentina was drowning in a cup of water".[1]

Therefore, the exchange rate policy had been "hijacked" by unconscious psychosocial dynamics in the sense that, having become a social defence, it served a purpose other than its purely economic function. The intensity of the resistance to change was precisely due to the socioanalytic role of the policy.

Unless socioanalytic dimensions of policies are acknowledged and understood, it remains likely that policy formulation and implementation will continue to be carried out in a vacuum, eliciting resistance to change, which will often be misdiagnosed. A framework incorporating psychoanalytically informed thinking and technical interventions when formulating and implementing public policies is, therefore, needed.

Theoretical framework and methodology

"Country-in-the mind" and socioanalytic map

Two basic principles of socioanalytic dialogue are (Boccara, 2010):

1.   Policy outcomes are influenced by social defences. The latter are, by definition, mobilised to fend off large group anxieties.
2.   Social defences are a function of shared societal narratives, called "country romance".

The notion that psychosocial dynamics can lead to policies being diverted from their original purpose is completely absent from public policy debates. As such, the idea of policies being used as social defences is one of the main contributions of socioanalytic dialogue. As a consequence, socioanalytic dialogue is based upon applying the concept of social systems as a defence against anxieties to the country level. As such, social defence is, in my view, one of two fundamental concepts that leaders and policy makers need to be made aware of in order to be able to understand how country-level psychodynamics issues have an impact on policies.

Societal behaviours are best understood in reference to shared narratives (Akerlof & Kranton, 2010; Akerlof & Shiller, 2009). As such, socioanalytic dialogue approaches countries, or cultures, as if they had character. This is similar to how Long (2008) approaches organisations. Furthermore, psychoanalytically informed organisational work also uses extensively the concept of "organization in the mind" (Armstrong, 2005). Applying the same idea to entire societies is also itself not new, since it has, for example, already been done in sociology by Benedict (1946) on Japan and by Fanon (1952) on the psychology of colonisation. However, these two authors did not focus on country-level unconscious dynamics.

Socioanalytic dialogue relies on two tasks, that of identifying:

- the internal mental representations by subgroups;
- the intergroups' projections and introjections.

The internal mental representations include the residents' perceptions of their country and the kind of society to which they are aspiring. These are respectively called the existing and ideal mental representations. They correspond to the shared narratives mentioned earlier. The intergroups' projections and introjections capture ways in which various sub-groups in a country view one another as well as their perceptions of how others view them. Taken together, the mental representations and intergroup projections and introjections are called the socioanalytic map of the country. It is shown in Figure 14.1.

We now turn to illustrating some applications of the concepts above to various country settings.

In the case of Russia, a significant share of the population, particularly the leadership, might have internalised that only top-down authoritarian approaches can, by successfully spurring innovation and creativity, transform the economy. Although this might reflect

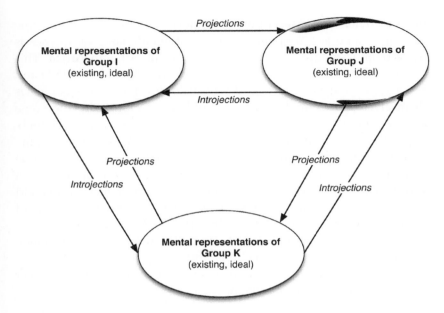

Figure 1. Socioanalytic map of the country. (Source: www.socioanalytic dialogue.org)

political calculations to maintain the *status quo* in the distribution of power, it is likely that deeper psychological forces are also influencing the debate. In a briefing on Russia, *The Economist* (13 March 2010) noted that, "In Russia's history, it is Peter the Great and Stalin that are considered the great modernizers rather than Alexander II, who abolished serfdom, or Mr. Gorbachev, who opened up the country". As such, the "Russia in the mind" might include mental representations of an authoritarian state, which is also idealised. This would, in turn, influence policy choices on modernisation.

    In Sub-Saharan Africa, even in countries where the impact of the slave trade was lessened by the geography, there nevertheless seems to exist a profound humiliation. This humiliation is in relationship to the huge scars that are, in large part, the consequences of the historical interactions between European traders and colonisers and the local populations. To the detriment of the African continent's ability to move forward, the humiliation often remains repressed. Recent history and portrayal of Africa might have increased, through introjection, the intensity of these feelings. This is facilitating the emergence of social defences consistent with high levels of anxiety, and, in some regions, shame and despair. A major, but avoidable, consequence is the economic failure of some countries in Sub-Saharan Africa. This might be interpreted, as has already been done by Kabou (1991) and Etounga-Manguelle (1991), as a refusal to develop by the countries themselves. For example, poverty could unconsciously have become an internalised component of a nation's identity. Furthermore, there might also be unconscious collusion between Western and some African countries in which the latter may unconsciously fulfil a role on behalf of the West. Perceptions of their performance can become a way to validate other countries' sense of triumphalism and shield them from narcissistic injuries. This illustrates the application of projective identification to countries. This is the second of the two fundamental concepts that leaders and policy makers need to be made aware of: intergroups' projections and introjections might induce some populations within a country, or even entire countries, to act upon what is projected into them.

Policies in the age of contempt

Recent and rapid changes in the world, especially the global wave of dissent of 2011, could allow for an increased readiness to acknowledge the significant impact that societal unconscious processes might have on policies. Policies are the source of most tensions in countries. They also are what connect citizens to the state and to one another. Thus, disagreements on policies often provide fertile ground for large group unconscious dynamics.

As such, socioanalytic dialogue aims at identifying primarily the psychosocial issues and mechanisms that might have an impact on policies. In order to be able to do so, it is necessary to have a conceptual framework of what the linkages between country-level psychosocial dynamics and policies might be. The proposed framework is called: "Policies in the age of contempt" (Boccara, 2011a).

The framework incorporates the two basic principles of socioanalytic dialogue mentioned earlier. The specificity of the "Policies in the age of contempt" framework is due to the fact that it explicitly differentiates between two sources of anxieties: perverse societal dynamics, and structural changes in the environment. It is this specific feature

that renders the framework particularly relevant to today's psychosocial dynamics.

Since social defences are mobilised to fend off anxieties, one of the
main tasks of socioanalytic dialogue is to identify the anxieties, be
they already existing or induced by a policy being either proposed or
implemented.

First, there are anxieties induced by structural changes in the environment. They have already been mentioned earlier in reference to
major changes taking place in social and economic structures all over
the world. These changes have been aptly characterised by Stapley
(2006) as the "death of a way of life". From a socioanalytic dialogue
perspective, the decrease in connectedness between individuals due to
the increased preponderance of transaction-driven instrumental relationships particularly stands out. Connectedness's gradual disappear-
ance is experienced as destroying the containing function of society.
As a consequence, individuals might feel that their identity is under
threat and react accordingly. This, in turn, becomes one of the most
important psychosocial mechanisms leading a society to mobilise
regressed social defences.

Second, there are anxieties induced by perverse societal dynamics.
In a perverse social system, individuals are often treated with
contempt and denigrated as they are used instrumentally to satisfy the
needs of others (Long, 2008). Anxieties stemming from being denigrated, meaning subject to repeated narcissistic injuries, are of a different nature than those stemming from structural changes in the
environment. While the latter are perceived as affecting everyone in
the same way, anxieties induced by perverse societal dynamics,
because they only affect specific sub-groups, are often experienced as
personal attacks. As such, the social defences mobilised to fend them
off, including by rejecting the perverse dynamics themselves, can have
a sudden and significant impact on policies. Once group revulsion at
the perverse dynamics reaches a certain threshold, social defences
may become drastically altered as a consequence of groups deliber-
ately choosing to abandon the system. This is called "Exit".

The framework is illustrated in Figure 14.2.

We now turn briefly to the events leading to the Tunisian revolution, as they illustrate particularly well the framework.

Mohamed Bouazizi's suicide by self-immolation was an individual
act of despair rather than a planned political act. Nevertheless, it

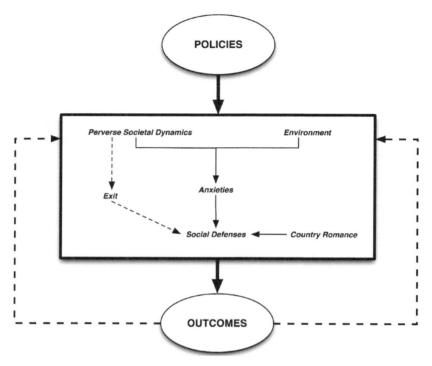

Figure 14.2. Policies in the age of contempt. (Source: www.socioanalytic dialogue.org)

triggered a revolution, only ten days elapsing between Bouazizi's death and President Ben Ali abandoning power and leaving Tunisia. Furthermore, the events that took place were not simply unexpected, but, rather, as shown by Benslama (2011), who analyses the events from a Lacanian perspective, inconceivable. Mental representations, both within the Arab world and outside, simply did not include groups able to take charge of their destiny and overthrow deeply entrenched dictatorships.

The far-reaching consequences of Bouazizi's act imply that there had to be, almost instantly, a strong identification with Bouazizi's state of mind. Therefore, his experiencing of the situation must also have been that of much of the disenfranchised population in Tunisia and, ultimately, elsewhere in the Arab world. As Ben Jelloun (2011) suggests, Bouazizi's humiliation, powerlessness, and disgust at the ways he was treated were also felt by many of his compatriots. As underscored by bloggers, for example Ben Mhenni (2011), and opposition politicians, the abuses of the power structures became the main factor behind citizens' mobilisation. The elites experienced pleasure at the expense of denigrated others, whose existence they were incapable of genuinely recognising. From socioanalytic dialogue's perspective, one of the most important characteristics of the perverse state of mind that flourished under Ben-Ali's regime is the contempt for the general population that individuals in power felt and shamelessly expressed. These aspects of object relations at the level of the entire society and their behavioural implications are precisely what the framework aims at capturing.

Bouazizi's act allowed individuals to repossess dignity, at a time when it was thought to have been lost forever. Empowered by the realisation that one could do away with the shame that one had intro-jected while in the role of the denigrated object, individuals deliber-ately chose to no longer participate in the system. This "Exit" is symbolised by two slogans that circled the globe: "Degage" (get out) and "Game over".

The level of perversion in Tunisia's Ben-Ali was so extreme that it allowed, almost overnight, powerful identifications to force social changes. As such, the same mechanism is not applicable elsewhere. Nevertheless, in several countries, a significant share of the popula-tion experiences the society as unfair and dysfunctional. Whether these individuals decide to react and, if so, how, can vary greatly. For example, "Exit" can signify a forced breakdown of the system through mass protests as in Tunisia, a retreat away from it with symptoms such as voters' apathy or disillusionment, or enactments of potentially dangerous fantasies. Regardless, "Exit" is likely to have a significant impact on social defences and, therefore, on policies.

As such, the framework is useful to think about psychosocial dynamics and policies in a world where perverse societal dynamics increasingly dominate.

Sequencing principles and "analytic" attitude at the country level

This section draws on Boccara (2010). Social defences are different from most psychological aspects traditionally encountered in econom-ics and public policy, since they are mostly unconscious. Unlike the consumption goods in economics, for which substitution or abstention are possible alternatives, there are no alternatives as far as anxieties are concerned: they must be alleviated. This provides the rationale for the first sequencing principle: for each anxiety resulting in a lack of sufficient containment of the society, social defences will be activated sequentially, until one is found capable to address it sufficiently well.

In most cases, it can be assumed that the defences in each sequence will be of an increasingly regressed nature. Freud talks of multiple determinism rather than sequential determinism, going along with the idea that the unconscious has no time. The idea of social defences mobilised in sequence may be right at the societal level, but this has not been established. However, this is a principle, rather than a theorem. For modelling purposes and discussions with policy makers, it is best to treat the mobilisation of social defences in a sequential manner. Sequential activation is what is seemingly observed in societies (e.g., a sequence of events leading to a deterioration in the political situation in response to policies met with resistance).

Furthermore, a policy can be used for social defence purposes rather than its stated objectives. This provides the rationale for the second sequencing principle, which is concerned with the transmission mechanisms leading a policy to fail: once basic needs are met, policies that can potentially satisfy social defence needs will be used for that purpose first, and it is only once the components of a policy that can be used as social defences have been mobilised for that purpose that agents will be able to allow the policy to work towards achieving its stated objectives.

These two principles cannot capture all the nuances of psychodynamics. They are only intended to create a bridge between psychodynamics and economics or public policy by providing guidance to modellers and policy makers. Together, the two principles capture the key characteristics of social defences that are relevant to policy making. These are: (i) the fact that they must be activated until the corresponding anxieties are sufficiently alleviated; and (ii) their primacy over other psychosocial behavioural responses. The two principles can explain seemingly irrational psychosocial dynamics such as a policy failing once it is used as a social defence, or policy paralysis once increasingly regressed social defences are activated.

The focus, so far, has been on the public policy relevance of selected concepts of psychoanalytic theory. We now turn to the applicability of the psychoanalytic process at the country level. As such, this section discusses what an "Analytical attitude at the country level" should entail by arguing, echoing principles increasingly emphasised by psychoanalysis since Kohut (1959), for empathic ability to be communicated to all sub-groups to allow each one of them to increase their awareness and understanding of all the key intergroups projections and introjections. Structural change, whether through economic reforms or social legislation, is often the impetus behind policies. This does not, however, imply that the concept of therapeutic action can be automatically extended to a country or its policies. However, it is a useful frame of reference to conceptualise what country-level change might entail. One way of approaching this in a manner consistent with the framework presented earlier is to characterise it as the increased ability of a country, through a shared understanding, to address psychodynamics issues that might be hampering it from reaching its policy goals. Internalisation and ownership of policies is widely considered a prerequisite to a nation's success in enabling far-reaching transformations. Echoing Winnicott (1965), socioanalytic dialogue refers to a nation finding its "true self". This formulation captures almost perfectly the socioanalytic dialogue rationale for promoting psychoanalytically inspired interventions in the formulation and implementation of policies.

Psychoanalytically informed ideas on listening and communicating techniques are also relevant (e.g., Albrecht Schwaber, 1998). Policies are often debated in settings (e.g., debates aimed at influencing political views, asymmetric processes between countries and their donors at times of crisis) that encourage what Arlow (1995) called "stilted listening". Although the contexts differ, psychoanalysis's natural appreciation of the subtleties of listening provides valuable insights that can, in turn, be applied to the policy-making realm. For example, one can purposely listen to what citizens are expressing without preconceptions, as if forgetting the context, in order to avoid missing alternative or hidden feelings. This is especially important when issues susceptible to triggering anxieties are brought up.

The complexities of each country are determined by that country's history, in particular its traumas, and its culture. These complexities can often be disentangled through inferring the existing intergroups' projections and introjections. Sub-groups' mental representation of others can often highlight how history and culture left their mark on a society while intergroups' projections and introjections will often presage conflicts and resistance to change. As such, they must not only be understood, but also, as indicators of existing or future splits in the society, be empathically communicated to others. In order to do so, it is necessary to experience, as if being transported into someone else's mind, the mental affects of each of the sub-groups. In other words, one needs to be able to travel along all the projections and introjections shown in the socioanalytic map of the country. Doing so successfully requires empathic availability. Therefore, the analytic attitude at the country level is defined as follows: unrestricted willingness and ability to temporarily experience, in order to be able to communicate them to others, each of the intergroups' projections and introjections as if they were our own.

Socioanalytic policy dialogue groups

Socioanalytic dialogue requires collecting and interpreting psychosocial data to infer the socioanalytic dialogue map of the country, which, in turn, informs the collection and interpretation of policy-specific psychosocial data. Group work with individual representatives of various sub-groups, or socioanalytic policy dialogue groups, is the technique of choice to infer the shared societal unconscious (individual level unconscious derivatives are not of interest and must, therefore, be differentiated from the societal level ones). Other data sources include historical material, legends and myths, media, and individual interviews.

The sampling strategy for socioanalytic policy dialogue groups is no different than that of focus groups used in opinion surveys (e.g., political campaign). However, the groups are expected to meet several times. The robustness of the societal unconscious across representative individuals is such that socioanalytic policy dialogue groups can be conducted with groups of approximately ten individuals. Sampling size is, therefore, unlikely to be a constraint. However, important decisions may follow and policy makers must have confidence in the results. As such, it is paramount to test the robustness of the derivatives of the societal unconscious by comparing data across various samples. Furthermore, some elements may be repressed in presence of others and capturing accurate psychosocial dynamics is likely to require initial segmentation of the sample by sub-groups.

Socioanalytic dialogue favours working with the notion of a societal unconscious rather than roles, because, conceptually, this captures all potential affects and defences (see also Chapter One of this book, on the associative unconscious). Thus, socioanalytic policy dialogue groups are not as structured, in terms of task or time boundaries as group relations events. Nevertheless, although the emphasis remains always on associations, discussions are sometimes organised around specific policy topics. However, great care must be given not to narrow too soon policy-specific discussions. Issues pertaining to a specific policy might have been displaced and themes, seemingly unrelated to a specific policy, could be missed.

Group relations has limited applications to policy-related country work. As emphasised by Kernberg (1980), these groups "do not provide a temporal dimension since they are not subject to certain group processes that take time to develop". They do not incorporate sufficiently the impact of leaders' personalities. They also do not capture adequately the impact of stable societal features and relations between these features and existing conflicts. Group relations can, however, be relevant when evaluating societal roles and issues of identity (Aram, Baxter, & Nutkevitch, 2009).

Unlike the case with individuals or organisations, country dialogue on issues such as culture, history, or psychology does not (except, as shown by Volkan (2006), when group identity is threatened and the society becomes highly regressed) often generate much resistance. This is called resistance diffusion. The intuition behind this is that individuals are almost always able to differentiate between individual and shared identities. As a result, country-specific issues can usually be discussed without individuals immediately experiencing country-level interpretations as personal attacks. A first wall of resistance is breached when individuals are able to hear what is being said. Furthermore, sovereignty and the multiple comparisons that are made worldwide, across various indicators of wellbeing between nations, also contribute to resistance diffusion.

Until now, societal level data on affects, anxieties, and defences has never been collected as part of public policy work. Socioanalytic dialogue's premise is that doing so systematically would not only allow for a better understanding of complex societal dynamics, but could also be used as background for country-level interventions aimed at promoting genuine ownership and internalisation of policies. As such, collecting the relevant data and undertaking dialogue should never be undertaken without an analytic attitude at the country level. Listening for societal unconscious dynamics in a rigid fashion, by selectively focusing on specific aspects, precludes a complete and accurate understanding of societal dynamics.

In order to illustrate the methodological aspects above, what follows describes some of the technical aspects and policy relevant findings of the first socioanalytic policy dialogue group. It was planned and conducted in the Washington, DC area (see "Young professionals and the work place within", www.socioanalytic dialogue.org). The group itself consisted of ten individuals and met nine times for an average of three hours each time over the October 2009–May 2010 period. The goal was to explore young professionals' mental representations of work and of their roles in societies.

The socioanalytic policy dialogue group relied on a combination of experiential learning (participants systematically reflecting on their reactions to what is being said as a way to exploring new meanings), freely flowing discussions (with interpretations which, in turn, had to be validated), and other techniques (e.g., drawings). Thus, the socioanalytic policy dialogue group did not prioritise a specific mode of intervention but rather utilised a variety of interventions (often several during the same meeting), which all had in common their reliance on psychoanalytic principles adapted to groups. The tasks were not strictly defined or adhered to. They were, instead, largely determined each time by the group. Similarly, although participants were aware of boundaries (e.g., choice of topics, meetings not addressing individual unconscious issues), these remained fluid.

One of the most important findings was that what initially seemed to be pride in one's work and organisation was, in fact, the reaction to being validated by others. It was, therefore, a borrowed pride. The majority of participants were able to offset their disillusion, even despair, at work with the fact that outsiders, who had a better than reality perception of the participants' workplace, admired them. Thus, the borrowed pride played a defensive role by facilitating coping at work and allowing the young professionals to find meaning, which otherwise was utterly missing.

Although the data generated by the socioanalytic policy dialogue group were found to be consistent with those of comprehensive workplace surveys (based on much larger data sets and much costlier undertakings), they provided subtler information on mental representations, which the large surveys did not capture. For example, survey questionnaires, regardless of their design, could not have identified that pride in one's work and organisation was, in fact, pride in how one was perceived by others.

This is important, since motivation and, therefore, productivity is affected by the nature of the pride that may exist in the workplace. Genuine pride will have a positive impact on productivity (positive identification with the organisation) whereas "borrowed" pride, playing the role of a coping mechanism or defence, will not.

Country examples

Bolivia is the first country where socioanalytic dialogue was applied (Boccara, 2011b). The work was undertaken in Bolivia while the methodology was still being developed. As such, it constitutes a psychoanalytically based evaluation, as opposed to an intervention, of a country and of its policies. Although there has already been, albeit rarely, policy discussions informed by country-level psychodynamics issues, socioanalytic dialogue interventions on either the entire policy framework or on specific policies have not yet been undertaken. The field is still in its infancy. Thus, in order to illustrate further the methodology, the concluding section discusses, using Chile as an example, the applicability of socioanalytic dialogue to a country.

Undoing traumas in Bolivia

Historical traumas are of particular importance since, by definition, they are events whose intensity is such that societies are unable to adequately address or mourn them. As a result, historical traumas are often accompanied by magical wishes of going back to times prior to their occurrences. These wishes might themselves be expressed by attempts through rituals, words, or thoughts, to symbolically erase what has happened. This symbolic erasing constitutes an undoing. Up until now, Bolivia seems to be unable to adequately mourn its past, in particular developments associated with the exploitation of silver in Potosi. As such, "Undoing Potosi" is the main social defence operating in Bolivia today. As a consequence, the country seems stuck in a regressive search for the identity of origin. This, in turn, translates into policy makers feeling pressured to introduce new policies in a bid to replace all the old ones, as if a panacea to all ills plaguing the country had been found. This never fails to disappoint and the country, in a compulsion to repeat fashion, starts all over again. Each occurrence is always believed, at first, to be the last.

"Undoing Potosi" also led to two startling developments, the 2001 Census and the 2009 Constitution. The 2001 Census questionnaire on ethnic identity only listed pre-Columbian ethnic groups to choose from. It had, therefore, "omitted" the *mestizo* category, to which two thirds of the population belongs. It was followed by the 2009 Constitution, which transformed the Republic of Bolivia into the Plurinational State of Bolivia, comprising exactly the thirty-six original indigenous nations that existed at the time of the arrival of the Spaniards. From a socioanalytic dialogue perspective, the 2001 Census is a precursor to the 2009 Constitution, which, in turn, is considered to be a significant enactment. The 2009 Constitution is the outcome of social defences mobilised in response to wishing to undo, through rebirth, the traumas of the past. Both the Census and the Constitution are, it is hypothesised, in the mind, a complete return to the idealised past during which only pre-Columbian inhabitants occupied the land.

Mestizaje (the mixing of races as a result of the Spanish colonisation) and the subjugation of one group by another imply complex and unstable identifications. For example, victimisation and shame due to the Indian aspects of one's identity co-exist with guilt and, possibly, a wish to repair due to the Spanish aspects of one's identity. As a consequence, the society is often ambivalent. This ambivalence translates into frequent policy reversals and inconsistencies in policies. The resolution of the conflict that emerged from these internalised representations required the collective guilt to be projected outward into a feared, envied, and hated bad object, whose function was to despoil. The fear and hate of this despoiling object was found to be essentially shared by all, irrespective of ethnic affiliation. The phenomenon of convergence of social defences is discussed in Boccara (2011b). Also found in the USA, it is believed to be more prevalent than differences across population groups in most countries would suggest.

The resulting wish to deprive the "other" implies that economics (e.g., access to resources) is perceived as a zero-sum game. This is not conducive to economic growth. The wish to deprive the "other" is also present in politics (e.g., access to power) and in governance (e.g., access to information). This is not conducive to respecting and being able to enforce democratic principles.

Because of *mestizaje*, ethnic affiliations are no longer available as markers of identity and, as a consequence, "remembered" economic and institutional arrangements of the idealised past are instead chosen as substitute markers of identity. As a consequence, resistance to change is high, since there is a propensity to reject policy proposals that are perceived as attacks on the rescued identity. This implies strong preferences for left-leaning economic policies (pre-Columbian Andean societies were based on a welfare system of risk sharing), which are idealised, and for an autocratic state, reminiscent of the times of the Aymara kingdoms and, more particularly, of the Incas.

Understanding the past and creating the future in Chile

Throughout most of 2011, Chile was affected by protracted and some-times violent protests on higher education. In addition, as shown by the most recent Latinobarómetro (2011) survey data, the country appears to be suffering from an internal collapse in basic trust and hope. This suggests the presence of psychosocial dynamics that are likely to be misunderstood and have the potential to have a significant negative impact on the country's policy framework.

For example, the protests could also be the result of an uncon-scious transmission of defiance across generations. The older genera-tion did not (it was impossible) protest against the Pinochet regime and ended up being unable to voice its anger since the transition to democracy, starting with the plebiscite of 1990, went smoothly. Presi-dent Pinera represents the first time a right-leaning political party has been in power again, since the left-leaning Concertación had been power ever since Pinochet had relinquished his. As such, it is quite possible for the current protests by the younger generation, acting on behalf of the older, to be also motivated by their expressing their parents' anger, which had never found a proper outlet during and after the Pinochet years. Curiously, for an education-driven protest, the younger generation chose to come down the streets of Santiago banging pots and pans, exactly as was done during the Pinochet era. The difference is that, during those times, the use of kitchen wares made sense, since the protest was against the liberal economic policies of Pinochet which were squeezing the middle and lower classes' ability to make ends meet (i.e., feed themselves).

Furthermore, as a more advanced economy in Latin America, Chile is more susceptible to the issues brought up in the policies in the age of contempt framework. As the population becomes more assertive, it will be more likely to react to their experiencing the contempt of the elites, the survey pointing to perceptions of elites being unwilling to "share" the wealth they were able to accumulate, in large part because of the widening gap in economic opportunities.

However, contempt is unlikely to constitute the whole explanation, because, in spite of the country being the most successful economy in the continent, Chile is an outlier with most indicators of wellbeing and future expectations coming far below than those of the other countries. The high level of preoccupation with inequality suggests that the population is disgusted with the society and its economic system. This disgust is likely to be the source of the despair, which is strikingly revealed by the data. The survey shows that trust in institutions and in the future is eroding. But something deeper and more worrying must also be occurring, since the survey shows that Chile is also suffering from an erosion of basic trust. Neither disgust with, nor mistrust of, the system can explain this, since they do not automatically lead to individuals losing trust in their neighbours. Once basic trust disappears, a society is unlikely to be able to contain its individuals and anxieties are likely to increase rapidly. This can lead to citizens wholly rejecting what is provided by the state (e.g., health and education policies, judicial system), as the latter becomes a contaminated object. This is a form of "Exit", with citizens essentially disavowing all policies. At this stage, a major policy transmission mechanism, citizens' participation, is missing.

Chile's collective mourning work of some aspects of its past might not yet be sufficiently robust. Unfinished mourning is likely to complicate tremendously the psychosocial environment in which policies are chosen and implemented. Furthermore, since we are discussing issues that are, at least in part, unconscious, they can be difficult for policy makers to identify and, therefore, address.

With the education protests as a background, socioanalytic dialogue work in Chile could allow various constituencies to internalise the nature and role of the existing social defences. This internalisation could, in turn, be the catalyst to a national conversation on the underlying issues. The goal would be to reduce splitting across constituencies and decrease the likelihood that regressed social defences would be mobilised.

Conclusions

This chapter has argued that complex and changing country-level behavioural issues, particularly those related to the societal unconscious, should be assessed and incorporated in public policy analysis. As such, the chapter presented a framework, socioanalytic dialogue, and discussed its main methodological aspects. The chapter has also illustrated the concepts and their applications through several country examples.

The most important conclusions are twofold: countries, like individuals, can be thought of as having character, societal behaviours being best understood in reference to shared narratives, the "country romance"; one of the most significant risks to policies today is having countries, through their institutions, captured by perverse societal dynamics, characterised by society-wide interpersonal relationships whose dominant feature is contempt.

The examples of Bolivia and of Chile illustrate the applicability and potential impact of socioanalytic dialogue. In the case of Bolivia, undertaking work on economic identity would probably be a profound and robust way to set the stage for reparative leadership by assisting various groups in relinquishing victimisation aspects of their identity. In the case of Chile, it would probably contribute towards increasing the capacity of the nation to mourn the causes and consequences of the societal fracture experienced by the country prior to, and during, the Pinochet regime.

More generally, the increased awareness and understanding of country-level psychosocial issues, as long as they are sufficiently internalised, should decrease the need, and, therefore, the likelihood, of societies adopting regressed social defences. This would, in turn, decrease instances of policies failing and, as such, increase the likelihood of countries reaching their policy objectives in a manner consistent with a genuine internalisation and ownership of their goals.

Note

1.   The author was Director of Sovereign Ratings at Standard & Poor's at the time and covered all the events leading to the Argentinian default.

References

Akerlof, G., & Kranton, R. (2010). *Identity Economics: How our Identities Shape our Work, Wages, and Well-Being*. Princeton, NJ: Princeton University Press.

Akerlof, G., & Shiller, R. (2009). *Animal Spirits: How Human Psychology Drives the Economy and Why it Matters for Global Capitalism*. Princeton, NJ: Princeton University Press.

Albrecht Schwaber, E. (1998). From whose point of view? The neglected question in analytic listening. *Psychoanalytic Quarterly, 67*: 645–668.

Aram, E., Baxter, R., & Nutkevitch, A. (Eds.) (2009). *Adaptation and Innovation: Theory, Design, and Role-Taking in Group Relations Conferences and their Applications*. London: Karnac.

Arlow, J. (1995). Stilted listening: psychoanalysis as a discourse. *Psychoanalytic Quarterly, 64*(2): 215–233.

Armstrong, D. (2005). *Organization in the Mind*, R. French (Ed.). London: Karnac.

Benedict, R. (1946). *The Chrysanthemum and the Sword*. New York: Houghton Mifflin, 2002.

Ben Jelloun, T. (2011). *Par le Feu*. Paris: Gallimard.

Ben Mhenni, L. (2011). *Bloguese pour un printemps arabe*. Paris: Editions Indigene.

Benslama, F. (2011). *Soudain la Revolution*. Paris: Editions Denoel.

Boccara, B. (2010). Policy making and its psychoanalytic underpinnings. Paper presented to the ISPSO Annual Meetings, 2010. Accessed at: www.socioanalyticdialogue.org, 20 August 2012.

Boccara, B. (2011a). Policies in the age of contempt. Unpublished paper presented at the United Nations. Accessed at: www.socioanalyticdialogue.org, 20 August 2012.

Boccara, B. (2011b). Undoing traumas in Bolivia. Unpublished paper presented at the CIFAR Annual Meetings. Accessed at: www.socio analyticdialogue.org, 20 August 2012.

Etounga-Manguelle, D. (1991). *L' Afrique a t-elle besoin d' un programme d' ajustement culturel*. Paris: Editions Nouvelles du Sud.

Fanon, F. (1952). *Peau Noire, Masques Blancs*. Paris: Editions du Seuil. English translation: *Black Skin, White Masks*. New York: Grove Press, 2008.

Kabou, A. (1991). *Et si l'Afrique Refusait le Developpement?* Paris: L'Harmattan.

Kernberg, O. (1980). *Regression in Groups, Internal and External Reality*. New York: Jason Aronson.

Kohut, H. (1959). Introspection, empathy, and psychoanalysis: an examination of the relationship between mode of observation and theory. *Journal of American Psychoanalytical Association, 7*: 459–483.

Latinobarómetro, Informe (2011). Santiago de Chile (www.latino-barometro.org) 20.08.2012.

Long, S. (2008). *The Perverse Organization and its Deadly Sins*. London: Karnac.

Stapley, L. (2006). *Globalization and Terrorism: Death of a Way of Life*. London: Karnac.

The Economist (2010). Another great leap forward? 13 March.

Volkan, V. (2006). *Killing in the Name of Identity*. Charlottesville, VA: Pitchstone.

Winnicott, D. W. (1965). Ego distortion in terms of true self and false self. In: *Maturational Processes and the Facilitating Environment* (pp. 140–152). London: Hogarth Press.

CHAPTER FIFTEEN

Wonder and socioanalysis

Alastair Bain

"O" Poem On Being at Soapy Bore

("O" is Wilfred Bion's symbol for ultimate reality)

> Being different.
> How different?
> Can't ask.
> You can but no answer.
> 'O' can be been
> But never known.
>
> Heart of Dreaming
> By its throb.
> Lived
> Not known.
>
> Pages whipped from my hand
> The wind.
> Pages torn
> By the wind.
> And browned

By the riverbed.
Pens disappeared.

Nothing to write with
No pages to write on.
Forced into being.

Log burning
In riverbed
Sit around.
Dreams around.

Tree
Casting shade.
Shade moves
With the sun.
We move
With the Shade.
Around the tree.

And across the riverbed
On burning afternoons
To t'other side.
Where more shade.
We work and play
And in the coolness of evening
Go back to the burning log.
Dreaming around.

Evening pleasure
Walking barefoot in the riverbed.
Middle of the day
Only aboriginal children revel
On the burning sand
And show us the coolness
Under the sand
And point to the water under the riverbed.

Same Being
Many names

Criss crossing origins
But Here

And Now.
Whither?
Not Now.
Later.
Later never arrives
In the Present.

Now
Being.
No names.
Just here.
Heart
Throbbing.

Dreamers
Sleeping in a circle[1]
Around
The burning log
Sand pouring from
Their heads.

Wonders of the galaxy and bush flowers reflected.

(Poem by Alastair Bain, 2012)

The "Heart of Dreaming" conference took place in September 2009. Soapy Bore is part of an Aboriginal community in Utopia, 350 kilometres north-east of Alice Springs, Northern Territory. The conference was held in a dry, sandy riverbed of the Sandover River. There were twelve participants, from Melbourne, Sydney, Hobart, London, and Utopia.

The experience of wonder at the Soapy Bore Conference in 2009 and socioanalysis generally indicates that wonder is about the transformation of being, whether for an individual, group, community, or organisation. At Soapy Bore, this is perhaps most evident because of the extreme conditions that are referred to in the poem, which resulted in us being stripped of things we thought we knew, such as programmes, pencils, paper, and being exposed directly to wonder.

Socioanalysis is "the activity of exploration, consultancy, and action research which combines and synthesises methodologies and theories derived from psycho-analysis, group relations, social systems thinking, organisational behaviour . . . and social dreaming" (Bain, 1999). Socioanalysis is rooted in *wonder*, and, like social dreaming, it is subversive of the establishment order, whether the mind, the group, or what is thought to be known, through always remaining open to exploration and to asking "But what else is there?" besides what is already stated to be known. (Interestingly, Bion never refers to "wonder", although it is at the heart of what he is doing.) To do this requires an unsaturated mind, a mind that Keats identifies as "without any irritable reaching after fact and reason" (Keats, 1817). An unsaturated mind is based in the now, or present. With memory, desires, past and future, and knowledge it becomes saturated, and not open to the experience of "O", ultimate reality.

This mind, I suggest, is the same mind as the "beginners mind" (Suzuki, 1970) in Zen Buddhism, and the mind of mystics generally.

Sir Francis Bacon is reputed to have said: "When Wonder ceases, Knowledge begins". I would suggest that knowledge these days more frequently tends to become property, usually owned by an individual, a university, a drug company, a corporation, or the state. "Knowledge is Power" as Sir Francis Bacon is also reputed to have said. And through intellectual property laws, trademarks, patents, copyright, and so on, it is also money, meaning money paid to you for :knowledge" or property that somebody else needs. The accent is on ownership, and for those that do not own, they pay.

I would also suggest that knowledge in the forefront of the mind limits wonder. The application of "knowledge" is perhaps at the heart of the conservative, bureaucratising, and risk averse behaviour of universities, corporations, and the state.

Wonder, however, cannot be owned and appropriated for personal, corporate, or public gain. Wonder opens knowledge to other dimensions, which give birth from "not knowing". The matrix in social dreaming is akin to a womb awaiting conception. Dreams, like semen, fertilise the matrix and, through associations and connections, *shared* meanings are grown. These meanings are not owned, in the sense that knowledge may be owned—they are an expression of wonder and become part of our *being*. At Soapy Bore, one notes, there is no individual ownership of land; rather, people belong to the "country". The elements—wind, heat and desert—beat out of us our supposed knowledge about things and left a space for wonder to arise and for heart and being to be constantly created.

Wonder is also at the heart of philosophy, as Socrates says, "It looks as though Theodorus' sketch of your character was accurate, my friend. I mean this feeling—a sense of wonder—is perfectly proper to a philosopher: philosophy has no other foundation, in fact" (Plato, 2004, p. 37).

In Greek mythology, Thaumas is a wondrous being and Iris is the daughter of Thaumas (Plato, 2004). Iris is the personification of the rainbow and messenger of the gods. As the sun unites earth and heaven, Iris links the gods to humanity. She travelled with the speed of wind from one end of the world to the other, and into the depths of the sea and the underworld.

Those who were at the International Group Relations Conference in 2002, will remember the marvellous rainbows over Louttit Bay at Lorne. Iris would seem to be the goddess of socioanalysis

At the beginning of the Brazilian Lectures, Bion tells a story:

> I shall start with a fable, in the guise of an historical account, of the Royal Cemetery at Ur. On the death of the king the entire court processed into an excavation, since called 'The Death Pit', and there, dressed in their finery and jewels, took a drug from a small cup later found by each body.

> Four hundred years later, without any publicity, the tombs were robbed. It was a courageous thing to do because the Cemetery had been sanctified by the death and burial of the Royal Family. The robbers were the patrons of the scientific method; the first who dared to break through the ghostly sentinels of the dead and their priestly attendants. (Bion, 1973, p. 11)

The tomb robbers, through greed and wonder, become "patrons of the scientific method".

The problem with knowledge is that it can become, as Bion noted, a carapace or shell from which the world is made sense of. While knowledge is indispensable for our functioning, unless it is cleansed and bathed in wonder it can stifle us. The socioanalytic methodologies you will read about in this book need to be constantly refreshed through wonder or otherwise they simply become applied knowledge, which might be useful for making money through teaching or consultancy, but they will not extend our purview.

I want to finish this short chapter by talking about the liberating aspects of wonder for the group, especially when revealed through social and organisational dreaming. It leads to a different form of connection between people that is not hierarchic, but has an authority generated through shared meaning.

I have written elsewhere at more length about the different concepts of authority, one based in hierarchy and the control of anxiety, the other based in wonder and exploration leading to the authority of the *sangha*—people on the same path, in this case the social dreaming path (Bain, 2006).

Note

1.   The "Dreamers sleeping in a circle" and other images in the poem come from a dream of Peter Hetrelezis's at Soapy Bore.

References

Bain, A. (1999). On socio-analysis. *Socio-Analysis*, 1(1): 1–17.

Bain, A. (2006). Sources of authority: the double threads of anxiety and wonder. In: A. N. Mathur (Ed.), *Dare to Think the Unthought Known*. Tampere: Aivoairut.

Bion, W. R. (1973). *Brazilian Lectures 1*. Sao Paulo: Imago Editoria.

Keats, J. (1817). Letter to George and Thomas Keats, 23 December. In: M. B. Forman (Ed.), *John Keats, Letters* (4th edn) (pp. 260–261). London: Oxford University Press, 1952.

Plato (2004). *Theaetetus*. London: Penguin.

Suzuki, S. (1970). *Zen Mind, Beginner's Mind*, T. Dixon (Ed.). New York: Weatherhill.

CHAPTER SIXTEEN

Using and creating socioanalytic methods

Susan Long

T he methods in this book all open up a path to the unconscious, through connections, amplifications, associations, and patterns. While socioanalysis may, at times, focus on the repressed, the foreclosed, or the denied experiences of groups, organisations, or society (see, for example, Hirschhorn, 1988; Long, 2008, Sievers, 2003; Stein, 2008), the focus in this book is on accessing the associative unconscious as a path not just to the pathology of the system, but to its creative potential.

Socioanalysis (systems psychodynamics) is a young discipline. In terms of the Peircean philosophy of science, discussed in Chapter One, it works largely within the first, yet most creative stage of scientific discovery when data is created through an inquisitive state of mind, patterns are discerned, and working hypotheses are formed to guide further exploration. It is a science of subjectivity, devoted to understanding how subjectivity works collectively in groups, organisations, and society, recognising that the collective comes before the individual and that subjectivity and mind are formed and shaped in the social (Long, 2001).

Methods for exploring subjectivity in groups and social systems are needed because subjectivity has a huge influence on the ways that humans behave. It is the foundation for both pathological and creative possibilities and actions. But subjective experience is not easily explored. It is predominantly accessed by exploring a person's conscious experiences, yet immediate and conscious experience is shaped and transformed by a huge number of factors and so is not as transparent as we might like to believe. Elsewhere, I have outlined some characteristics of experience that emphasise its subjectivity, range of complexity from simple to transformed, whether symbolised or not, how it is linked to behaviour, and its reflexivity (Long, 2004). Experience is a broad term covering states-of-mind ranging through conscious and unconscious. Lacan (1977), for example, understands that experience is registered through three main paths, the Symbolic, the Imaginary, and the Real, while Kleinian socioanalysts pay attention specifically to paranoid–schizoid and depressive states of mind.

The complexity of accessing subjective experience has been approached by dynamic psychology through projective techniques— the Rorscharch Ink Blot Test or the Thematic Apperception Test, for example. These are based on the assumption that impulses, defences, and other inner phenomena are projected into the external world and perceived to exist there. One idea of the projective test is that the psychological defences of the ego will be circumvented by applying directly to the perceptual experience. This is not based predominantly on the content of the perception, but on less consciously manipulated aspects of perception. The subject in essence reports on his or her own inner state, while thinking that he or she is simply seeing something "out there".

The socioanalytic methods described in this book owe something to this idea, in so far as they circumvent consciously defended conceptions through appealing to perceptions, drawings, dreams, and other non-verbal phenomena. This is done in an open manner and, I would say, with respectful curiosity. Instead of personalising the unconscious, the central purpose is to access hidden thoughts and feelings that are understood to "belong to" the group. In other words, they belong to the symbolic system that is shared in a given organisational or societal grouping. Individuals are discouraged from thinking that they are simply seeing or thinking something that is personal; they mostly intuitively understand—through the ways that these methods are used—that their experience also holds something for others. Of course, this means that the methods are used by those trained in their use and with a professional background that includes education in the research, concepts, and theories involved.

The tension between immediate experience and its transformation in thinking

Humans, as long as we know, have been fascinated by immediate experience and the workings of the mind on that experience. The whole discernment of what is real and what is illusion rests on the sense of reality as experienced—to see it with your own eyes, to hear with your own ears, is compelling. And humans have evolved to rely on that immediate experience for survival. Yet, much immediate experience is lost.

> Experiences form the basis of psychic life; we are continually in experience. Yet if we are to learn from our experience, we must first have access to what is often ephemeral, unsymbolised, dismissed, or confusingly complex. (Long, 2004, p. 105)

All experience is ultimately emotional experience (Bion, 1977). Beyond immediate emotional experience, the capacity to have memories, to conceptualise, to make judgements, to develop theories challenges experience and illustrate that it can be (at some levels) illusory. For one, experience is constantly being transformed and conscious access to immediate experience is difficult. Second, the evidence that different individuals have alternative, sometimes contradictory, perceptions and experiences supports the individuality, subjectivity, and potential illusory condition of experience (at any level), let alone the evidence from theories of psychological defence, delusory ideation, and unconscious processes. Immediate experiences, while indicating an internal "truth", dance in the shadows and transform themselves at a rapid rate as soon as we try to grasp them.

Bion recognises this when he says,

> I suggest that thinking is something forced on an apparatus, not suited for the purpose, by the demands of reality and is contemporary with, as Freud said, the dominance of the reality principle. A modern analogy is provided by the fact that the demands of reality not only forced

the discovery of psycho-analysis, but have led to the deflection of verbal thought from its original function of providing restraint for motor discharge to the tasks of self knowledge for which it is ill-suited and for the purpose of which it has to undergo drastic changes. (Bion, 1962, p. 57)

Bion's theory of thinking outlines some of those drastic changes and the human struggle with them (Grotstein, 2007; Symington & Symington, 1996).

Additionally, the recognition that each person is but a small part of a much broader social system—of an even broader ecological system—with a limited perspective of the whole tells us that a broader social and external "reality" is far more complex than can be grasped from isolated individual fleeting experiences. This is the perspective of systems theory.

Because of all these factors, understanding the collective "mind" or symbolic matrix of meaning is not easy. We can only pursue it with some degree of hope that, in glimpsing a social reality, we can avoid pathological social states and come closer to finding creative paths into the future.

What can be said of the internal realities of a social system? The analogy given at the beginning of this book—that each person in a social system, be it a group, an organisation, or society, is like one piece of a jigsaw puzzle, different from every other piece and from the whole, yet needed for the whole picture to emerge—should be recalled. The puzzle is multi-dimensional, complex, and dynamically changing. But each piece is important. Each experience counts towards the whole, each thought adds to the matrix of human thinking and endeavour. It is not that immediate experience is irrelevant or always illusory, but it must be placed in a context, whether the context of a person's life history, the context of the current group, or the context of the multifarious states-of-mind available for creating or registering experience.

The tension between any singular experience and the capacity to think both logically about it (in relation to the demands of reality) and systemically (in relation to an understanding about the connectedness of things and the social basis of psychology) is the very stuff of psychoanalysis and socioanalysis. Moreover, the philosophical question of whether or not there is a reality beyond the mind is not of relevance here. The tension is that one spoken of by Bion about the ill-equipped capacity to think about ourselves—an ill-equipped capacity deeply rooted in our social systems as well as those individuals emergent from these systems. All thinking, from alpha element to scientific theory, is flawed, but it is most of what we have available to access and utilise (in the world) the fundamental "O" of our experience as individuals and in organisations.

The techniques or methods of psychoanalysis emphasise that this tension is not resolved simply by presenting the mind with logic or data from a supposed bigger picture. Mutative interpretations only work anyway when the patient (or client organisation) is so close to making the interpretation themselves that it does not matter: as Shakespeare said, "ripeness is all" (King Lear). The primary psychoanalytic method involves exploration of the experience in order to find its context; to expand the experience and find the repressed; to amplify the experience (a term taken from Gordon Lawrence's work in the social dreaming matrix) and find its connections, reverberations, and patterns, and so to allow the primary emotional experience to be accessed and reworked. This is the method of free association. The analyst and patient together find meaning in the associations. Through this method, and the meaning making of the analytic pair, the conscious and, especially, the unconscious contexts of the patient's symptoms are uncovered. Logic is not impressed on the mind, but as much as possible is discovered. A wider picture or, perhaps better put in terms of the "talking cure", a more comprehensive narrative is found, even though this follows the centrepiece of the analysis, which is not so much the logic found as the emotion reworked.

So it is with socioanalytic methods. In depth, these methods work by accessing, through the associative unconscious, the central emotional experiences to be found in a social system and its context and to open up the potential for their transformation, perhaps from a pathological to a more normal position, perhaps even to a position redolent with creative potential. The reflective spaces created by these methods allow people to feel safe enough to reconnect with emotional experiences that lie at the heart of their work together and from there to think about how their work might be done more satisfactorily (see Chapter Two). But even when this degree of depth is not achieved, these methods provide insights into the social system through the attention paid to the mental matrix.

Creating socioanalytic methods

As has been said, the methods in this book all open up a path to the unconscious, through connections, amplifications, associations, and patterns. In socioanalysis, the interest is not in the individual, but in the matrix of thought that is the associative unconscious of the system under study. From this perspective, thoughts and feelings come from the deep structure and dynamics of the system through the individual. It is not that the individual is denied; his or her thoughts and feelings, of course, have personal resonance and derive from personal experience. But the thoughts and feelings are also *of* the social system while *in* the individual (Armstrong, 2000)—some more strongly than others. The use of reflective space, reflection groups, and matrices allow the social content to be revealed.

The history of the development of each of these methods has been touched on in the book and the various chapters have given case examples of their use. Each method was begun and developed in response to a particular need felt by practitioners as they worked with groups and organisations. Organisational role analysis was developed at the Grubb Institute because of a need to embed the learning from group relations conferences more fully into everyday organisational life. The Listening Post developed from a desire to more fully substantiate ways of "picking up" societal preoccupations. Work drawings developed as a way of accessing more unconscious ways of seeing the organisation and the roles within it. Social dreaming began from recognising the value of a focus on the dream rather than the dreamer. Role biography and role history began as methods when I was teaching at a university. I found that, by discussing role biographies, students became more closely connected to how their own past experiences had influenced the work roles that they were currently in. Importantly at the time, the discussion of role biographies linked students from quite different cultures as they found stories that crossed national and language boundaries. The tasks and roles they described held the links, albeit that these were coloured by different national hues.

The problems faced by organisations and societies, while sometimes seeming to repeat history, are also ever changing within new contexts. So will the need to develop new methods for exploring those problems change over time.

There are a few points to hold in mind.

1. The body of theory and research behind these methods is large
    and complex. They did not develop in a vacuum. New methods
    will need to take the learning of the past into account.
2. The practitioners who developed and use these methods are
    skilled professionals who trained in formal programmes. There
    are several programmes around the world that educate and train
    students in socioanalytic and systems psychodynamic methods
    (see www.ispso.org). In Melbourne, the National Institute of
    Organisation Dynamics Australia (NIODA) takes such a perspec-
    tive, as do the Tavistock and Grubb Institutes in London.
3. Methods become stale and static if the thinking behind them is
    not regularly reviewed.
4. These methods are collaborative. They enable consultants/
    researchers to work with the people in the groups and organisa-
    tions studied. In fact, we could say that the methods are co-
    created by practitioners and group members, guided by the
    practitioners. Without this co-creation, the methods could not
    produce real working knowledge and learning.

    > These methods only work if the practitioner genuinely believes
    > the "other" is a potential co-creator of a shared reality, so the
    > outcomes can then include insight, creative possibilities and the
    > experience of meaningful co-operation. (Newton, 2012)

5. The methods are used in strict accordance with ethical principles
    that protect the rights of those involved. Respectful curiosity and
    wonder are the stance from which to come.
6. The methods should create the opportunity for the development
    of "working hypotheses" rather than "hypothesis testing". While
    hypothesis testing may come later, in much social systems based
    research the ever-changing, dynamic nature of the system means
    that its very exploration creates change.

Central to these methods is the impetus to explore the subjectivity
of the system and what this means for action on the part of people in
the system. This subjectivity is accessed through the experiences of
persons in their roles within their systems and contexts (Bazalgette,
2011). Increasingly, new theory is developed to aid this exploration
and to guide the development of new methods.

> These methods should be viewed as ways of creating shared knowing
> within groups, organisations and society at the very time when an

explosion of 'expert' knowledge in the world threatens our cohesion and masks the human need for interdependence. (Newton, 2012).

This book provides a philosophy of science for socioanalytic methods whereby new theories and methods may develop for shared knowing.

References

Armstrong, D. (2000). Emotions in organisations: disturbance of intelligence? Paper presented to the 17th ISPSO Annual Meeting, London.

Bazalgette, J. (2011). Leadership: the impact of the full human being in role. Grubb Institute of Behavioural Science Paper. Accessed on 12 August 2010 at: www.grubb.org.uk.

Bion, W. R. (1962). *Learning from Experience*. London: Karnac, 1984.

Bion, W. R. (1977). *Seven Servants: Elements of Psychoanalysis, Learning from Experience, Transformations, Attention and Interpretation* New York: Jason Aronson.

Grotstein, J. S. (2007). *A Beam of Intense Darkness: Wilfred Bion's Legacy to Psychoanalysis*. London: Karnac.

Hirschhorn, L. (1988). *The Workplace Within: Psychodynamics of Organizational Life*. New York: MIT Press.

Lacan, J. (1977). *Ecrits*. London: Tavistock.

Long, S. D. (2001). Working with organizations: the contribution of the psychoanalytic discourse. *Organisational and Social Dynamics, 2*: 174–198.

Long, S. D. (2004). Building an institution for experiential learning. In: L. J. Gould, L. Stapley, & M. Stein (Eds.), *Experiential Learning in Organizations: Applications of the Tavistock Group Relations Approach* (pp. 101–136). London: Karnac.

Long, S. D. (2008). *The Perverse Organization and Its Deadly Sins*. London: Karnac.

Newton, J. (2012). Personal communication.

Sievers, B. (2003). "Your money or your life?" Psychotic implications of the pension fund system: towards a socio-analysis of the financial services revolution. *Human Relations, 56*(2): 187–210.

Stein, M. (2008). Toxicity and the unconscious experience of the body at the employee-customer interface. *Organization Studies, 28*: 1223–1241.

Symington, J., & Symington, N. (1996). *The Clinical Thinking of Wilfred Bion*. London: Routledge.

INDEX

Abraham, F., 270–271
affect(ive), 91, 94, 99, 123, 216, 227, 234, 240, 290–291
aggression, 34, 190, 192–193, 209, 213, 218, 221
Ahlers-Niemann, A., 134, 138, 148
Akerlof, G., 282, 298
Albrecht Schwaber, E., 289, 298
Allport, G. W., 259, 272
Amado, G., 34, 43
Ambrose, A., 34, 43
Anderson, D. R., 15, 21
anger, 122, 158, 190, 263–264, 295–296
Angyal, A., 93, 104
anxiety, xxiv, 26, 31–33, 37–38, 42–43, 52, 60, 62, 73, 75, 79, 88, 98, 141–142, 162–163, 168, 171, 180, 189, 191, 193, 209, 214, 221, 239, 244, 259, 264, 270–271, 279–282, 284–285, 288–289, 291, 296, 306
    avoidance of, 98
    disabling, 33
    excessive, 209
    externalised, 33
    individual, 253
    intolerable, 98
    nuclear, 192
    performance, 208
    primitive, 94, 99
    psychotic, 33
    state, 193
    underlying, 27
Aram, E., xix–xx, xxix, 260, 271–272, 291, 298
Argyris, C., 237, 254
Arlow, J., 289, 298
Armstrong, D. G., 37, 43, 51, 66, 69, 88, 132, 149, 209, 215, 217, 223, 229,
235, 240, 246, 254, 259–260, 272, 274, 282, 298, 312, 314
Ashby, W. R., 35, 43
Australian Institute of Social Analysis, xx

Baglioni, L., 122, 126
Bain, A., xx–xxi, xxviii–xxix, 36, 43, 165, 176, 209, 223, 242, 255, 303–304, 306
Bamforth, K., 267, 277
Banet, A. G., 120, 126
Baxter, R., xix–xx, xxix, 260, 271–272, 291, 298
Bazalgette, J., 132, 149, 209–210, 224, 234–235, 313–314
behaviour(al), xx, 4, 7, 56, 91, 93, 99, 132, 146, 190–191, 196, 205–206, 219, 227–228, 237, 239, 259, 261–264, 267–268, 304, 308
    see also: unconscious
    assumption, 92
    expected, 266
    human, 249, 267, 308
    implications, 287
    interviewing, 101
    issues, 297
    organisational, xxi, 43, 183, 304
    overt, 25
    psychopathic, 168
    psychosocial, 288
    societal, 282, 297
    system, 94
Benedict, R., 282, 298
Ben Jelloun, T., 286, 298
Ben Mhenni, L., 287, 298
Benslama, F., 286, 298
Beradt, C., 113, 126
Beumer, U., 129, 151, 162, 178
Biberman, G., 71, 89

315